# LOST IN FLORIDA

LOST IN FLORIDA
*Prelude to Equipment Finance*

TRACKS OF THE MOHEGAN
*A Second Engine Mystery*

THE HISTORY OF EQUIPMENT FINANCE, VOLUME 1, 1832-1833
*Literature, Law, Coal in the Time of Cholera*

THE HISTORY OF EQUIPMENT FINANCE, VOLUME 2, 1838-1840
*Locks & Canals and Baltimore & Susquehanna*

THE HISTORY OF EQUIPMENT FINANCE, VOLUME 3, 1841-1849
*Locks & Canals and Philadelphia & Reading*

THE HISTORY OF EQUIPMENT FINANCE, VOLUME 4, 1845-1897
*Boat Loans, Philadelphia Car & Equipment Trusts, Central of New Jersey*

THE HISTORY OF EQUIPMENT FINANCE, VOLUME 5, 1859-1900
*Bonds, Leasing Companies, Car and Equipment Trusts*

THE HISTORY OF EQUIPMENT FINANCE, VOLUME 6, 1873-1967
*Pennsylvania Railroad, GATX, Equitable Life, Conclusion*

ISLAMIC FINANCE AND THE SHARIʿAH
*The Dow Jones Fatwa and Permissible Variance
as Studies in Letheanism and Legal Change*

# Lost in Florida

*Prelude to Equipment Finance*

## Michael J.T. McMillen

River Stone Publishing Group

RIVER STONE PUBLISHING GROUP

RIVER STONE PUBLISHING GROUP is an imprint of RIVER STONE CAPITAL, LLC
Published 2022 by River Stone Publishing Group, Bethlehem, Pennsylvania
Printed in the United States of America

Copyright © 2022 by Michael J.T. McMillen
All rights reserved

ISBN: 978-1-957948-01-0
Library of Congress Control Number: 20222934173

McMillen, Michael J.T., 1950-
Lost in Florida: Prelude to Equipment Finance
Michael J.T. McMillen
Includes bibliographical references and index

Except as permitted by applicable statute, and without limiting rights under the copyright, no part of this publication may be reproduced, stored in, or introduced into a retrieval system, or transmitted, in any manner, in any form, or by any means, without the prior written consent of both the copyright owner and the publisher of this book, except by a reviewer quoting brief passages in connection with a review written for insertion in a magazine, newspaper, broadcast, website, blog, or similar outlet.

This title is available as:
ISBN (hardcover, color interior): 978-1-957948-00-3
ISBN (paperback, color interior): 978-1-957948-01-0
ISBN (paperback, black and white interior): 978-1-957948-02-7

LCSH

Railroads-United States-History-19th century
Railroads-United States-History
United States-History-Finance
Finance-United States-History

BISAC

History, United States, 19th century (HIS036040)
Transportation, Railroads, History (TRA004010)
Business & Economics, Finance, Financial Engineering (BUS027010)

# Dedication

Wallace Judson Huppler and James Stewart McMillen

*models and mentors in word and deed*

Cover Illustration: Nicolson Wood, *Traité pratique des chemins de fer de Nicolson Wood, traduit de l'anglais (deuxième édition) par MM de Montricher et de Franqueville, ingénieurs des Ponts et Chaussées et de Ruolz, Planches, Paris, chez Carillian-Goeury éditeur-libraire* (1834)

Cover design: Catherine Debbage

# Contents

| | | |
|---|---|---|
| Acknowledgements | | xi |
| Conventions | | xv |
| | Accessions and Collections | xv |
| | Footnotes and Endnotes | xv |
| | Reference Conventions | xv |
| | Sources and Credits | xv |
| | Views and Responsibilities | xv |
| **Part I** | **Proem** | 1 |
| 1 | Prologue | 3 |
| | Engines to Florida | 3 |
| | Pensacola as Prelude | 4 |
| | Perspective | 6 |
| | Endnotes: Chapter One | 7 |
| **Part II** | **Assessing Involvement** | 9 |
| 2 | Reflection | 11 |
| | Endnotes: Chapter Two | 14 |
| 3 | L&C Machine Shop | 17 |
| | The Machine Shop | 17 |
| | Opportunity, Innovation, and Risk | 18 |
| | Building Locomotives | 20 |
| | Selling Locomotives | 23 |
| | Endnotes: Chapter Three | 24 |
| 4 | Railroad Experience | 31 |
| | Generally | 31 |
| | Boston & Lowell | 32 |
| | Endnotes: Chapter Four | 33 |
| 5 | Cause for Caution | 35 |
| | Endnotes: Chapter Five | 38 |
| **Part III** | **Pensacola Schemes** | 43 |
| 6 | Capturing Pensacola | 45 |
| | Endnotes: Chapter Six | 48 |
| 7 | Restructuring and Financing Plan | 53 |
| | BUS Parties, With Plan | 53 |
| | Land Matters | 57 |
| | Diverging Interests | 58 |
| | Endnotes: Chapter Seven | 59 |
| 8 | Control | 63 |
| | Endnotes: Chapter Eight | 65 |
| 9 | Pensacola Associates and Friends | 67 |
| | Guardians | 67 |

|  |  |  |  |
|---|---|---|---|
|  |  | Thomas A. Biddle | 68 |
|  |  | Elihu Chauncey | 70 |
|  |  | Samuel Jaudon | 72 |
|  |  | Charles Augustus Davis | 76 |
|  |  | Sampson Vryling Stoddard Wilder | 79 |
|  |  | Morris Robinson | 82 |
|  |  | William Gibbs McNeil | 84 |
|  |  | Other BUS Relationships | 85 |
|  |  | George's Creek Coal & Iron | 86 |
|  |  | Conclusions and Questions | 89 |
|  |  | Endnotes: Chapter Nine | 89 |
| Part IV | Pensacola People | | 95 |
| 10 | William H. Chase | | 97 |
|  |  | Endnotes: Chapter Ten | 101 |
| 11 | Walter Gregory | | 103 |
|  |  | Endnotes: Chapter Eleven | 106 |
| 12 | Family Business | | 109 |
|  |  | Gregory Family Cottage Business | 109 |
|  |  | Expanding Opportunities | 114 |
|  |  | Endnotes: Chapter Twelve | 116 |
| Part V | Disintegration | | 119 |
| 13 | Call to Arms | | 121 |
|  |  | Defaults | 121 |
|  |  | Call to Contortions | 122 |
|  |  | Endnotes: Chapter Thirteen | 131 |
| 14 | Repudiations | | 133 |
|  |  | Florida Judiciary Committee Report | 133 |
|  |  | Repudiation and Persistence | 134 |
|  |  | Endnotes: Chapter Fourteen | 136 |
| 15 | Engines Enigma | | 139 |
|  |  | Walker Anderson | 139 |
|  |  | BoP Commissioner's Report | 141 |
|  |  | Endnotes: Chapter Fifteen | 143 |
| Part VI | Resurrections | | 147 |
| 16 | Envoi as Prelude | | 149 |
|  |  | Envoi | 149 |
|  |  | Prelude | 150 |
|  |  | Endnotes: Chapter Sixteen | 152 |
| Bibliography | | | 155 |
|  | Principal Document Accessions and Collections | | 155 |
|  | Abbreviations | | 156 |
|  | Credits for Figures | | 157 |
|  | Credits for Maps | | 158 |
|  | Citations to Laws | | 159 |
|  | Sources Referenced | | 159 |
| Index | | | 201 |

## Maps

| | | |
|---|---|---|
| | About the Graphic Designer | 208 |
| | About the Author | 209 |

Maps

| | | |
|---|---|---|
| 1 | Pensacola, Territory of Florida | 44 |
| 2 | Proposed Railroad System | 52 |
| 3 | Graham Map of Proposed Railroad | 57 |

Table

| | | |
|---|---|---|
| 1 | Share Holdings in Bank of Pensacola | 64 |

Figures

| | | |
|---|---|---|
| 1 | Patrick Tracy Jackson | 10 |
| 2 | Stephenson *Planet* Class Engine, 1834 | 20 |
| 3 | *Bristol* Locomotive Engine | 22 |
| 4 | Camden & Amboy, 1834 | 30 |
| 5 | Bank of Pensacola Bond, 1835 | 54 |
| 6 | Nicholas Biddle, 1843 | 66 |
| 7 | Bank of the United States | 68 |
| 8 | Thomas A. Biddle | 69 |
| 9 | Samuel Jaudon | 72 |
| 10 | William Bainbridge | 74 |
| 11 | James DePeyster Ogden & Charles Augustus Davis, 1839 | 77 |
| 12 | *Cider Making*, William Sidney Mount, 1840-1841 | 78 |
| 13 | Sampson Vryling Stoddard Wilder, circa 1808 | 80 |
| 14 | Sampson Vryling Stoddard Wilder | 81 |
| 15 | Morris Robinson | 83 |
| 16 | William Gibbs McNeill | 84 |
| 17 | Fort Pickens and Fort McRae | 96 |
| 18 | William H. Chase | 99 |
| 19 | Egeria at the Fountain | 105 |
| 20 | Walter Gregory Monument, Spring Grove Cemetery | 108 |
| 21 | Dudley S. Gregory | 110 |
| 22 | Richard Keith Call | 120 |
| 23 | Endorsement of Bank of Pensacola Bond | 124 |
| 24 | London Bond Agreement | 125 |
| 25 | Text of London Bond Agreement | 126 |
| 26 | Walker Anderson | 138 |
| 27 | *Still Engine #1* | 210 |

# ACKNOWLEDGEMENTS

This volume derives from primary source research for a history of the origins and development of equipment finance. It considers a transaction between The Proprietors of Locks and Canals on Merrimac River and the Pensacola Railroad just as the Panic of 1837 descended upon the United States. The transaction was a debacle for Locks & Canals, the Pensacola Railroad, and the other transactional parties. The transaction involved no elements of equipment finance. However, it served as the analytical prelude to transactions in which the first equipment finance structures were developed. Those stories are told in other volumes.

Background material on Locks & Canals is from THE HISTORY OF EQUIPMENT FINANCE, VOLUME 2, 1838-1840: LOCKS & CANALS AND BALTIMORE & SUSQUEHANNA. Background material on the visit of Patrick Tracy Jackson with Horace Binney, and the 1842 and 1843 transactions that gave rise to that visit, is from THE HISTORY OF EQUIPMENT FINANCE, VOLUME 3, 1841-1849: LOCKS & CANALS AND PHILADELPHIA & READING.

Work on this study, and the pleasures of paper, expanded our home library to the limit of graceful accommodation within our physical capabilities. It also engendered appreciation for electronic research that allowed us to transcend physical limits. Many electronic advances are courtesy of research libraries, archives, and educational institutions. I am especially grateful to the libraries of the University of Pennsylvania Carey Law School and the University of Pennsylvania, followed closely by the institutions acknowledged here and in the first section of the Bibliography. Other advances in electronics allowed me to digitally capture thousands of pages of fragile paper originals that grace the many libraries and archives that I have indulged, and have indulged me, during research for this study.

The pandemic induced by SARS-CoV-2 was disruptive in many ways, including in the conduct of research and the ability to obtain high documents and high-resolution images. I am grateful for those who persevered in assisting me through the pandemic, especially library and archival staffs.

I have accrued a great many debts during research and writing for this study. My gratitude goes out to the individuals and institutions that so graciously provided guidance, criticism, assistance, and resources. These include:

Christopher T. Baer, Richard K. Bates, Kurt R. Bell, John K. Brown, Albert J. Churella, Lucas R. Clawson, Alvin Dong, Bill Draper, Hannah Elder, Martha

Capwell Fox, Michael Knoll, Patrick M. Malone, Brian McCall, Addison L. McMillen, Karin Laine McMillen, Martha Mills, Malissa Murphy, Joseph Parsio, Laurel A. Racine, Daniel M. G. Raff, Philip Scranton, Iren L. Snavely, Jr., Jeffrey S. Wilkey, and Jeffrey S. Wood; and the staffs and services of:

Baker Library of Harvard Graduate School of Business, Berks History Center Museum and Henry Janssen Library, Boston Public Library (including the Norman B. Leventhal Map & Education Center), British Library (including the Mechanical Curator Collection on Flickr), Curtis, Mallet-Prevost, Colt & Mosle LLP, Debevoise & Plimpton LLP, Digital Commonwealth, Florida Supreme Court, The Free Library of Philadelphia, The Frick Collections, Hagley Museum and Library (especially the Archives and Manuscripts Department), Historical Society of Pennsylvania, HathiTrust at the Hatcher Graduate Library of the University of Michigan and participating libraries, Historical Society of Phoenixville Area, Jenkins Law Library, Lehigh County Historical Society, The Library Company of Pennsylvania, Library of Congress (including the Marion S. Carson Collection), Lowell National Historical Park, Massachusetts Historical Society, The Metropolitan Museum of Art, The National Canal Museum, National Gallery of Art, National Library of Medicine of the United States of America, National Museum of American History, National Museum of Industrial History, National Portrait Gallery (London), National Portrait Gallery of the Smithsonian Institution, New York Art Resources Consortium (The Brooklyn Museum, The Frick Collection, and The Museum of Modern Art), New York Historical Society, The New York Public Library (including the Rare Book Division, the Lionel Pincus and Princess Firyal Map Division, The Miriam and Ira D. Wallach Division of Arts, Prints and Photographs, the Emmet Collection of Manuscripts Etc. Relating to American History, and the Robert N. Dennis Collection of Stereoscopic Views), Railroad Museum of Pennsylvania, Reading Area Community College, Reading Railroad Heritage Museum, State Archives of Pennsylvania of the Pennsylvania Historical and Museum Commission, Rutgers, The State University of New Jersey, State Library of Pennsylvania, Rare Collections, University College London, Centre for the Study of the Legacies of British Slavery, University of Massachusetts, University of Pennsylvania, University of Pennsylvania Carey Law School Library, and Worcester Art Museum.

My apologies to any that I have neglected to mention.

I am grateful to Patrick M. Malone for his insights, enthusiasm, direction, precision, and encouragement as well as vast knowledge so freely shared. And for his patience and assistance in orienting me within nineteenth century industry. Few memories are more cherished than my first journey to the Baker Library in Pat's company. I recall with special fondness the day that, seated across from Pat, I held in my hands for the first time the materials described by George Sweet Gibb in *Three Early Railroad Contracts*.

Christopher T. Baer was kind enough to guide me through the early phases of archival research, to indulge a raft of questions, many rudimentary, and to nurse me to many more sophisticated discussions. He graciously allowed me access to his private collection.

My heartfelt thanks to Marsha Mills for technical assistance, for the many kindnesses, and for the candy showered on Addison.

The staff of the Archives and Manuscripts Department of the Hagley Museum and Library brought life to archival work in Addison's eyes. That contribution will have a long history.

Special gratitude is owed to John K. Brown for encouragement regarding the evolving role of locomotive and other rolling stock builders as financial intermediaries and insights regarding capital equipment.

Benjamin Tandowski has my eternal gratitude for his post-prandial suggestions regarding search engines: my life will never be the same.

Catherine Debbage deserves special thanks for the cover of this volume and the other volumes in the series.

I think often, with gratitude, of my parents and their contributions to this study. My father, J. Glenn McMillen, first interested me in the study of history. He turned a blind eye to my late-night (often all night) reading while huddled, with flashlight, in my bedroom closet and gave freely of his history books to nurture those sessions. He was always available to discuss how past occurrences influenced events of the day and surmise with me as to how each might influence future affairs. My mother, Margaret H. McMillen, schooled me in precision, attention to detail, discipline, circumspection, the indominable spirit, and the importance of knowledge and insight regarding self and others. Responding to my first semester of college education, in a single day she applied her knowledge and insight in showing me the path to salvage my academic progression; for that I am forever grateful.

In every moment I am grateful to my wife, Karin, and my son, Addison, for their criticism, humor, and perspective. They make the music. Never confuse a direct line of sight with a straight path of execution. No knowledge is wasted; have fun; do your best.

———

My grandfathers, Wallace Judson Huppler (Hupp) and James Stewart McMillen (Mac), each mentored, nurtured, and inspired, including with respect to topics addressed in this study. These men, from quite different perspectives, inculcated the principles that are so dear, encouraged exploration, and taught of freedom and choice and attendant responsibilities. Each with sensitivity, civility, gentility, gentle rigor, firm hands, a warm heart, extraordinary patience, and adept inspirational nudging (often with fleeting look or sidelong glance). This book is dedicated to the memory of these two men.

    Michael J.T. McMillen
        Washington Township, Pennsylvania
        April 13, 2022

# Conventions

### Accessions and Collections

The principal accessions and collections used for the study from which this book derives are described in the bibliography.

### Footnotes and Endnotes

Both footnotes and endnotes are used in this book. Generally, footnotes are for text-related observations, perspective, and context, and endnotes are used for sources and related information. Endnotes are placed at the end of each Chapter.

### Reference Conventions

Bond and loan issuances are sometimes referenced by issuance and maturity dates: [issuance date]~[maturity date]. Unless otherwise noted, interest and dividend rates are per annum and commission percentages are of the face amount or par value. References to outstanding bond amounts are prior to discounts, commissions, charges, and fees. A reference to a "$" is to the United States dollar at the time. Unless otherwise specified, the terms "locomotive" and "engine" each refer to a "locomotive engine".

### Sources and Credits

To enhance accessibility, full journal citations are used. Sources in the bibliography are alphabetical by citation name and then year of publication. Abbreviations and credits for figures, maps, and tables, are at the beginning of the bibliography.

### Views and Responsibilities

Views expressed in this book are solely mine and not reflective of the positions of any institution with which I am or have been affiliated. Without reservation, and despite the best efforts of others to keep me on the path, all errors and misconceptions, whether of fact or interpretation, are solely mine and solely my responsibility. I have received no financial consideration or support relating to research for or writing of any aspect of this book or this study.

# PART I

## PROEM

# Chapter One

## Prologue

**Engines to Florida**

The Proprietors of Locks and Canals on Merrimack River commenced involvement with locomotive building in 1832 when it purchased two engines from Robert Stephenson in England and assembled them in Lowell, Massachusetts. As a Locks & Canals director, Patrick Tracy Jackson was intimately involved in the initiative, though his primary business commitment at the time was development and construction of the Boston and Lowell Rail-road Corporation. In 1834 L&C retained George Washington Whistler to manage locomotive building. In 1835, L&C built its first locomotive, for the Boston & Lowell. L&C built at least ten locomotives during that year. Eight were sold in Massachusetts and two in New York. By 1836, engine building was a principal business of the L&C machine shop. Fourteen or fifteen engines were built. Two went to the Pensacola Railroad as part of an order for locomotives, railroad cars, and related equipment. The others went to railroads in New England.[1]

In 1836 Locks & Canals agreed to build and sell to the Pensacola Railroad locomotives, cars, wheels, axles, and parts. Kirk Boott was then L&C agent and treasurer. Appointed agent in 1822, he held the position until his death on April 11, 1837. Patrick Tracy Jackson was a director and shareholder of L&C when the transaction was approved. His influence within L&C was significant, and sometimes dominant. The degree of Jackson's involvement and influence in approving the Pensacola Railroad transaction is unclear.

The engine sale to the Pensacola Railroad contravened L&C practices. L&C sold engines in the northeastern United States to railroads owned, controlled, or operated by people known to Jackson and members of the L&C board of directors, usually other Boston Associates.[A] Not to the distant wilds of the Territory of Florida.

---

[A] Boston Associates were merchants from Boston's elite and wealthy families, and a few individuals from other occupational and social groups. In the earliest years, they were men who moved to Boston and surrounds. These included Francis Cabot Lowell (Newburyport), the Jacksons (Newburyport), Amos and Abbott Lawrence (Groton), Nathan and William Appleton (New Ipswich), the Cabots (Beverly), and the Thorndikes (Beverly). By 1845 the group consisted of about eighty men. They were bound by business interests, friendships, and intermarriage. They became known as the

Not to an undertaking—still conceptual—that had not initiated construction of its road or other infrastructure. Not to a railroad owned by a newly established bank formed by unfamiliar Florida real estate speculators. L&C usually sold engines for cash on delivery. Payment deferrals were uncommon. The Pensacola Railroad was afforded an unsecured payment deferral despite knowledge that payment would not be made until the railroad became operational, some years hence.[2]

L&C delivered two engines to the Pensacola Railroad in the winter of 1836-1837. Likely the transaction would have been a misadventure even if the Panic of 1837 had not occurred. The Panic and its aftermath ensured a calamity. For all involved. A perfectly orchestrated symphony of defaults. Essentially every party defaulted, save L&C.[3]

**Pensacola as Prelude**

After resigning as agent of Boston Manufacturing Company in 1827, Patrick Tracy Jackson devoted his attention to personal investments. In 1828 he founded and acted as agent of Appleton Manufacturing Company. In April of 1828 he became involved in developing bituminous coal deposits near Lycoming Creek in Pennsylvania, primarily for iron production. That investment collapsed in 1840. The assets of Lycoming Coal Company were sold at auction. Between 1830 and 1835 Jackson founded, constructed, and managed the Boston & Lowell railroad. He was immersed in his Pemberton Square real estate development project in Boston from 1835 to 1838.

Following the death of Kirk Boott in 1837, Jackson was invited to assume the role of agent and treasurer of Locks & Canals. He accepted in April 1838. Whereupon he inherited responsibility for the Pensacola Railroad indebtedness to L&C, which was then in default.

Jackson marked the Pensacola Railroad transaction as the beginning of his education in the art of equipment financing. The transaction became a saga and ended a debacle. Jackson, ever the adept manager, harvested the bitter fruit: the

---

"Boston Associates", a term coined by Vera Shlakman in 1935. In the early 1800s they transitioned from merchants to manufactury, particularly in the textile industry in Waltham and Lowell where, by 1850, they operated thirty-five mills; about one-quarter of all regional spindles. But their investments were much broader, including insurance, banking, manufacturing, railroads, and mining. They served as board members and officers of companies in which they invested. They appointed company treasurers (then a particularly powerful position), policy officers, and purchasers of cotton, raw materials, equipment, and supplies. Their skill sets lay in the collection, organization, and management of capital pools and manufacturing and other business processes.

learning that could be, and was, applied to later transactions for sales of locomotives, cars, and other rolling stock.[B] Equipment vendors needed more robust structural and contractual protections. Protections that were sensitive to the emerging role of locomotive builders as providers of credit, and later financing and financial intermediation services, to railroad customers.

Starting with a sale of locomotives to the Baltimore and Susquehanna Railroad Company in 1839, Jackson began developing the elements of what became the principal equipment finance structure. The structure was modified and refined in two transactions with the Philadelphia and Reading Rail Road Company. In 1842 L&C built running gear for 600 coal cars for the P&R pursuant to the Running Gear Contract. In 1843 L&C built 12 locomotives, 450 wood coal cars, and 150 brakes for the P&R under the Engines Contract. Almost immediately after execution of these two Rolling Stock Contracts, the P&R defaulted in making payments under each. The defaults continued for years, well beyond the final payment dates under the contracts. Which resulted in further modifications to the structure.

Progressive development of the equipment financing structure involved experimentation with conditional sale, an agency structure, trust structures, collateral security structures, and various payment arrangements. P&R payment defaults induced further structural modifications. Jackson was forced to balance short-term financial realizations from the exercise of rights and remedies against disruptions to relationships and revenue generation capabilities that would result from exercising those remedies. The realization that exercising remedies would be counterproductive inspired further modifications in the transactional structure.

The structure developed by Jackson for the Rolling Stock Contracts was sound. It was adopted by Schuylkill Navigation Company in 1845 and comprised the core of its boat loans from 1845 to 1868. It was the basis for car trust and equipment trust structures of Lehigh Coal & Navigation in 1868 and 1869: The Railroad Car Trust of Philadelphia and The Lehigh Equipment Trust of Philadelphia. Those were adopted and copied by the Central Railroad Company of New Jersey. Car and equipment trust structures came to dominate railroad equipment financing.

---

[B] In this book, "rolling stock" refers to locomotive engines, tenders, coal and other cars, carriages, wagons, and other vehicles used on a railroad, and (less conventionally) railroad parts and equipment, including running gear. Running gear refers to components of a railway vehicle that run passively on the rails (such as wheels, axles, axle boxes, springs, vehicle frames, and other carrying parts of a truck or engine). In the age of steam locomotives, the distinction between running gear and driving gear was more pronounced than now, when all axles are driven.

By 1868 Jackson's structure, as refined, formed the core of what now constitutes "equipment finance". Equipment finance is a harmonized body of structural elements and techniques of implementation for financing the acquisition (by building, manufacture, construction, purchase, or use) of equipment, alone or as a part of a larger project, in which (in the pure case) the source of funds and recourse afforded the financier for repayment of the financing are limited to revenues generated by the equipment, either as operating income or disposition proceeds.[4]

While the Pensacola Railroad transaction did not involve elements of equipment finance structures as now known, it was the birthing ground for those structures. Other books in this study examine the origination and development of equipment finance.[5]

**Perspective**

As the aftermath of the Panic of 1837 diminished the business of the Locks & Canals machine shop, Jackson determined that the shop and related assets should be sold or converted to a twist mill. The most significant impediment to sale was the P&R debt under the Rolling Stock Contracts. It had long been, and remained, in default. Ultimately, the machine shop was sold. But the unpaid debt remained a burden on L&C. A specter of business past.

On December 10, 1845, before sale of the machine shop, Jackson journeyed to Philadelphia to seek the advice of Horace Binney, a prominent lawyer. The L&C board of directors desired guidance regarding the disposition to a third party of the P&R debt under the Rolling Stock Contracts. True to character, Jackson expanded the consultation. He sought to enhance the value of the P&R receivable to L&C and any potential assignee of that receivable. Because Jackson and other Boston Associates had become holders of P&R debt and equity, the plan also initiated steps to force the P&R to address its massive floating debt overhang.[C]

---

[C] In the early nineteenth century, "floating debt" embodied two concepts: the excess of current liabilities over assets; and short-term debt that was periodically refinanced (the latter being the contemporary definitional focus). The interest rate on floating debt in the nineteenth century was fixed, but tenors were short, allowing rates to vary or float over the short term. Funded debt had longer tenors, usually more than one year or one business cycle, with a fixed rate for the term. Accounting practices permitted railroad asset values to be increased by discounts given on bonds (usually 20-50% of the face amount; sometimes more), interest on bonds, notes and other indebtedness, and deficits from early operations. Asset values were highly inflated; and liabilities significantly understated.

Jackson and Binney devised an elegant plan to address Jackson's concerns. The plan forced payment of the P&R debt and reduction of the floating debt; without litigation or formal initiation of remedies, although the threats of each remained a factor in ensuring the plan's success. The plan did much more. It initiated a process that resulted in financial restructurings of the P&R from 1845 through 1849.

For perspective, the story begins in 1845, just after Jackson's visit to Horace Binney, as Jackson reflected on his involvements with equipment sale and financing transactions between 1836 and 1845. Beginning with that which was lost in Florida.

### Endnotes: Chapter One

[1] Use of the term "building" follows the convention of Roe & Lytle (1941), at 1. "We shall use the term *building* to cover the production of machines or other articles one at a time, or in numbers so limited that the methods of production are unchanged. By *manufacturing* we shall mean production in lots, by special-purpose equipment and usually with corresponding parts interchangeable."

Factors affecting the building concept, from financial and operational perspectives, were many, especially in an environment in which technology and design changed rapidly and continuously, as was the case with locomotives and other rolling stock in the nineteenth century. They included large capital costs of the product (capital equipment), narrow specialized markets, bespoke production to specifications provided by customers (such as railroads), inability of the producer to amass inventories and anticipate customer demands, a general inability to influence customer demands and requirements (with exceptions, such as Baldwin's flexible beam truck), and individualized production management. For some relevant considerations in the context of locomotive building by the Baldwin Locomotive Works, Brown (1995-1), with a summary at xxv-xxxii and detailed discussion in subsequent chapters.

For L&C engine sales, see endnote 14, Chapter Three.

[2] Discussion of the Pensacola Railroad transaction takes up a thread left hanging by George Sweet Gibb in Gibb (1947). For the conduct of business with known counterparties, Lamoreaux (1996), addressing banking in the nineteenth century, and Lamoreaux, Raff & Temin (2003). For the term "Boston Associates", Shlakman (1935). For the Boston Associates, Dalzell (1987), Prince & Taylor (1982), Schakenbach (2011), Barkin (1981), especially at 463-66 (addressing management, entity control, and the treasurer's role), Goodman (1966), Gregory (1975), Cox (2012), Hartford (2001), Jaher (1972), Rich (1975), and, tracing beyond the Civil War, Maggor (2017).

[3] For the Panic of 1837, see Lepler (2013), Roberts (2013), McGrane (1965), North (1961), especially at 66-74 and 177-215, Temin (1969), especially at 113-71, Kim & Wallis (2005), Wallis (2001), McFaul (1972), Howe (2007), at 502-4, Lepore (2018), at 421-71, Rousseau (2002), Palmer (1837), Gilbart (1840), BHS 1837 Panic (1933), Oberg (1985),

Dorfman (1951), Adams (2011-1), Adams (2011-2), Rezneck (1935), Priest (1973), Cole (1928), Charvat (1937), Hansen (1915), and Perkins (1931).

[4] This is a practitioner's definition. Equipment finance techniques are used primarily for capital equipment, broadly defined. Definitions of capital equipment vary with focus, financial practice, and jurisdiction. For present purposes, the definition adopted by John K. Brown serves well: "those mechanisms sold to secondary companies for use in their final production of goods or delivery of services." Brown (1995-1), at 251, Introduction note 1, and Brown (1993), at 7.

In practice, many definitions include parameters relating to useful life, per-unit cost, and other factors. See, for example, the procurement-related definition of the Office of Finance & Treasury of Princeton University, available at https://finance.princeton.edu/buying-paying/buy-supplies-and-equipment/capital-equipment?msclkid=b945f168b19e11ec94e281faf65db7f6.

> Capital equipment is an article of nonexpendable, tangible property with a useful life of more than one year, and an acquisition cost of $5,000 or more per unit. The $5,000 threshold includes: The item itself; Expenditures necessary to put the item in place; and Ancillary charges such as taxes, duty, protective in-transit insurance, freight, and installation costs.

Compare the procurement-related definitions of equipment at 2 C.F.R. § 200.33 and capital asset at 2 C.F.R. § 200.12. The Uniform Commercial Code of New York, § 9-102(33), defines equipment, as "goods other than inventory, farm products, or consumer goods", and is dependent upon definitions of the other terms. From a U.S. tax perspective relating to determinations of capital gains and losses, consider the definition of a capital asset at 26 U.S. Code § 1221, and the definition on the public website of the United States Internal Revenue Service: "Almost everything you own and use for personal purposes, pleasure, or investment is a capital asset." https://www.irs.gov/publications/p544#en_US_2021_publink100072479. From an international accounting perspective, consider International Accounting Standard 16 of the International Accounting Standards Board, which applies to property, plant, and equipment (broadly, fixed assets). For property owned by the U.S. federal government, consider Statement of Federal Financial Accounting Standards (SFFAS) 6: Accounting for Property, Plant, and Equipment, which defines property, plant, and equipment as "Tangible assets that (1) have an estimated useful life of 2 or more years, (2) are not intended for sale in the ordinary course of business, and (3) are intended to be used or available for use by the entity." Computer software is separately treated, including under SFFAS 10: Accounting for Internal Use Software. There are many other legal, tax, accounting, economic, and financial definitions of equipment, direct and through other related concepts.

[5] McMillen (2022-2), McMillen (2022-3), McMillen (2022-4), and McMillen (2022-5).

# Part II

## Assessing Involvement

Figure 1: Patrick Tracy Jackson

## Chapter Two

### Reflection

Patrick Tracy Jackson chose to take the train from Philadelphia to Boston on the morning of December 11, 1845. He was returning after a December 10 consultation with the eminent lawyer Horace Binney regarding two contracts—the Rolling Stock Contracts—between Locks & Canals and the Philadelphia & Reading. Train travel was the most expeditious alternative; but entailed approximately 16 hours of travel on different railroads and ferries sandwiched around an overnight stay in New York City. Jackson used the time to reflect on his meetings with Binney and the history of L&C's involvements in sales of locomotives and other rolling stock to railroads.[1]

Settling in for the ride, Jackson felt a bit wistful. He recalled his horseback rides between the Lowell and Waltham manufactories and his family home in Boston. Horseback passage was tranquil time, conducive to savoring the nuance and delicacy of sounds and smells and the intricacies of opportunities, risks, and decisional factors. Time to reflect, reconsider, deliberate, and plan. That which was thought known may not have been. The vantage of hindsight might yield clarification.

Jackson did not brood over imperfections in past decisions, although his memory for them and their implications was long. He was a practical man, well-suited to his managerial roles as a director and the treasurer of Locks & Canals and other companies. He sought to extract lessons from judgmental errors for application in the benefit of L&C and the other entities that he served. Jackson sought solutions.

The December 10 meeting with Binney was productive. Binney and Jackson devised a plan, in four movements, to address the P&R's defaulted debt under the Rolling Stock Contracts. They defined the plan and its progression. Refinements would come with implementation. Jackson was confident of the outcome. An outcome he had been unable to achieve after almost four years of near constant attention to the debt. He felt a sense of solace. For the first time in years.

Horace Binney was every bit the perceptive, penetrating, practical lawyer of his reputation. The visit with Binney upended much that Jackson thought he understood about his own work. In minutes, Binney dissected and then reharmonized the arrangement under the Rolling Stock Contracts. Artfully.

Without drama. Avoiding, for the moment, the dreaded collision of interests that litigation or asset seizure would entail. The plan ensured that L&C emerged with dignity and absolute power. The threat of remedies remained. If, when, and how the threat might proceed to force was completely within L&C's control, which increased the likelihood of achieving the desired result without the trauma of legal action.

The plan's elegant simplicity was apparent in its earliest phases, the first of which was completed before Jackson's homeward journey began. Jackson carried the seminal agreement. On December 10, immediately after meeting with Binney, the agreement was executed by John Tucker, the P&R's president, and William McKee, a trustee appointed by the P&R under the Engines Contract. It remained to be executed by Nathan Appleton and William Sturgis, the two trustees appointed by L&C. Jackson also carried a letter of capitulation from Tucker. Jackson would present both documents to the L&C board of directors at a December 13 meeting. Appleton and Sturgis would sign at that meeting, allowing Jackson to move to other steps in the plan. One of the remaining three had already been achieved, orally. It needed only to be formalized.[2]

After four years of grappling with the P&R debt, Jackson glimpsed resolution. L&C could rid itself of involvement with the debt in a later step in the plan. As importantly, the plan addressed other issues of relevance to L&C, most notably the P&R's enormous floating debt overhang. As well as devaluing the P&R debt, the floating debt threatened equity and debt investments that Jackson and other Boston Associates had made in the P&R since 1841.

The plan derived from the transactional structure of the Rolling Stock Contracts, which improved on the structure used in an 1839 sale of engines to the Baltimore and Susquehanna Railroad Company. The impetus for developing the Baltimore & Susquehanna structure was the debacle experienced by L&C in its sale of locomotives to the Pensacola Railroad in 1836.

In May of 1836 L&C agreed to sell to the Pensacola Railroad six locomotives, twelve passage cars, and wheels, axles, springs, and other iron work for one hundred burthen cars. Two engines were delivered in the winter of 1836-1837.[3]

Economic havoc from the Panic of 1837, Crisis of 1839, and Collapse of 1842 rendered default by the Pensacola Railroad inevitable. Systemic economic events were beyond L&C's control. Jackson was comfortable with that assessment. He did not capitulate to the systemic changes. The thought never crossed his mind. Capitulation was antithetical to all that was Patrick Tracy Jackson. His thoughts were on management of the adversities. That was where both his successes and his failures lay.[4]

Jackson drifted over the stream of events after onset of the Panic. In 1837 the Pensacola Railroad ceased all activities, including payments. The Bank of the United States,^A which played a leading role in the Pensacola transactions, surrendered to liquidation in 1841. By 1842, on the eve of executing the Running Gear Contract (the first of the two Rolling Stock Contracts), bank closures swept the country. Two days before execution of that contract, Samuel Bradford, the P&R treasurer, made a notation in his correspondence book, accentuated with three exclamation marks. The Pennsylvania Township and Mechanics Bank had that day closed its doors "*sine die*". Reportedly, the Manufacturers and Mechanics Bank had closed as well. As anticipated, bank shutterings were widespread.[5]

Jackson recalled the status of the Pensacola Railroad debt as L&C embarked on the Rolling Stock Contracts. The debt was $10,383.26 from July 31, 1837 through July 31, 1839, on an original purchase price of approximately $13,000 for two locomotives. No payments had been made since 1837 and interest was accruing. The debt was not included on L&C's financial statements for 1840. Jackson reinstated the debt on the 1842 financial statements, slightly reduced to $9,783.23. Yielding to the increasingly dismal prospects, Jackson classified the debt as "doubtful". That brought total doubtful debts for 1842 to $22,660.16, accompanied by an annual profit of $105,744.40 (an increase over previous years).[6]

Other reflections during the trip to Boston focused on factors that induced L&C's involvement in the Pensacola transaction. Confidence in the capabilities of L&C and Jackson's experiences with building locomotives and railroads were influential factors. Trust in some transaction participants, especially those associated with the BUS and Nicholas Biddle, was important. Which factors had been undervalued or inappropriately considered in the analysis? Clearly those relating to the Pensacola promoters and those pertaining to collateral security. Probably some regarding the BUS and people related to the BUS and Biddle. What lessons had Jackson taken from the Pensacola debacle in structuring the Baltimore & Susquehanna and Philadelphia & Reading transactions? There were many. All these matters Jackson revisited during his journey home.

Although still an L&C board member, Jackson was in retirement when the Pensacola Railroad transaction was arranged, focusing on personal investments. He

---

^A  References to the Bank of the United States (or BUS) are to The President, Directors and Company of the Bank of the United States created under PA Law (1836) No. 22 on February 18, 1836.

was taking losses—financial and emotional—on a project to develop bituminous coal fields near Lycoming Creek, Pennsylvania. He knew more losses would come on that project. To greater success, he completed construction of the Boston & Lowell railroad and stayed on in multiple roles after the first train ran on May 27, 1835. Jackson then focused on his Pemberton Square real estate development project in Boston. It was an offshoot of the need to develop stations and storage for the Boston & Lowell. Jackson suffered significant financial losses on the Pemberton Square project in 1838, and more in 1840.

The business and financial condition of Locks & Canals declined after the death of Kirk Boott on April 11, 1837. The L&C directors invited Jackson to forsake retirement to manage L&C. Losses on the Lycoming and Pemberton Square projects induced Jackson to accept. He became agent and treasurer in April of 1838.

By the time of his visit with Horace Binney, Jackson was again focused on retirement. He proffered his resignation as L&C treasurer on August 30, 1845. Like his previous resignations, the matter was referred to a committee, comprised of William Sturgis and John A. Lowell. The resignation was accepted on September 16, effective December 1. After thirty years of involvement with L&C and entities in Waltham and Lowell, Jackson was stepping away from day-to-day management of the businesses he conceived and nurtured.

Despite effectiveness of the resignation, on December 6 the L&C board directed Jackson to meet with Binney in Philadelphia regarding the P&R debt under the Rolling Stock Contracts. At the time, Jackson was no longer L&C treasurer; that position was held by John T. Morse. Jackson continued as a member of the board of directors. The duty of the debt stayed with Jackson.[7]

**Endnotes: Chapter Two**

[1] In 1845 there were two primary routes from Philadelphia to New York. One via the Camden & Amboy, leaving Philadelphia in the morning, with a steamboat between South Amboy and New York. The trip took approximately 5½ hours. Another involved a combination of railroads (and ferries) comprised of the New Jersey Railroad, the New Brunswick & Trenton, and the Philadelphia & Trenton, leaving Philadelphia around 4:30 p.m., taking approximately 4½ hours.

There were four primary routes from New York to Boston. The Long Island Railroad ran from Brooklyn to eastern Long Island, with a steamboat to Allyn's Point, and then railroad lines through Norwich and Worcester. Travel time was approximately 10½ hours. A second route was via steamboat from Battery Place to Stonington and the Boston & Providence or, in season, a steamboat direct to Newport and Providence with a connection to the Boston & Providence. A third line was comprised of a steamboat from New York to New London and Allyn's Point and railroads through Norwich and Worcester. The fourth route was a steamboat from New York to New Haven and railroads through Hartford, Springfield, and Worcester. Travel time for each of the last three routes was approximately 13½ hours.

See Disturnell (1846), with route tables and travel times. For the Camden & Amboy, see Dunbar (1915-III), at 991-96, and for the Boston & Providence and Boston & Worcester, Dunbar (1915-III), at 996-1007.

2. The December 10 agreement is in L&C Minutes (December 13, 1845) and Binney's hand-written draft is at HA 1520, Box 1220, Folder 9022.

3. For the rolling stock, Pensacola RR AR (1836).

4. For agreement on the Pensacola Railroad contract by early May of 1836, Jack Downing Letter (1836, May 30), likely penned by Charles A. Davis, and Pensacola Gazette (1836, May 7).

5. Samuel Bradford was born in Boston in 1803. He was a close friend of Ralph Waldo Emerson and William H. Furness, from childhood until their respective deaths. Bradford worked with the Boston merchant and auction house of Whitwell, Bond & Co. from 1816 until 1825 when he formed a short-lived mercantile partnership with J. W. Storer in Portsmouth, New Hampshire. He returned to the Boston importing house of Sewall, Williams & Co., which failed soon after his return. Bradford then relocated to New York and joined Davenport, Wycoff & Barnes as a bookkeeper, living with William Emerson, the brother of Ralph Waldo. Shortly thereafter he started a crockery business, which was soon wound up.

In 1830 Bradford's sister was invited to Philadelphia by Thomas A. Biddle. Bradford accompanied his sister. On March 31, 1830, Biddle offered Bradford a position with the Little Schuylkill Navigation and Railroad Company, in which Biddle had an interest. Bradford was secretary and treasurer of the Little Schuylkill until May 23, 1844. Bradford was elected secretary and treasurer of the P&R on January 8, 1838. He held both offices at the P&R until April 1856, when he resigned as secretary, continuing as treasurer until 1881. He worked closely with Patrick Tracy Jackson on the Rolling Stock Contracts.

By 1841 the trustees of the BUS owned essentially all stock and unsecured bonds of the Little Schuylkill. The bonds were sold to other Philadelphia bankers. On September 7, 1841, Edwin Smith and Bradford were appointed trustees of the Little Schuylkill, managing for the benefit of the bondholders until May of 1852.

For Bradford, Bradford (1880), with the Little Schuylkill offer at 66 and 68 and P&R involvements at 68-9. For Bradford's note on the bank closings, P&R Corr. (March 1, 1842), at 318.

6. The L&C work logs and financial statements reference the "Pensacola Railroad" receivable. Gibb (1947), at 12, surmised it was charged off as a bad debt. That is likely; but not definitively determined. The debt was $220 on July 31, 1836 (L&C Minutes (September 27, 1836)) as L&C began work. For the debt through 1839, L&C Minutes

(October 20, 1838 and October 26, 1839). For its absence on the 1840 statements, L&C Minutes (September 18 and 20, 1840). For the reduced Pensacola Railroad debt, doubtful debts, and profits for 1842, L&C Minutes (September 20, 1842).

Gibb (1950), Appendix 6, at 641, does not include the Pensacola Railroad as a railroad for which L&C built locomotives (Appendix 6 is based upon a list provided to Gibb by Charles Fisher). Brown (1959), at 11, identifies two L&C engines as acquired by the Pensacola Railroad in 1836. Brown's determinations of L&C production and delivery match those of L&C in 1836 and for all but one year in the 1835-1840 period (where the variation is two engines). The carried receivable is consistent with the sale price, in late 1836, for two engines. Von Gerstner (1842-1843), at 744-45 and note 39, indicates that the Pensacola Railroad possessed two engines in the spring of 1839.

[7] For Jackson's resignation letter, L&C Minutes (August 30, 1845). For acceptance of his resignation, L&C Minutes (September 16, 1845). For the direction to meet with Binney, L&C Minutes (December 6, 1845).

## Chapter Three

### L&C Machine Shop

**The Machine Shop**

The determinative factor in the decision to sell rolling stock to the Pensacola Railroad was the need of the Locks & Canals machine shop for work to absorb available capacity. L&C began experiencing a diminution in work in 1836. It was worrisome, but not ominous. The Pensacola Railroad contract was irresistible temptation. The equipment was to be delivered by February 1, 1837.[1]

Thoughts of the Locks & Canals machine shop gave Jackson a pause in pride. It was Jackson's jewel.

Jackson recalled how the mechanics who comprised the machine shop, originally housed in Boston Manufacturing Company, were interviewed, hired, and originally worked at Jackson's Broad Street counting house. The mechanics, including the brilliant chief mechanic, Paul Moody, moved to Waltham in November of 1813 when Jackson acquired the failing paper mill of John Boise on the Charles River and built a new brick mill for Boston Manufacturing. Jackson and Moody established the machine shop to create and build the unique machinery required for the integrated textile manufacturing operations conceived by Francis Cabot Lowell. When hired, Moody was only thirty-four, but already had over twenty years' experience with textile machinery. During his time with the machine shop, which lasted until his death in July 1831, Moody was recognized as a leading American mechanic and Jackson and Moody developed a close friendship and deep mutual respect. Through their prodigious efforts, the L&C shop became one of the premier machine shops in the United States.[2]

Jackson nurtured the shop and arranged its expansion into the building of locomotives and other rolling stock. He arranged its passage from Boston Manufacturing into, successively, Merrimack Manufacturing Company and, in 1823, Locks & Canals. At its transition into L&C, the machine shop employed over three hundred mechanics.

The three-quarter mile Pawtucket Canal around Pawtucket Falls was selected as the expansion site when Boston Manufacturing outgrew the water power capabilities at Waltham and no alternative site could be located on the Charles River. Merrimack Manufacturing was founded as the expansion vehicle. Jackson remembered fondly his determination, with Nathan Appleton, to expand manufacturing away from coarse cotton goods to calicoes and finer quality goods. Competition in coarse goods was increasing, and prices were dropping. The country's westward expansion raised the standard of living, and thus demand for more refined products.[3]

In 1821 and 1822 Jackson orchestrated the acquisition of Locks & Canals, which owned the Pawtucket Canal. L&C remained dormant until, in 1825, Jackson implemented a restructuring. The restructuring enabled L&C to acquire the machine shop as well as real estate, water power rights, and mill privileges that had been purchased by and on behalf of Merrimack Manufacturing in and near East Chelmsford.[4] Guided by Jackson and compatriots, the City of Lowell was created by Merrimack Manufacturing and L&C. Those were seminal events in establishment of the Lowell operations.[5]

**Opportunity, Innovation, and Risk**

Patrick Tracy Jackson had an acute sense of opportunity. Especially in areas where technology impacted power. He was a product of the scientific and technological spirit that influenced Oliver Evans and was propagated by Evans in his book, THE YOUNG MILL-WRIGHT AND MILLER'S GUIDE.[6] Innovation was pervasive. For Jackson, innovation related to his beliefs regarding personal responsibility and initiative. He did not have to clearly foresee the innovation associated with a new opportunity. He acted on the belief that innovation would come. Jackson's successes with textile manufacturing, waterpower, mill power, dams, waterwheels, construction, and lighting, and his involvements with Paul Moody's many innovations, solidified his beliefs, his sense of confidence, and his focus on power and its application in manufacturing, transportation, and communication. Jackson internalized the principle that the only constant is change and, concomitantly, the inevitability of innovation.

Jackson was comfortable with risks that accompanied innovation and change. His risk tolerance had always been high. He had learned to accept—even relish— risk associated with opportunity. His merchant activities laid the base, including his time in India, Cape Town, and the Cape of Good Hope. Early experiences in overcoming financial adversity emboldened him. The Waltham and Lowell textile ventures were rife with risk and rendered plentiful rewards. His sense of confidence and tolerance for high levels of risk derived from his successes, combined with his belief in personal action, personal responsibility, and the ability to innovate and manage.[7]

Not all viewed his risk tolerances as prudent. Nor had all his risk taking been judicious. Witness Francis C. Lowell bailing him out in earlier years, with some scolding, and his experiences with Lycoming coal and Pemberton Square. Some characterized Jackson as a reckless speculator, a plunger, even a gambler. But, in his own mind, Jackson was untroubled, and usually undeterred, by risks assessed. They could be defined, analyzed, and managed.[8]

Jackson took risks—including large risks—in areas he adjudged to hold potential for future development: manufacturing, transportation, communication, and power. The endeavors in which he took the plunge were usually discreetly defined and circumscribed projects. The nature of the risks was relatively determinable. Occurrences could not be predicted, of course. Some occurrences were preventable. Many risks and occurrences were manageable. Risk was the nature, even the essence, of business. To Jackson, business was about management of tractable risks.

Jackson's approach to risk—including identification, assessment, and management—contrasted with that of William H. Chase, the lead promoter of the Pensacola Railroad and related ventures. The contrast should have given L&C, including Jackson as a director, more pause.

Chase's work in building forts for the United States Army Corps of Engineers showed him to be competent, perceptive, and, in most engineering matters, attentive to detail. He was certainly ambitious and confident. His Pensacola plans were expansive, even grandiose. Development of an entire New City in Pensacola, a new railroad across the south, a new bank in Pensacola, and a series of canals. Restructuring of cotton sales of a large region. The development of the entire Gulf of Mexico, militarily and economically. Chase's different undertakings were interrelated, each feeding into the others. On a scale and set of assumptions that was uncomfortable for Jackson.

Chase's plans were general, conceptual, and, at times without definitional detail. Often there was inadequate circumscription of risk by element or project. Undertakings were indiscrete; each element bled risk into each other element. Chase seemed a baronial promoter enamored of his conceptions and either relatively uninformed regarding the necessities of realization or overly confident. In any case, he bolted ahead on his projects, at times without prudent planning. An example was the building of Fort McRee without adequate investigation of its physical foundation. An engineering failure, it was cracking by the Civil War.

Nevertheless, Locks & Canals was in need. The opportunity lay within L&C's competence: building locomotives and other railroad equipment. It entailed risks familiar to L&C. The enormity of the risks was not decisive, nor was the involvement with unproven technology. Jackson had learned to manage risks of that scale and type. He was a master of processes within that nexus. Building locomotives was risky, as was building railroads. Jackson had enthusiastically mastered each. These experiences inclined L&C toward a decision to build locomotives for a distant railroad in May of 1836.

Figure 2: Stephenson *Planet* Class Engine, 1834

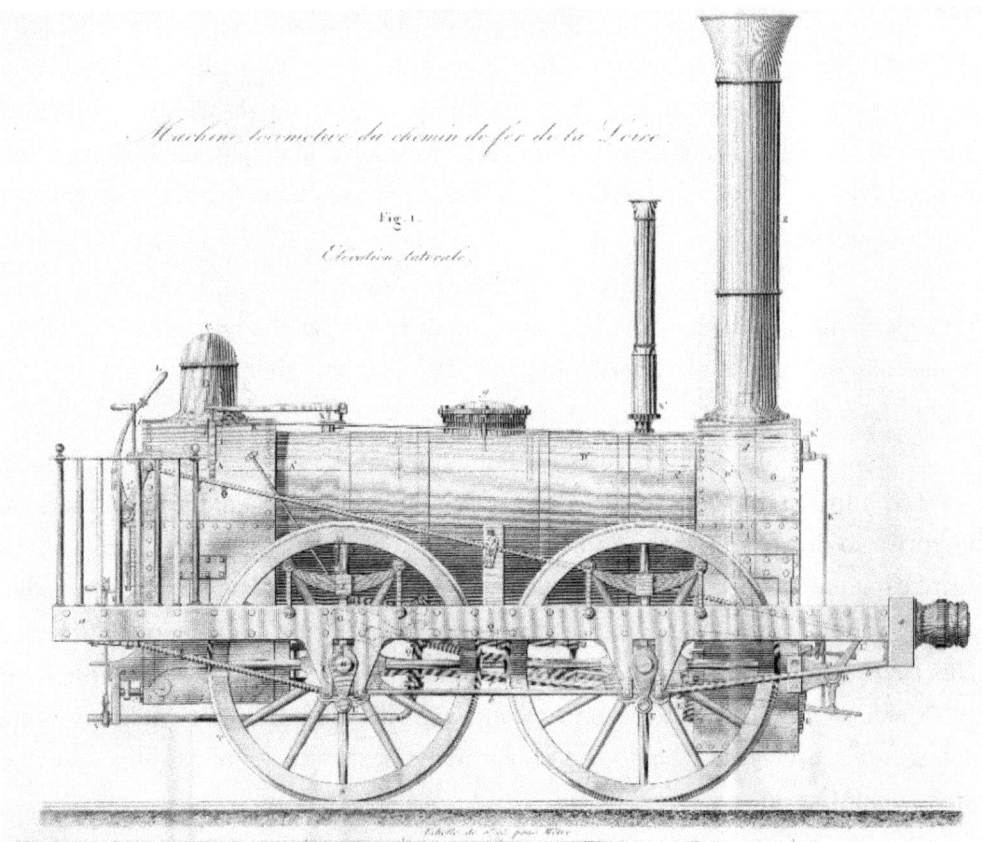

**Building Locomotives**

By the early 1830s, Jackson believed that steam and railroad transportation presented boundless opportunities. The locomotive engine presented the most immediately realizable opportunity; and facilitated realization of associated opportunities, such as coal and iron. Building locomotives was a process Jackson understood. Akin to building textile machinery, it was a circumscribed undertaking amenable to control by mechanics, as engineers were then described.

L&C commenced involvement with locomotive engines in 1832 when Jackson imported two *Planet* class 2-2-0 steam locomotives from Robert Stephenson of Newcastle-on-Tyne, England. The L&C machine shop assembled them in East Chelmsford. Figure 2 is an illustration of a Stephenson 0-4-0 *Planet* class locomotive engine from 1834. Figure 3 is an illustration of a *Planet* class locomotive, the *Bristol*, built for the Western Railroad. Figure 27 is an illustration of a *Planet* class engine (the *Baltimore*) built by L&C in 1837 for the Baltimore & Susquehanna.[A]

After acquiring the Stephenson engines, L&C began building its own. The first was completed in June 1835 for the Boston & Lowell. The intention was to name that engine the *Jackson*, after Patrick Tracy Jackson. The name was a tad inappropriate in the Whig community in which L&C operated. The more so given Jackson's affiliations: he served as chairman of the Whigs of Boston by 1838. The engine was christened the *Patrick*.[9]

The *Planet* class became the model, for about ten years, for engines built by L&C and some U.S. builders.[B] The engines built for the Pensacola Railroad were *Planet* class 2-2-0 engines, modeled on the *Bristol*, shown in Figure 3.[10] Three of the eight built for the Baltimore & Susquehanna from 1837 to 1839 were of the *Planet* class: the *Pennsylvania* (No. 16), the *Osceola*, and the *Pittsburgh*. The other five were 0-4-0 engines: the *York* (No. 17), the *Howard* (No. 19), the *Baltimore* (No. 22), the *Susquehanna* (No. 24), the *Pittsburgh*, and the *Maryland*. Of the 0-4-0 group, the *York* and the *Pittsburgh* were built in 1839; the others in 1837.[11]

Indicative of the commitment to locomotive building, in April 1834 L&C engaged an experienced railroad man, George Washington Whistler, to supervise building. In August of 1835, L&C authorized construction of additional facilities for engine building.[12]

---

[A] The Whyte notation for classifying steam locomotives by wheel type refers to, sequentially, the leading, driving, and the tailing axles, and the number of wheels on each axle. A 4-4-0 has 4 wheels on two leading axles, 4 wheels on two driving axles, and no tailing wheels. The system was developed by Frederick Methvan Whyte of the New York Central Railroad in 1900. During most of the nineteenth century, three types of arrangements were favored in the U.S.: 4-2-0, 4-4-0 (the most popular), and 4-6-0.

[B] *Old Ironsides*, Matthias W. Baldwin's first locomotive engine, was built in 1832 on the *Planet* class model. The *E. L. Miller*, Baldwin's second engine, built for the Charleston and Hamburg Rail Road Company on February 18, 1834, differed from *Planet* class engines. It had six wheels, one pair of 54-inch driving wheels at the rear of the firebox, 10x16 inch cylinders, a horizontal boiler, a Bury dome firebox, a wooden frame outside the wheels that supported the boiler, a four-wheeled center-bearing swiveling or "bogie" truck that formed a flexible unit, and a half-crank axle at the back of the firebox. Baldwin used this design for many years, and it was copied by many other builders.

Figure 4 shows the *Planet* and related passenger carriages in 1834. It was built for the Camden & Amboy railroad, possibly under the supervision of Robert L. Stevens.

Figure 3: *Bristol* Locomotive Engine

Whistler was well known to Jackson, having assisted with building the Boston & Lowell. Before joining L&C, Whistler, a graduate of the U.S. Military Academy, worked for the Baltimore and Ohio Railroad Company, the Baltimore & Susquehanna, the Paterson and Hudson River Railroad Company, the New York, Providence and Boston Rail Road Company, and others. He worked on designing the first wood-fired steam locomotive in the U.S. He left L&C in 1837 and moved to Stonington, Connecticut to build another railroad. While in that endeavor, Whistler began consulting with the Western Railroad Company, becoming its chief engineer in 1840.

One of Whistler's five sons with Anna Matilda McNeill (his second wife) was named after William Gibbs McNeill. McNeill was Whistler's brother-in-law and a fellow engineer. McNeill participated in the Pensacola Railroad endeavor, aligned with the BUS and Nicholas Biddle. Jackson knew McNeill intimately; and respected him. McNeill worked with Jackson at the Boston & Lowell and the Boston and Providence Rail-Road Corporation. McNeill also worked at the Baltimore & Ohio. One of Whistler's sons was named after Kirk Boott, one of Jackson's closest associates at Locks & Canals. Another son, James Abbott McNeill Whistler, was then only seven years of age but demonstrated an aptitude for painting.[13]

**Selling Locomotives**

While Jackson harbored no doubts about building engines, he had misgivings about selling engines to the Pensacola Railroad. Sale to a Florida railroad was contrary to L&C's customary practices. Because of the underdeveloped state of transportation and the high costs of transporting large equipment, regional sales were the norm in the 1830s and 1840s.

In 1835, at least ten engines were placed in operation by L&C. Eight were sold in Massachusetts and two in New York. In 1836, fourteen or fifteen engines were built, with all but two going to New England customers. Those two went to the Pensacola Railroad. In 1837 four engines were sold to the Baltimore & Susquehanna, with the remainder sold in New England. During 1838, eleven engines were delivered, and nine were on hand. Fifteen were built in 1839 and six in 1840. Locomotive sales were $83,800 for 1838. The price for a locomotive was $6,500 to $11,000. L&C usually sold at the lower end of that range. L&C profit on an engine priced at $7,000 was $2,200, or 31%.[14]

By 1838 L&C was the third largest U.S. locomotive builder (32 engines to 15 railroads in six states, with only two—those sold to the Pensacola Railroad—being sold outside New England, New York, and Maryland). Only the Baldwin Locomotive Works (78) and the Norris Locomotive Works (34) built more engines than L&C. Over half of all locomotive builders went out of business after the Panic of 1837 and its sequelae. By 1840 there were only six to ten.[15]

By the end of 1839, in addition to four engines for the Baltimore & Susquehanna, L&C built engines for the Boston & Lowell (the *Suffolk* and the *Medford*), the Boston & Portland (the *Meteor* and the *Berwick*), the Boston & Providence (the *King Philip* re the *Attleborough*), the Boston & Worcester (the *Meteor*), the Eastern Railroad Company (the *Piscataqua* and the *Naumkeag*), the New Bedford and Taunton Railroad Company (the *Taunton*), the Taunton Branch Railroad Company (the *Rocket*), and the Western Railroad (the *Hampden*, the *Berkshire*, the *Hampshire*, the *Worcester*, and the *Suffolk*). L&C and George Washington Whistler built the 9-ton engine used for opening the Baltimore & Susquehanna line. The engine pulled two passenger cars, carrying 140 passengers, two miles up an ascent of 84 feet in seven minutes, a rate of almost 19 miles per hour. "This was by no means equal to the full power of the engine. Its maximum, I believe, has never been tested."[16]

In its thirty years of building locomotives, L&C built fewer than 150. Notwithstanding the 1837 Panic and its aftermath, L&C built 43 engines and more than a thousand coal cars between 1839 and 1845, as well as running gear, brakes, and other rolling stock. Even in 1836, when it inked the agreement to sell engines to the Pensacola Railroad, L&C's prospects for building locomotives were encouraging.

### Endnotes: Chapter Three

[1] For the L&C equipment, Pensacola RR AR (1836), issued as of July 1, 1836. The report indicated that, in March 1837, the Pensacola Railroad ordered 1,500 tons of iron rail, with plates and spikes, for October 1, 1837 delivery, expecting that 500 tons would be laid in each of October and November. Disposition of the iron is addressed in Chapter Thirteen, under "BoP Commissioner's Report".

[2] For the machine shop's history, Gibb (1950), with its sequential passage at 55-8. For Boston Manufacturing machinists at Broad Street and early development of the machine shop, Unger (2013), at 1-57. For Moody, Connors (2014), Bagnall (1884), Gibb 1950, at 26-39, Jeremy (1973), especially at 45 *et seq.*, and *Moody v. Fiske* (1820) (one of Moody's patent infringement actions). Moody was buried in Lowell on July 8, 1831: Lowell Vital Statistics (1930), at 214.

Boston Manufacturing was incorporated on February 23, 1813, pursuant to MA Law (1813) Ch. XCII. Jackson made the largest investment ($20,000). Between them, two of Jackson's brothers took $15,000. Francis C. Lowell invested $15,000. Lowell and the Jacksons controlled 50% of the stock. Nathan Appleton and Uriah Cotting each invested $5,000. Benjamin Gorham and Warren Dutton, each a brother-in-law of Jackson, took $5,000 between them, in equal amounts. See Gibb (1950), at 9, and Dalzell (1987), at 5-73.

3   The Nathan Appleton version posits that Moody identified the site. Patrick M. Malone's skepticism seems apt. It is difficult to imagine that Patrick Tracy Jackson and others were unaware of the potential of Pawtucket Falls and the condition of L&C given that Jonathan Jackson, Patrick's father, was the first president of and a stockholder in L&C, located at Pawtucket Falls. Johnathan still owned 15 shares at his death in 1810. Appleton's version is Appleton (1858), at 17-9. For Malone's observations, Malone (2009) at 21-2. For the 15 shares held at death, Jonathan Jackson Will (1806), listing of assets, at 390. Malone (2009) provides a view of L&C and the textile, manufacturing, and engineering enterprises at Lowell.

    The Merrimack Manufacturing articles of association were written on December 1, 1821, three months after it commenced acquiring L&C shares and lands in East Chelmsford. Six hundred shares were authorized. Appleton and Jackson each obtained 180, each of Kirk and John W. Boot obtained 90, and Paul Moody obtained 60. Merrimack Manufacturing was incorporated on February 6, 1822 by Kirk and John Boott and William and Ebenezer Appleton, pursuant to MA Law (1822) Ch. XLVI. Those individuals sold some of their shares to investors prior to incorporation to finance the purchase of L&C shares, land, and mill powers and pay construction costs: Gregory (1975), at 178-81. MA Law (1822) Ch. XLVI, § 3, provided that each shareholder was personally liable for Merrimack Manufacturing's debts incurred while the person was a shareholder, including after that person no longer held the shares.

4   For acquisition and transfer of stock, land, and mill powers of L&C, Gregory (1975), at 173-93. L&C was acquired by stealth in the fall of 1821, using, as agents, Thomas M. Clark of Newburyport, an L&C director, and Henry Andrews, of Boston, to acquire 352 of the 600 outstanding shares. Land and mill powers were acquired by stealth, except from a few local persons who learned of the development plans, forcing purchases at high prices. Thereafter, the stock, land, and mill powers were transferred to Jackson, Nathan Appleton, Kirk and John Boott, and Paul Moody. They were transferred to the directors only after Merrimack Manufacturing was chartered in February 1822. The directors held the shares and assets in trust for the next three years. Transfer of shares and assets to trustees was a frequent technique in the nineteenth century. See Morley (2016), Silberstein-Loeb (2015), at 193, and Mahoney (2000), at 884.

    For the progression of events from the perspective of the L&C board of directors, see L&C Minutes (November 14 and December 11 and 26, 1821, and January 8 and 17, February 4, and March 4, 1822). For the statutory authorization to acquire Merrimack Manufacturing real estate, water power, mill powers, and other estates in Chelmsford, Dracut, and Tewksbury on January 27, 1825, see MA Law (1825) Ch. XLVII. This law did not charter or incorporate a new L&C entity. For the 1825 revitalization of L&C, Gregory (1975), at 183-84 (asserting formation of a new L&C of the same name). For

Gibb's position, Gibb (1950), at 67-9. For Clark's position, Clark (1924), at 30 (the reference to "1882" is an error).

This author's reading of a source cited by Gregory (at 184, footnote 44) is consistent with revitalization of the original L&C (rather than a new L&C); see Appleton (1858), at 27-8, describing an allocation of 1,200 shares in the existing L&C to holders of that number of shares in Merrimack Manufacturing and "the expediency of organizing the Canal Company, by selling them the land and water power not required by the Merrimack Manufacturing Company." And see *Lowell v. L&C* (1843) and Gibb (1950), at 69, each recognizing the sale to L&C (as part of an asset transfer) of $60,000 of stock in L&C held by Merrimack Manufacturing. That stock sale generated a tidy profit for Jackson, Boott, Moody, and others involved in the 1821 L&C acquisition. After the asset transfer, L&C held the machine shop, stock in L&C, and certain real estate, water power rights, and mill privileges previously held by Merrimack Manufacturing.

[5] L&C was incorporated under MA Law (1792) Ch. XV. Lowell was chartered as a municipal corporation on April 1, 1836: MA Law (1836) Ch. CXXVIII. The city was named after Francis Cabot Lowell who, with Jackson, Boott, and others, transformed East Chelmsford into a hub of the American textile industry. For the city charter and related documents, Lowell City Documents (1846). In 1826 Lowell had 3,000 residents. By 1836 it was 18,000, and by 1840 21,000. By 1844 there were eleven primary textile manufacturers in Lowell, as well as other companies.

Formation of city of Lowell is discussed in Miles (1845), Appleton (1858), Cowley (1868), Waters (1917), Coburn (1920), Persey (1990), Merrill (1946), and Gregory (1975), at 173-93. See also Morris (2012), at 97-103, and Malone & Parrott (1998). For the populations in 1826 and 1833 and short descriptions of the eleven companies in 1844, Merchants' Magazine (1844, May), at 426-27, noting that L&C employed 1,000-1,200 people.

[6] Evans (1795), of which fifteen editions were published, the last in 1860 being edited by Thomas P. Jones, Superintendent of Patents in 1829 and Patent Officer examiner in 1837 and 1838. Oliver Evans was a talented inventor and ardent advocate for rights of inventors and patentees. He worked in the areas of textile cards, milling (including the introduction of leather belts in the automation of flour production), high pressure steam engines, dredging, refrigeration, and integrated continuous production systems, among others. His patent disputes established legal precedents. Of the first five patent law cases considered by the U.S. Supreme Court, four involved Evans (two were the same case): *Evans v. Jordan & Morehead* (1815), *Evans v. Eaton* (1818), *Evans v. Eaton* (1822), and *Evans v. Hettich* (1822) (the first case before the Supreme Court was *Tyler v. Tuel* (1810)). The first private law of the U.S. congress extending a patent related to an Evans patent, the third issued in the U.S. This patent was one of the most litigated in U.S. history and the subject of twelve reported court decisions between 1807 and 1822 (the case survived the death of Evans in 1819). See Devine (1983) and Frederico (1945).

[7] For Jackson's merchant activities, including his time in India, Cape Town, and the Cape of Good Hope, Porter (1937), at 592-772.

⁸ Jackson was involved in a venture with Joseph and Henry Lee that failed in 1811, bringing Jackson to the brink of bankruptcy. Lowell, while in Europe, wrote Jackson on November 16, 1811, bluntly advising against haste in building his fortune, incurrence of excessive indebtedness, and endorsements of indebtedness of others. See Dalzell (1987), at 9, quoting portions of the letter.

⁹ For Whyte's classification system, Whyte (1900), at 374, and, for naming conventions in other countries and before acceptance of the Whyte notation, Gaskell (1952). For favored wheel arrangements, Cupper (2001-1). For Jackson's confirmation of initial engine building and the purchase from Stevenson (Jackson's spelling), Jackson-Stevenson Letter (1839). One Stephenson engine was sold to the Boston & Providence and the other was used by L&C. Letter of Jackson to Stephenson, February 9, 1839, quoted in Brown (1959), at 20. For the first L&C-built locomotives, Clark (1924), Hay (1975), an unpublished paper kindly made available by Patrick M. Malone, and Brown (1959), at 11, 18, 20, 21, 22, 23, 24, 25, 30, 31, 32, 40, 44, 48, 49, 50, 60, 71, 74, and 75. For Jackson as chairman of the Whigs of Boston, Boston Courier (1838, November 5) and Boston Courier (1838, November 8). For Robert Stephenson and his father, George, Smiles (1868).

The *Patrick* was the first of six 2-2-0 engines built by L&C for the Boston & Lowell in 1835 (the others being, sequentially, the *Lowell*, the *Boston*, the *Merrimack*, the *Concord*, and the *Nashua*). In 1835, L&C built two engines for the Boston & Providence (the *Lowell* and the *Providence*), one for the Buffalo and Niagara Falls Railroad Company (the *Buffalo*), and one for the Paterson & Hudson (the *Whistler*).

¹⁰ Hildreth (1959), at 402, identified the *Bristol* (built for the Western Railroad) as the model for engines built by L&C for the Pensacola Railroad. See also Clark (1924), at 46.

¹¹ For the *E. L. Miller* and matters in the footnote, Sanford (1924), at 9-10 and 20, and Baldwin History (1920), at 14-6. For the four 1837 engines, Brown (1959), at 17-8, Taber (2008), at 241, Hay (1975), at 3, and Treasury Steam-Engines Letter (1838), at K-3. Brown (1959) identifies six engines delivered by L&C to the B&S in 1837: the *Pittsburgh* and the *Osceola*, each being a 2-2-0 with 11x18 inch cylinders and 54-inch drivers, the *Maryland*, the *Susquehanna*, and the *Howard*, each being a 0-4-0 with 12x18 inch cylinders and 48-inch drivers, and the *Baltimore*, an 0-4-0 with 11x16 inch cylinders and a 54-inch driver. Taber (2008), at 241, lists the same six as Brown and observes that the *Howard*, the *Osceola*, and the *Baltimore* were probably rebuilt to 4-2-0 and many were replaced by larger engines before the 1854 reorganization into the Northern Central. Brown and Taber state that one additional engine was delivered by L&C in 1838 (the *Pennsylvania*), and one in 1839 (the *York*). The 1838 delivery is not mentioned in the B&S statement to the Maryland Committee on Internal Improvements; it may be an engine that was built in 1837 and put on the road in 1838, as indicated by the Northern Central AR (1857), at 36 (also listing the other engines, as stated in the text). Von Gerstner (1842-1843), at 241, mentions all eight engines (not by name). See also White (1968-1), at 8, with a picture of the *Baltimore* on a B&S advertising flyer shown on 9, and observing, at 8 and 10, that L&C was building the same engine in 1839.

12   Whistler's arrangement with the Western Railroad continued until 1842, when he moved to Russia, acting as the consulting engineer of the St. Petersburg to Moscow railway together with his son, George W. Whistler, Jr. Whistler was born in Fort Wayne, Indiana on May 19, 1800 and died on April 7, 1849 in St. Petersburg. A short biography of Whistler is Vose (1887). See also Fisher (1947), BHS Whistler (1926), and Drake (1879), at 975. For development of anthracite-fueled engines, see Warner (1940).

13   James Abbott McNeill Whistler was born on July 10, 1834 in Lowell.

14   For regional sales, Gibb (1947), at 94-5, and Appendix 6, at 641 (which does not list engines built for the Pensacola Railroad), and White (1968-1), at 15-6. Eight Massachusetts engine sales are identified in Brown (1959), at 21 and 22 (six for the Boston & Lowell and two for the Boston & Providence; at 25 and 50 two are identified for New York (one for the Buffalo & Niagara Falls and one for the Paterson & Hudson). Five are identified for Massachusetts and two for New York in Treasury Steam-Engines Letter (1838), Gibb (1947), at 94, and Appendix 6, at 641, and Hay (1975). For 1836 sales, Brown (1959) identifies fourteen total: at 22 (two for the Boston & Portland), 24 (one for the Boston & Worcester), 40 (one for the Long Island Railroad), 48-9 (six for the New York, Providence and Boston Railroad Company), 60 (one for the Philadelphia, Wilmington and Baltimore Railroad Company), 71 (one for the Taunton Branch), and 11 (two for the Alabama, Florida and Georgia Rail Road Company, the legal name of the Pensacola Railroad). Treasury Steam-Engines Letter (1838), Gibb (1947), at 94 and 641, and Hay (1975) specify a total of fifteen.

For locomotive prices and financing arrangements, McMillen (2022-4), (Chapter Thirty, discussing the PR-BW Engines Contract (1844), the PR-BW Engines Contract (1845), and the PR-BW Engines Contract (1846)), Gibb (1947), at 11, Gibb (1950), at 95, von Gerstner (1842-1843), at 302-033, and Fisher (1947), at 40. Von Gerstner and Gibb each indicate a price of $7,000 for 12-ton L&C engines in 1838. The price was $6,500 in 1839 and 1843, especially after Baldwin's 1842 patenting of the flexible beam truck. The Western Railroad purchased L&C locomotives for $10,750 in 1840 and from Ross Winans in 1841 for $11,000: Fisher (1947), at 40 and 41, respectively. For the profit on early engine sales, Gibb (1947), at 11-2, and Gibb (1950), at 95.

15   For the 1838 status of L&C, Gibb (1947), at 11-2, and Appendix 6, at 641 (Appendix 6 lists two engines sold to the Marietta & Cincinnati between 1835 and 1840, although it is unclear what railroad is referenced as the Belpré (later Marietta) and Cincinnati Railroad Company which was incorporated on March 8, 1845). Production and relative status data are determined from Treasury Steam-Engines Letter (1838) and Knight & Latrobe (1838). Information regarding the Boston & Lowell is in Knight & Latrobe (1838), at 11-3. See the listing of engines and their builders in Brown (1959) and Taber (2008), at 21. For Winans, Sagle (1947) (listing Winans-built locomotives) and White (1963). Baldwin's firms had different names through the years, including Baldwin & Whitney. See Baldwin Catalogue (1907) for the names and principals from 1831 to 1907. Use of the moniker "Baldwin Locomotive Works" began in 1867 in connection with the reorganization of the company following the death of Matthias W. Baldwin in 1866. Joy

(1878), at 635. For the Baldwin Locomotive Works, see Brown (1995-1), Baldwin Works (1897) (a company history), Soloman (2010), White (1968-2), and Clark (1966). Biographies of Matthias W. Baldwin are Calkins (1867) and Kelly (1946). For the Norris Locomotive Works, see White (1984), Brown (1959), at 9-10 and in each railroad entry, and Dewhurst (1950).

Regarding other builders in the 1830s and early 1840s, see Batson (1970) (starting in late 1833), Becker, Fisher & Jackson (1930) (starting in 1832), Bell & Fisher (1929) (starting in 1838), Dome (1970) (starting in 1838), Hart (1946), at 1-2 and 9-119 (1946) (including, at 25-35, discussion of locomotives built between 1836 and 1871), Firm Histories (2007) (a comprehensive historical survey in brief descriptions, with some discussion of early builders), Sagle (1972) (Mt. Clare Shop, for repairs, from 1829), White (1980-1) (Miller and the *Best Friend of Charleston*), Fisher (1942), White (1980-2) (including Harlan & Hollingsworth (also Betts, Harlan & Hollingsworth) of Wilmington: "perhaps the first firm to establish itself specifically as a railroad car builder"), White (1980-3) (Holmes Hinkley and Boston Locomotive Works), White (1984) (Norris Works), White & Edson (1974) (from 1837), White (1968-1), and Colvin (1902), a survey of early builders. Cupper (2007-2) is an index of articles on early builders appearing in RAILROAD HISTORY and RAILWAY & LOCOMOTIVE HISTORICAL SOCIETY BULLETIN. And see Brown (1874) and, for engravings of early engines, White (1972). For locomotives built before 1839 for the B&S, von Gerstner (1842-1843), at 667. For locomotives built in 1839, Brown (1959), at 18, 21, 22, 23, 24, 31, 44, 71, 74, and 75. For L&C-built locomotives in 1835-1845, Gibb (1950), at 641, Appendix 6. Brown (1959) identifies 22 engines for 1839-1840.

For diminution of locomotive building during the 1837 Panic and its aftermath, White (1968-1), at 13 and Appendix A at 449 (positing ten), and Brown (1995-1), at 12 (positing eight) and at 9 (noting that Baldwin produced only nine engines in 1840, down from a high of 40 in 1837), and Gibb (1950), at 93-4 (positing six).

16   A&ER AR (1838), at 123.

Figure 4: Camden & Amboy, 1834

## Chapter Four

### Railroad Experience

**Generally**

Experience with the development of railroads was another factor that inclined L&C to sell rolling stock to the start-up Pensacola Railroad. That experience resided primarily in members of the L&C board of directors, especially members that served as railroad directors. L&C directors who worked with railroads other than the Boston & Lowell had direct involvements with operations and policy formulation. Directors who served the Boston & Lowell functioned more in a review capacity because Patrick Tracy Jackson made essentially all operational and policy decisions, although judiciously conferring with directors.[1]

Jackson was immersed in developing transportation systems as well as building transportation equipment, usually with other Boston Associates and most avidly, but not exclusively, when Massachusetts businesses benefited. Early involvements were part of an effort to promote Boston in competition with New York and Philadelphia, and in implementing the Massachusetts railroad initiative as the internal improvements debate tilted toward the railroads and away from canals.[2]

Boston Associates who worked with Jackson on railroad projects included William Sturgis, John Bryant, Nathan Hale, Abbott Lawrence, William Appleton, Nathan Appleton, George W. Pratt, George Lyman, and Joseph F. Loring, among others. Their projects included the Boston & Lowell, the Boston & Worcester, the Western Railroad, and, later, the Philadelphia & Reading. Jackson, Bryant, William Appleton, Lyman, and Loring served as Boston & Lowell directors on a board that, during construction, included more capitalists than most railroads. Jackson and Loring were directors of the Boston & Providence. Nathan Hale and, after the construction phase, John Bryant were directors of the Boston & Worcester. Thomas B. Wales was a director of the Boston & Providence and the Western Railroad.[3]

Jackson and, through the machine shop, L&C were involved in developing the Western Railroad, the first trunk line in the U.S., which was conceived to connect Boston with the Hudson River and Albany. The machine shop built the first engines purchased by the Western Railroad, in 1839. The purchases were arranged by George Washington Whistler, as the railroad's consultant from 1837 to 1840 and its chief engineer from 1840. By 1842 L&C built twelve engines for the Western

Railroad, although the railroad started purchasing engines from Ross Winans in 1841 and, pursuant to a subcontract, from Matthias W. Baldwin.[4]

The Western Railroad expanded rapidly in 1843 and 1844 and needed the services of a machine shop. More, it desired to have its parts and equipment built by a company whose equity investors and management overlapped with its own. Locks & Canals served that need and that desire.

**Boston & Lowell**

Jackson's involvement with the Boston & Lowell was more directly relevant to decision making regarding the Pensacola Railroad. Jackson conceived of, built, and managed, the Boston & Lowell. Chartered on June 5, 1830, it opened for travel, with a single track, on June 24, 1835. The second track was completed in 1841. Leading roles in its establishment were taken by Jackson, Kirk Boott, George Washington Whistler, and (at Jackson's behest) L&C.[5]

The Boston & Lowell was Jackson's obsession. Its conception, birth, completion, and operation evidenced his masterly strategic and organizational skills, the same skills that brought success to Boston Manufacturing, Merrimack Manufacturing, and L&C. Completion of its first track in 1835 induced Jackson into his first retirement from L&C and related businesses at Waltham and Lowell.[6]

Jackson was so deeply and dominantly involved in the Boston & Lowell that he held three positions simultaneously during its first three years of existence: president, treasurer, and agent. He relinquished the presidency after three years of operations and the agent position after five, continuing as treasurer. He received no salary until he held only the treasurer position.

During the time he held two of the three positions, Jackson was the sole chief executive, the chief policy maker, and the sole operational executive. That arrangement, and Jackson's legendary attention to detail, ensured that few decisions of consequence were made without his review and assent. For example, the board of directors originally chose 35 pounds per yard English rail in a fish-belly pattern, "but later voted that Jackson should use his own judgment". The organizational structure, and the board structure (four of its five directors were outsiders), ensured that Jackson acted on his own initiative with respect to most matters. Given Jackson's political instincts and bent toward consensus decision making on major issues, his determinations rarely veered from those of the directors, which further enhanced his authority, not only within the Boston & Lowell but in virtually every organization in which he functioned.

Examples of the freedom exercised by Jackson were many. Unlike those responsible for construction of other railroads who were limited to expenditures estimated by the construction engineer, Jackson's construction expenditures were unrestricted. During the operations phase, Jackson made all operating decisions other than passenger fares. Jackson often negotiated arrangements for acquisitions of, and then acquired and contracted for, lands and rights of way in his own name. The board of directors subsequently assumed the contracts. In conducting bids for roadbed grading, Jackson kept prices paid to contractors secret from his board of directors, the justification being an ability to drive better bargains with bidders. Jackson's involvement with detail at times led to missteps. For example, he chose stone rather than wood sleepers, not allowing the engineer to make the determination. After realizing that their lack of flexibility adversely effected both comfort and the mechanical condition of the trains, Jackson candidly admitted his mistake to the stockholders.[7]

———

Experience in building railroads and in servicing the needs of railroads in their early operational years gave L&C comfort regarding the types of issues that would be encountered with a start-up like the Pensacola Railroad. L&C, including Jackson as a director, could not have been more mistaken in analogizing the Florida railroad to the Boston & Lowell or railroads built or managed by Boston Associates.

———

### Endnotes: Chapter Four

[1] See Kennedy (1951-1), at 71-2, and endnote 6 of this Chapter and associated text.

[2] For the internal improvements debate, see Rubin (1961), Taylor (1951), Goodrich (1960), Goodrich (1961), Larson (2001), Heydinger (1954), and Goodrich (1950), and, with respect to railroads within Massachusetts, Kirkland (1945). And see Moulton (1914) and Keller (1985). Poor (1860) provides summaries of railroad and canal development, company-by-company, in each state.

For railroad development, Bradlee (1918) and Kirkland (1945). For railroad projects of the referenced investor group and early Massachusetts railroads, Kennedy (1951-1), Kennedy (1951-2), Kennedy (1951-3), Kennedy (1951-4), and Gregory (1975), at 276-80. Additionally, for the Boston & Worcester, Dalzell (1987), at 88, and Gregory (1975), at 185-87, and for railroads in Western Massachusetts, Fisher (1947), Kirkland (1945), and MA R&C Report (1838). For the B&P, MA Law (1831) Ch. LVI. Jackson, Nathan Appleton, John E. Thayer, and other Boston investors took an active stock ownership role in the P&R in part to support the Rolling Stock Contracts.

[3] Many other important interconnections existed. Benjamin Ropes Nichols, a founder and shareholder of the Boston & Providence, served as legal counsel and clerk of both the Boston & Lowell and the Boston & Providence, of which Sturgis and John A. Lowell were directors. Nichols was a vice president of the Massachusetts Hospital Life

Insurance Company of Boston. Other vice presidents included Sturgis, Nathan Appleton, Abbott Lawrence, John A. Lowell, and Francis C. Lowell. Nichols was also a director of the Suffolk Bank of Boston, whose directors included William and Amos A. Lawrence, John A. Lowell, and Patrick Tracy Jackson. Nichols was a director of the National Insurance Company of Boston, with John A. Lowell and George B. Blake. Nichols was responsible for preservation of the records of the Old Colony of Plymouth.

For positions of Nichols and other Boston Associates, MHS (1880), Kennedy (1951-3), at 200, and Adams (1848), at 24 and 26. For the Old Colony of Plymouth, MA Law (1820) Ch. XCIX.

4  For the Western Railroad, Fisher (1947) (L&C-built locomotives at 82; westward expansion at 40-5). The Western Railroad was established by MA Law (1833) Ch. CXVI.

5  The official opening of the Boston & Lowell was June 1, 1835: Dover Gazette (1835, June 2) and NY Spectator (1835, June 4).

6  The Boston & Lowell was established under MA Law (1830) Ch. IV. See Boston Courier (1832, January 16), at 1, for its first stockholder and director meetings on March 4, 1831. Kirkland (1945), at 161, describes the B&L offering as "one of the most cautious and somber prospectuses ever written [and] based the hope of a 'small rent' of 6 per cent primarily on business between Boston and Lowell." See B&L Committee Report (1831). For opening of the B&L's first track, B&L AR (1836), at 17, and for completion of the second track, B&L AR (1841), at 8. For the B&L, Bradlee (1918) and SA (1888). The status of the B&L as of 1836 is described in Knight & Latrobe (1838), at 11-3, as of 1838 in von Gerstner (1842-1843), at 298-312, and, as of 1892 and providing a summary of its growth as of 1838, in Van Oss (1893), at 289-344. B&L AR (1844), at 8-9, includes two tables showing capital expenditures, revenues, expenses, dividends, and other data for each year from 1835 to 1844.

7  For Jackson's positions, Kennedy (1951-1), at 64, and for his salary, Kennedy (1951-3), at 201. Jackson received $1,000 annually as treasurer. For stone sleepers and discretionary freedoms, Kennedy (1951-2), at 84-7, 93, 95, and 96, Kennedy (1951-4), at 227, Kennedy (1951-1), at 62, 66-8, and 72, and Kennedy (1951-3), at 190. For harmony with directors and operational freedom, Kennedy (1951-1), at 72, and Kennedy (1951-3), at 96 (deferral on rails) and citing B&L board minutes for October 5, 1831 and January 19, 1833. For the lack of spending restrictions and Jackson entering into contracts, Kennedy (1951-2), at 87 and 93, respectively. For secrecy of contractor payments, Kennedy (1951-2), at 93, citing the B&L board minutes of January 2, 1832.

Even when functioning as a builder, Jackson focused on operational elements. After execution of the Running Gear Contract, Jackson determined which springs were used for the running gear. He rejected the plans of Wirt Robinson in favor of Ray's patent springs: see Emlen's letter to Jackson, P&R Corr. (April 14, 1842), at 343, letters to Davenport & Bridges, Bradley & Rice, and Thayer & Brother, at 343-44.

## Chapter Five

### Cause for Caution

While default by the Pensacola Railroad was unavoidable, losses sustained by Locks & Canals could have been mitigated had the transaction been better structured. Elements raising caution about L&C involvement in the transaction were many.

During his journey from Philadelphia to Boston in December 1845, Jackson catalogued the cautionary elements, most of which existed before the 1837 Panic. The engine sale to Florida was well outside L&C's customary regional markets and entailed greater shipping risks and costs. The transaction was proposed by an enthusiastic promoter, William H. Chase, during Chase's December 1835 visit to the north promoting the Pensacola Railroad and related schemes. Essentially all those schemes derived, directly or indirectly, from federal government largess for construction of forts and military projects in the Gulf of Mexico. The railroad was a start-up. It had not built even the most rudimentary infrastructure. Some roadbed grading was done prior to delivery of the engines, but not an inch of track was laid. There was no revenue base; and none would exist for years. Meanwhile, the railroad would incur large debts for infrastructure construction, much of which would be superior to L&C's payment claims. Those circumstances necessitated deferred payment credit to the Pensacola Railroad and an expectation of perduring debt.[1]

Debt, especially debt in a depression, troubled Jackson. In marked contrast to needful insolvent railroads, but of fundamental importance to those railroads, L&C had almost no debt. Under Jackson's watchful eye, L&C was a meticulously managed entity that survived on its cash flows. For building engines and other rolling stock, L&C was dependent upon financially stressed railroads for cash flows.

Jackson's approach to debt was simple: abstinence and avoidance.[A] In the early years of L&C engine building, the abstinence-and-avoidance principle as applied to customers worked well. Engines were sold for cash. Ever the realist, Jackson knew from constructing the Boston & Lowell and from textile operations that some debt

---

[A] That position was harmonious with the Massachusetts charter provisions that discouraged construction loans and its prohibition of bonded debt for railroad construction. By charter, the state could purchase the railroad after a period. It was thought the state's purchase price would equal only the authorized capital plus interest and not amounts derived from other sources of construction financing, such as loans.

incurrence was necessary. Like other Massachusetts railroads, Boston & Lowell debt was tightly controlled and rapidly retired with new equity. Given the state of the economy, Jackson acknowledged that some credit to railroad customers was necessary while the railroad completed infrastructure construction, acquired rolling stock, and ramped up operations. Jackson was forced to revisit controls on railroad debt structuring and management. He was apprehensive because he had no control, and no direct means of influencing control, of Pensacola Railroad debt. Actuality exceeded foreboding. The Panic of 1837 and its aftermath wreaked havoc with L&C's attempts to minimize and manage customer indebtedness.[2]

More broadly, as Jackson was keenly aware, the ability of a railroad to pay for infrastructure construction, engines, and other rolling stock was related to bond markets. Due to vetoes of bills to fund portions of the National Road and related determinations that the U.S. federal government was not to be involved in financing internal improvements within its states, it was left largely to the states to finance those improvements. Prior to the 1830s, European investors had little appetite for private entity debt issuances, and even less interest in the stock of private entities, about whom they had little information. European acceptance of state bonds increased throughout the 1830s. Europeans favored sovereign debt over private entity debt. Bonds were placed by banks (especially the BUS) and merchants (who were becoming merchant bankers). State and city bond issuances in northeastern and mid-Atlantic regions were intended to increase the competitive position of a state or city in trading with western regions. Baltimore was an example familiar to Jackson because of L&C engine sales to the Baltimore & Susquehanna.[3]

Many sovereign entity bond issuances were made in support of internal improvements, especially canals and railroads. Others were made to develop state banks, especially in southern states, with states reserving the right to acquire bank stock. Some, especially in the south, combined those approaches, allowing issuances to fund both a bank and, through bank investments, internal improvements. The Pensacola Railroad transaction was an example of that type. It included a right of the Territory of Florida to acquire stock in the Bank of Pensacola.

The objective of state or city involvement was to bolster private entity initiatives with a sovereign credit, by way of either substitution or enhancement. In some transactions, the sovereign issued bonds and passed issuance proceeds to the private entity, taking back private entity bonds, often as a mirror-image payment mechanism and sometimes as collateral security. That was a credit substitution mechanism. In a variation familiar to Jackson because of L&C's 1839 sale of engines to the Baltimore & Susquehanna, a sovereign passed its stock or bonds to the private entity, allowing the private entity to sell the sovereign securities in the markets. Each arrangement increased appeal in European markets.

In other arrangements, the sovereign guaranteed, and thereby enhanced, a private entity bond issuance. The Pensacola Railroad transaction was of that model: modulated because the issuance funded both a bank and a railroad. That complicated L&C's analysis. The risks and their management were extenuated, encompassing people having only indirect involvement with the railroad, namely transactional participants associated with the BUS and Nicholas Biddle. Those participants controlled the Bank of Pensacola which issued bonds to fund the Pensacola Railroad. The bank controlled the railroad through stock ownership and common directors. Locks & Canals held no interest in the Bank of Pensacola or the Pensacola Railroad.

Factors influencing the decision to sell engines to the Philadelphia & Reading were quite different and correlated more with the views of bond market investors. Railroads of the anthracite region, such as the P&R, were an exception to the lack of investor interest in private entity bonds. Railroads of this type were smaller, more circumscribed projects whose bonds could be analyzed based on the railroad's projected profitability. Which allowed some railroads to issue bonds, often convertible into common stock, without sovereign enhancement or substitution.[B] Examples included the P&R, the Philadelphia, Wilmington and Baltimore Railroad Company, the Camden & Amboy, and the Delaware and Raritan Canal Company, and subsidiaries such as the Philadelphia and Trenton Railroad Company. Pennsylvania anthracite transporters used English sterling as well as U.S. dollar issuances. Most were sold through Philadelphia with the BUS and Thomas Biddle and Company playing leading roles. Samuel Jaudon was made BUS London agent for the express purpose of placing bonds in the European markets.[4]

William H. Chase, the principal promoter of the Pensacola Railroad and related ventures, attempted to characterize the Pensacola Railroad as a project analyzable based upon its profitability (supplemented by U.S. federal government largess). He extolled Alabama and Georgia cotton, implying that, for analytical purposes, it was akin to coal for an anthracite railroad. That was alluring to investors and rolling stock builders with interests in cotton. Such as Nicholas Biddle, the BUS, Patrick Tracy Jackson, and Lowell entities like Locks & Canals.

Bond markets for state issuances were narrow during the 1837 Panic, recovered in 1838, and closed with the Crisis of 1839. Markets for many private railroad

---

[B] A few entities, such as Lehigh Coal & Navigation, financed their undertakings primarily with common stock sales.

issuances suffered greatly from and after the Panic. By 1841, a few states and territories, including Florida, Pennsylvania, and Michigan, began repudiating their bonds or bond guarantees, exacerbating market rejection of sovereign issuances.[5]

Boston, which had surplus capital and avoided debt leverage and bond issuances, was becoming the center for railroad financing in the 1840s. John Elliot Thayer and John Murray Forbes took leading roles in placing railroad debt in Boston markets, including for the P&R. Thayer served as a member of the P&R board of managers. It was rumored he might succeed Elihu Chauncey as P&R president. He did not. John Bryant and William Sturgis (Bryant & Sturgis) were also prominent in debt placements, including for the P&R.[6] Nathan Appleton played an important strategic investment role, and David A. Neal and Nathaniel Thayer participated. The London investor, McCalmont, Brothers & Company, was involved, both directly and through its New York correspondent, John Gihon & Company. John Tucker, a partner in Gihon & Company did become president of the P&R. The role of McCalmont Brothers was expanding, and the firm played an increasingly influential role in the P&R's affairs.[7]

The list of troubling considerations went on. Jackson's inclination was to conduct business based on personal relationships. Beginning with the Boston Associates and radiating outward. The Pensacola transaction involved no Boston Associates. It did involve a group of bankers and financiers known to Jackson and the L&C directors. These were current and former officers and directors of the Bank of the United States and individuals from Philadelphia and New York that were associated with the BUS and Nicholas Biddle. Jackson and L&C directors had worked and co-invested with many from this group, including Elihu Chauncey, Charles A. Davis, and William Gibbs McNeil.

The second group was comprised of Floridians, most visibly William H. Chase and Walter Gregory. L&C's knowledge of the Floridians was limited. That was deemed acceptable, though far from ideal. It was adjudged that individuals related to the BUS, who were shrewd financial strategists and rigorous in controlling investments, would constrain and control the Floridians. That judgment proved imprudent and investigation of the Floridians inadequate.

### Endnotes: Chapter Five

[1] On April 9, 1836, the Pensacola Railroad solicited contractors for road embankment work: Pensacola Gazette (1836, April 9-2). BoP Commissioner's Report, at 442-43, contains a statement of expenditures to April 2, 1840. The five largest were $200,000 for

grading, $160,00 for rails, $52,000 for machinery, $46,000 for the engineering department, and $40,000 for timber. Total expenditures were just over $564,000.

² Regarding footnote A, see Kennedy (1951-1), at 69-70, citing April 10, 1837 minutes of the Boston & Lowell board of directors regarding assessment of the state purchase payment obligation. The B&L charter legislation, MA Law (1830) Chap. IV, section 12, allowed the state to purchase the railroad after ten years of operations at

> the amount expended in making the said Rail Road, and the expenses of repairs, and all other expenses relating thereto, with interest thereon, at the rate of ten per cent. per annum, deducting all sums received by the Corporations from tolls or any other source of profit, and interest, at the rate of ten per centum per annum thereon.

Use of equity and limited use and rapid reduction of B&L debt is apparent in the financial statements: B&L AR (1834), B&L AR (1836), B&L AR (1837), B&L AR (1838), B&L AR (1839), B&L AR (1840), B&L AR (1841). Jackson was a director in 1841. Equity was $540,000 in 1833 and there was no indebtedness. Equity was $1.5 million in 1837 and debt was $37,393.32. Equity was $1.65 million in 1839 and no debt was listed.

³ See Hulbert (1904) (at 17-25, for the National Road; stagecoach and freight traffic is described at 119-41), Dunbar (1915-II), at 691-716, Hulbert (1903), Hulbert (1901), Searight (1894), Young (1904), Jordan (1948), Raitz (1996), Baker (2002), and Howe (2007), at 86.

President Madison vetoed the Bonus Bill, and federal funding of internal improvements, on March 3, 1817, his last day in office. Richardson (1900), volume I, at 584-85. On May 4, 1822, President Monroe vetoed an act authorizing toll gates and collections on the National Road as an unwarranted extension of congressional power to make appropriations, thereby establishing the federal position on state highways that endured until the mid-twentieth century. On May 27, 1830, President Jackson vetoed a bill funding the Maysville Turnpike extension in the 60-mile portion from Maysville to Lexington, Kentucky. This veto ended discussion of direct federal participation in internal improvements, because of the difficulty of obtaining a constitutional amendment. The Maysville Road bill was a compromise put forth approximately two weeks after defeat of a federal bill to construct a 1,500-mile road from Buffalo to New Orleans through Washington, D.C. Notwithstanding his Maysville Road veto, Jackson approved an appropriation for surveys and extension of the Cumberland Road just three days later and an appropriation for construction of a road from Detroit to Chicago on May 31, four days later. In connection with Ohio's 1803 admission to statehood, the U.S. Congress provided that 5% of the proceeds from sales of public lands in Ohio were to be spent on construction of roads to and through Ohio, with 40% spent on federal projects and 60% disbursed by the state legislature for state roads within Ohio. The state funds seem to have been diverted to political purposes.

For Monroe's veto of May 4, 1822 and a related paper stating his views on internal improvements, Richardson (1900), volume II, at 142-43 and 144-83. See also Young (1904), at 66-77, and Taylor (1951), at 19. The Jackson veto of May 27, 1830 is discussed at Remini (1981), at 251-56, Taylor (1951), at 20, and Jackson (1966). Baker (2002) discusses the Maysville Road bill and its history. See Taylor (1951), at 18-22 regarding appropriations, citing, at 19, Gephart (1909) with respect to the diversion of funds from Ohio land sales. For federal funding of river projects, including appropriations on and after 1819 and constitutional arguments, Lippincott (1914). Many rivers were navigable waters, and thus within the federal authority, and/or constituted boundaries between states.

4   Chandler (1954), at 248-53. Jaudon's agency appointment was made on September 22, 1837 and commenced on November 8. BUS Investigation (1841), at 12 and 16. Jaudon was succeeded as BUS cashier by Joseph Cowperthwaite, who became a BUS director in June 1840. Cowperthwaite was elected a P&R director on August 16, 1837. He resigned on September 20, just prior to appointment as the BUS cashier. Hare (1909-1914), at 10.

5   Preferences of New England investors, especially Bostonians, for common stock continued until around 1848 when state-guaranteed bonds were used to construct the Western Railroad. This well served New England when bond markets closed after the 1837 Panic. New England recovered before other regions and experienced exceptional profitability in the 1840s.

For state debt and territorial and state repudiation of sovereign debt, McGrane (1935), Florida being discussed at 232-44, Kim & Wallis (2005), at 742-44, English (1996), Ratchford (1941), Wallis, Sylla & Grinath (2004), Grinath, Wallis & Sylla (1997), Fishlow (1965), at 103-13, and Taylor (1951), at 338-45.

6   Sturgis was a banker, merchant, textile director, and railroad investor and director. He was born in 1782 in Barnstable, Cape Cod. He spent twelve years at sea, engaged in the fur trade of the northwestern U.S. with China. Trading led to relationships with northwestern American Indians and a life-long interest in their populations and languages, as evidenced by his writings. After returning to Boston, he formed a partnership with John Bryant, which lasted more than fifty years. Bryant & Sturgis became a leading, and for many years the dominant, merchant and ship owner in the Pacific trade among the U.S., China, and Hawaii. It dominated the California hide and tallow trades from 1829 to 1841. Sturgis left the China trade at the time of the Opium War (1840-1842). He then concentrated on U.S. inland investments, especially in railroads, in which he held many directorships. His mercantile and railroad activities have been characterized as low leverage, quick turnover, a relatively low profit percentage, and avoidance of speculative risk. Sturgis served as the Boston representative in the Massachusetts legislature until 1845. He was an honorary member of the Massachusetts Mechanics' Charitable Association and a member of the Massachusetts Historical Society.

For Sturgis, see Loring (1864), Merchants' Magazine (1865, March), Morison (1920), Larson (1935), Busch & Gough (1996), Barragy (1975), and, with respect to tribal languages, Archaeologia Americana (1836). For the interest of Sturgis in Indian populations and languages, see his *Diary, or Journal of his First Voyage* and *Three*

*Lectures upon the North-west Coast*, Sturgis (1978) containing portions of each. He also authored Sturgis (1822) and Sturgis (1845).

[7] McCalmont Brothers and Gihon & Co. became principal financiers of the P&R. McCalmont Brothers was deeply involved in securing English iron rails for the P&R, and thereafter expanded its role. Chandler (1954), at 254-59, Ratchford (1941), at 79-80, and McMillen (2022-4), Chapter Eight. Boston investors came to control the Philadelphia, Wilmington & Baltimore, reorganizing the railroad in 1847, reducing its debt from 57% to 34% of total investment, and appointing William A. Swift as president. L&C benefited by building engines for railroads in which the investments were made.

Thayer also played a primary role in arranging contracts for the building of locomotives and coal cars for the P&R. Thayer, with Albert H. Dorr, arranged the Rolling Stock Contracts. Thayer and Dorr arranged and negotiated the D&B Cars Contract (1842) with Davenport & Bridges, the D&B-F Cars Contract (1842) with Davenport & Bridges and Albert Fuller, and the B&R Cars Contract (1842) with Bradley & Rice, each for coal jimmies, and the D&B Iron Car Contract (1844) with Davenport & Bridges for the first iron coal cars.

# Part III

## Pensacola Schemes

# Map 1: Pensacola, Territory of Florida

## Chapter Six

### Capturing Pensacola

For Patrick Tracy Jackson, the Pensacola Railroad saga began with the Bank of Pensacola, a real estate development company (later formalized as the Pensacola Land Company and then as two different entities, each known as the Pensacola City Company), and the ambitions of William H. Chase, Walter Gregory, and a group of Florida businessmen. The confluence also engulfed Locks & Canals, the Pensacola Association, the Philadelphia & Reading, the Bank of the United States, friends of the BUS and Nicholas Biddle, the Territory of Florida, the State of Florida, and Territorial and State repudiations of its guarantee of Bank of Pensacola bonds.

The extravagant plans of the Floridians were alluring. The conception was drawing cotton and timber from Alabama and Georgia through the port of Pensacola and, via canals and railroads, connecting the ports of Pensacola and Mobile to the Mississippi delta as well as the Atlantic seaboard. The cotton was to flow into both domestic and foreign markets, a course of obvious interest to textile manufacturing operations at Waltham and Lowell and parties, such as Nicholas Biddle, intent on controlling cotton pricing. The timber was primarily for building naval and defense facilities.[1]

The Bank of Pensacola was born an unwanted child. Preference in Pensacola was for a branch of the BUS. Petitions to establish a BUS branch circulated throughout the 1820s and 1830s. Governor Andrew Jackson petitioned secretary of state John Quincy Adams for a BUS branch in 1821. In 1831 the Florida Legislative Council petitioned the BUS to establish a Pensacola branch. Each to no avail. Amidst these entreaties, the Territory of Florida passed acts, in 1824, 1825 and 1826, to incorporate a bank in Pensacola. Governor William Pope Duval vetoed each. The Territory's Secretary, George Walton, refused to consider the acts, prompting the Legislative Council to seek a writ of mandamus compelling Walton's consideration.[2]

Finally, The President and Directors of the Bank of Pensacola was incorporated in 1831, over Governor Duval's veto. Its originally authorized share capital was $200,000, comprised of 2,000 shares, each of $100 par value. No shares were issued until May 16, 1833, when stock subscriptions were opened and closed on the same day. Share issuances on that day were to Walter Gregory (1,705 shares) and eleven Pensacola residents (45 shares in total). Gregory, who relocated to Pensacola in connection with establishment of the Bank of Pensacola and his share purchase, owned 621 shares for his own account, the remainder being beneficially owned by other investors. Two hundred fifty shares were reserved for the Territory of Florida but not issued. Ten percent ($7,000) of the required purchase price was paid for Gregory's shares.[3]

The Bank of Pensacola commenced business in November 1833. The long delay was due to an inability to obtain stock subscriptions and continuing efforts to obtain a BUS branch. Even after incorporation of the Bank of Pensacola, a committee comprised of Hanson Kelly and others sought to obtain a BUS branch and abandon the Bank of Pensacola charter. The BUS branch was not forthcoming. The Bank of Pensacola charter expired. The charter was renewed by a new act, which was vetoed by Governor Duval, and then passed over his veto. At the opening of the Bank of Pensacola, Walter Gregory was president and James Catlin was cashier.[A] Its board of directors was comprised of Walter Gregory, Hanson Kelly, Henry Hyer, Charles C. Keyser, Joseph Forsyth, J. Jervison, Jr., and George W. Barkley.[4]

William H. Chase began accumulating land holdings in "New Pensacola" or the "New City" area of Pensacola around July of 1834. The principals in the real estate undertaking, in its early years, were Chase, Gregory, John A. Cameron,[5] and Thomas M. Blount,[6] each a transplant Floridian. Chase, with his brother George (also a Bank of Pensacola shareholder), promoted the real estate development to northern investors. As important drivers of projected increases in Pensacola land values, the marketing brochures cited development of the Pensacola Railroad, development of a terminal and trans-shipment facility at the Pensacola port, and the large amount of U.S. federal government support for forts, a naval base, and other military facilities near Pensacola. The real estate transactions were not conducted through a formal entity. They were transactions by individuals sharing a vision. Formalization of the real estate endeavor came in 1835.[7]

Conflicting agendas tore at the Pensacola Railroad from its inception. The railroad was separately incorporated in each of Florida and Alabama. The Florida, Alabama and Georgia Rail Road Company (FA&G) was incorporated by the Florida legislature on February 14, 1834. The Alabama, Florida and Georgia Rail Road Company (AF&G) was incorporated in Alabama on December 13, 1834. In February 1835, the Florida Legislative Council assented to the Alabama incorporation, repealed the 1834 Florida chartering act, and allowed the AF&G to extend its line to Pensacola Bay. The "Pensacola Railroad" was the AF&G. William H. Chase was elected president.[8]

---

[A] The artist George Catlin, brother of James Catlin, married Clara Bartlett Gregory, the sister of Walter Gregory, in 1828.

Walter Gregory, while president of the Bank of Pensacola, was a sponsor and shareholder in both the AF&G and FA&G. The incorporating commissioners included some individuals involved in the New City real estate initiative: Gregory, Chase, Cameron, and Blount. The commissioners also included a broader array of Florida investors, including Walker Anderson, Jasper Strong,[9] Henry Hyer, Hanson Kelly, James Catlin, and John Innerarity. The shares in the Pensacola Railroad (AF&G) were subscribed in December 1834. For the sale of $1.5 million of stock, and as permitted by the charter, only $3,750 was paid in cash ($0.25 per share).

Obtaining a charter in Alabama did not mean the AF&G was entirely welcome in Alabama. The AF&G's initially authorized road ran to Columbus but was stymied in its efforts to penetrate to Montgomery and the Alabama interior. Those efforts were blocked by opposition from the city of Mobile, at the mouth of the Alabama River. In 1837, Mobile obtained a legislative requirement that the consent of two-thirds of the stockholders of the Montgomery Rail-road Company was necessary to extend the AF&G road to Montgomery County. Those stockholders eventually relinquished the right to block the extension.[10]

As originally conceived, the Pensacola Railroad was to operate between Pensacola and West Point on the Alabama border. The 1836 marketing materials for the real estate venture described a grand vision for the railroad, as depicted in Map 2 and Map 3 (pages 52 and 57). A westward branch was to run from Pensacola to Mobile. The main line was to run from Pensacola north to Montgomery, with branches to Tuscaloosa and Columbus. In Montgomery, the line would split into a northern branch to Nashville and an eastern branch to Athens and Augusta, with a connecting line to Charleston, on the Atlantic Ocean. A separate southern line was proposed between Brunswick, Georgia, on the Atlantic Ocean, and the Apalachicola River, where a new canal would connect through Lake Wimico to St. Andrews Bay on the Gulf of Mexico. Another canal would connect St. Andrews Bay with Choctawhatchee Bay.[11]

Each of the Bank of Pensacola, the Pensacola Railroad, and the New City development venture was capital starved. On January 1, 1835, a capital call was made on the Bank of Pensacola shares. Gregory's 1,750 shares drew in $45,927, which was inadequate to the needs of the bank, of no assistance to the Pensacola Railroad, and of no abetment to the New City undertaking.[12]

Chase and Gregory sought to raise additional debt and equity financing. Chase was then an officer in the Army Corps of Engineers with responsibilities for the construction of Forts Pickens, Barrancas, and McRee. As such, he had access to northern financial interests, including at the port of Philadelphia. Walter Gregory also had northern contacts. He was from a financially successful family in Albany,

New York, where he spent his youth. His wealthy brother, Dudley S. Gregory, was the mayor of Jersey City. William Chase and Walter Gregory were successful in interesting a group of investors and financiers in Philadelphia, New York, Boston, and Jersey City.

### Endnotes: Chapter Six

1. Indicative of the magnitude of the opportunity, U.S. production of cotton, in bales, increased from 731,452 in 1830 to 1,426,891 in 1837 and 4,541,285 in 1859, and U.S. production as a percentage of total cotton consumption in Europe and the United States was 80.1% in 1831-1835, 82.4% in 1836-1840, and 86.7% in 1841-1845. Gray (1933), at 1026, Table 40, and 693, second table, respectively.

2. *A Petition is in Circulation at Pensacola for the Establishment of a Branch of the Bank of the United States at that Place*, 4 LOUISVILLE PUBLIC ADVERTISER 2 (October 13, 1821), Dovell & Richardson(1955), at 9-16, and, for the mandamus action, Pensacola Gazette (1826, April 8).

3. For the Bank of Pensacola incorporation, FL Law (1831). BoP Commissioner's Report, at 438, states that Gregory was from Boston. Walby (2014), at 23-4 (without source citation), asserts that Gregory's involvements in the bank resulted from a meeting in Boston with Chase, probably when Chase was marketing bank stock and promoting real estate development. By coincidence, Gregory then held a mortgage on a Pensacola building. For Gregory's Pensacola mortgage, Walby (2014), at 23-4. See Ellsworth (1976) regarding a Walter Gregory house in Pensacola.

4. For the 1833 extension of the Bank of Pensacola charter, FL Law (1833) Ch. 699, as passed over Duval's veto. For Duval's veto, FL Law (1833) Veto Message. The Bank of Pensacola seems to have had difficulties getting its five directors together. In 1834, FL Law (1834) Ch. 820 was passed to allow the conduct of business with less than five directors, as the stockholders might "deem prudent and advisable."

    For the Bank of Pensacola directors at commencement, Pensacola Gazette (1833, July 5), which observed: "No longer will the towns of Alabama reap the benefits of our agricultural labor, impoverishing and driving our residents from their homes." For an example of amendments to extend the subscription period for Bank of Pensacola stock, see FL Law (1833) Chap. 699, which is also set forth in 9 PENSACOLA GAZETTE 1 (July 12, 1833). For the efforts of Hanson Kelly and others to obtain a BUS branch and abandon the Bank of Pensacola charter, *United States' Bank*, 7 DAILY NATIONAL JOURNAL 2 (July 19, 1831).

5. Cameron was born in Mecklenburg, Virginia in 1788. He lived for a period in Fayetteville, North Carolina and represented that borough in the House of Commons from 1810 to 1812, when he joined the army to serve in the War of 1812. In 1825 he and James A. Patterson of Raleigh published the FAYETTEVILLE NORTH CAROLINA JOURNAL (the CENTINEL, renamed in 1826) as an outspoken supporter of Andrew Jackson. After

losing an 1829 election on a Jacksonian platform, Cameron sold the newspaper and went to Washington seeking a government position. Jackson appointed him consul to Vera Cruz. He later moved to Florida and was appointed a judge in the Western District. As a judge, he complained to Washington that his responsibilities were too great and his pay too little. He was a founder of the Pensacola Railroad, the Florida Insurance and Banking Company, the College of Pensacola, and Christ Episcopal Church in Pensacola. For Cameron, see Denham (1995), Dodd (1931), LC (1916), at 468, Pennington (1938), at 32, McFarland (1953), at 386 and 390 (regarding Cameron in North Carolina), FL Law (1834) No. 11, FL Law (1836) Ch. 973, and FL Law (1834) Ch. 774.

6  Blount was a leading Pensacola business figure and editor of the PENSACOLA GAZETTE. He was Escambia County Justice of the Peace in 1838. He served on the Legislative Council of the Florida Territory. As chairman of the finance committee and a member of the banking and judiciary committees, he was instrumental in passage of the 1835 Act (discussed in Chapter Eight) and restructurings of the Bank of Pensacola and the Pensacola Railroad. He served as a delegate from Escambia County to the convention to frame a constitution for the expectant, but still contested, State of Florida, working with Walker Anderson. For Blount, see Dodd (1931), at 225, 234, 235, and 238, Doherty (1959), at 354, Yonge (1933), at 173, Morris & Maguire (1980), at 310, Hoskins (1937), at 42 and 43, Hoskins (1938-1), at 242 and 250, and Hoskins (1938-2), at 131. For Blount as president of the Bank of Pensacola and Justice of the Peace, BoP Commissioner's Report, at 451-54.

7  Letters regarding development of the Pensacola navy yard are in Walby (2014), at 33-50. A letter to the Secretary of the Navy, dated March 1, 1837, was signed by Chase, Robinson, and Davis. An earlier letter from the Secretary of the Navy, dated December 29, 1836, is in Chase, Robinson & Davis (1837). Chase Brochure (1836) and Chase, Robinson & Davis Brochure (1837) were marketing brochures for the real estate project. Von Gerstner (1842-1843), at 743-44, describes the building of a hotel at a cost of $30,000 as part of that undertaking. For the land acquisitions, Dodd (1931), at 225-32, hinting at their complexities. For more flavor, including with respect to land titles, divisions, transmissions deriving from periods of Spanish control, and possible involvements of relatives of judges ruling on disputes relating to these matters, all in the context of one segment of one land tract, see *McGuire v. Blount* (1905), *McGuire v. Blount* (1903), and especially *McGuire v. Blount* Certiorari (1903). For a survey of crime in Pensacola, including during the period here considered, Denham (2011).

Richard Keith Call, during his years as a land speculator, acquired some land in and around Pensacola, although most of his land transactions were in Middle Florida. With James Innerarity he purchased 800 arpents on Santa Rosa sound (an arpent being 3,420 square meters, approximately 1 acre). With Henry M. Brackenridge he purchased 800 arpents on Escambia Bay. He purchased one lot in Pensacola. Doherty (1961), at 44.

8  For incorporation of the Pensacola Railroad in Florida and Alabama and assent to the Alabama incorporation, (a) FL Law (1834) Ch. 792, (b) AL Law (1834) No. 11, (c) FL Law (1835) No. 870, and (d) AL Law (1837) No. 76. For obtaining necessary rights in

Alabama, Campbell (1838), at 7-10, which discusses federal land acquisitions, and Hildreth (1959), at 397-400 and 403. Chase, on behalf of the Pensacola Railroad, sought 600,000 acres from the U.S. federal government, arguing the railroad would facilitate communication among New York, Washington, and Atlantic cities and New Orleans and Mobile and aid in defense of the Gulf of Mexico. He proposed the railroad transport troops, munitions, and war implements without charge. See PRR Petition (1835). An early article, in the spirit of boosterism, is ARJ (1835, April 4.

For the Pensacola Railroad and city of Pensacola, von Gerstner (1842-1843), at 744 (noting the total distance of the proposed road as 156½ miles, including to Montgomery), ARJ (1835, April 4), at 196-97 (the proposed railroad, bond financing by the Bank of Pensacola ("a bank now in high credit"), and Territorial guarantee), Hildreth (1959), Pettengill & Simmons (1952), at 15-17 (physical factors), Johnson (1965), at 109-12, Turner (2003), at 17-9 and 40, Dodd (1931), Dodd (1945), Doherty (1959), at 345-48, and Campbell (1838) (a detailed report on the anticipated line). The directors of the Pensacola Railroad in 1836 were Chase (president), Gregory, Cameron, Blount, Kelly, Robert Mitchell, and Robert Joyner: Pensacola Gazette (1836, January 9).

For context, there was active consideration, including public meetings in Pensacola, for annexation of the panhandle (particularly Escambia County) to Alabama. See for example, *Florida*, 58 NILE'S NATIONAL REGISTER (1840), at 147 (Hanson Kelly was chairman). Hildreth (1959), at 397-400, discusses difficulties experienced in Alabama. For the 1834 share subscription, Dodd (1931), at 232, citing the PENSACOLA GAZETTE, June 20, 1835. See also Dodd (1945), Rucker (1991), and Dysart (1982).

9  Jasper Strong was born on May 5, 1798 in Hartford, Vermont. He was an 1819 graduate of West Point and life-long business partner of William H. Chase. An example was ownership of the sloop *Ann Maria* together with his West Point classmate, Fred A. Underhill. The sloop operated out of New Orleans, with Chase as owners' agent. Strong married Underhill's sister (Widow Underhill, née Nixon). She died without issue and Strong married her sister, Eliza Julia Nixon, with whom he had two children, one named William Chase Strong. At the outbreak of the Civil War, Strong controlled approximately one hundred middle-aged slaves (all mechanics) who worked for the U.S. government at $1.50 per day.

Strong and Underhill secured the contracts for construction of forts in New Orleans and Fort Pickens in Pensacola. The Fort Pickens contract was for $900,000, with a profit to Strong and Underhill of $300,000. Underhill died, at age 29, during construction of Fort Pickens. Strong split the profit with Underhill's heirs. Strong died of yellow fever in Queeche, Vermont on November 6, 1864 at age 68. For Strong at West Point, Select Committee Report (1837), at 45 and 120, and West Point Reminiscences (1886), at 6. A short biography of Strong is Tucker (1889), at 464-65. For Strong, Chase, and the *Ann Marie*, New Orleans Ship Register (1942), at 8.

*Strong v. Willis* (1850) provides a glimpse of Jasper Strong's 1838 involvements in the New City project. Strong agreed to build a house for Alexander J. Dallas on lot number 276 for upwards of $6,000, depending upon construction costs. Dallas conveyed the lot to Strong and George Willis, as trustees, for the use and benefit of the wife and children of Dallas. Dallas died in 1844. The amount then due to Strong was $4,175.98. Despite being a trustee, Strong, as a creditor, sought to foreclose, attempting to renounce the trust and assail it as fraudulent. The text of the trust indenture is included in the opinion. Strong did not prevail.

10  See AL Law (1837) No. 76, which granted the Montgomery extension right, with required approvals.

11  The railroad plan is shown in the map at the end of Chase Brochure (1836), an offering document for the New City real estate project. In March of 1837, after the BUS-related parties became involved and $580,000 of lots had been sold (in January), a second offering document was circulated: Chase, Robinson & Davis Brochure (1837).

12  For the capital call, BoP Commissioner's Report, at 439.

Map 2: Proposed Railroad System

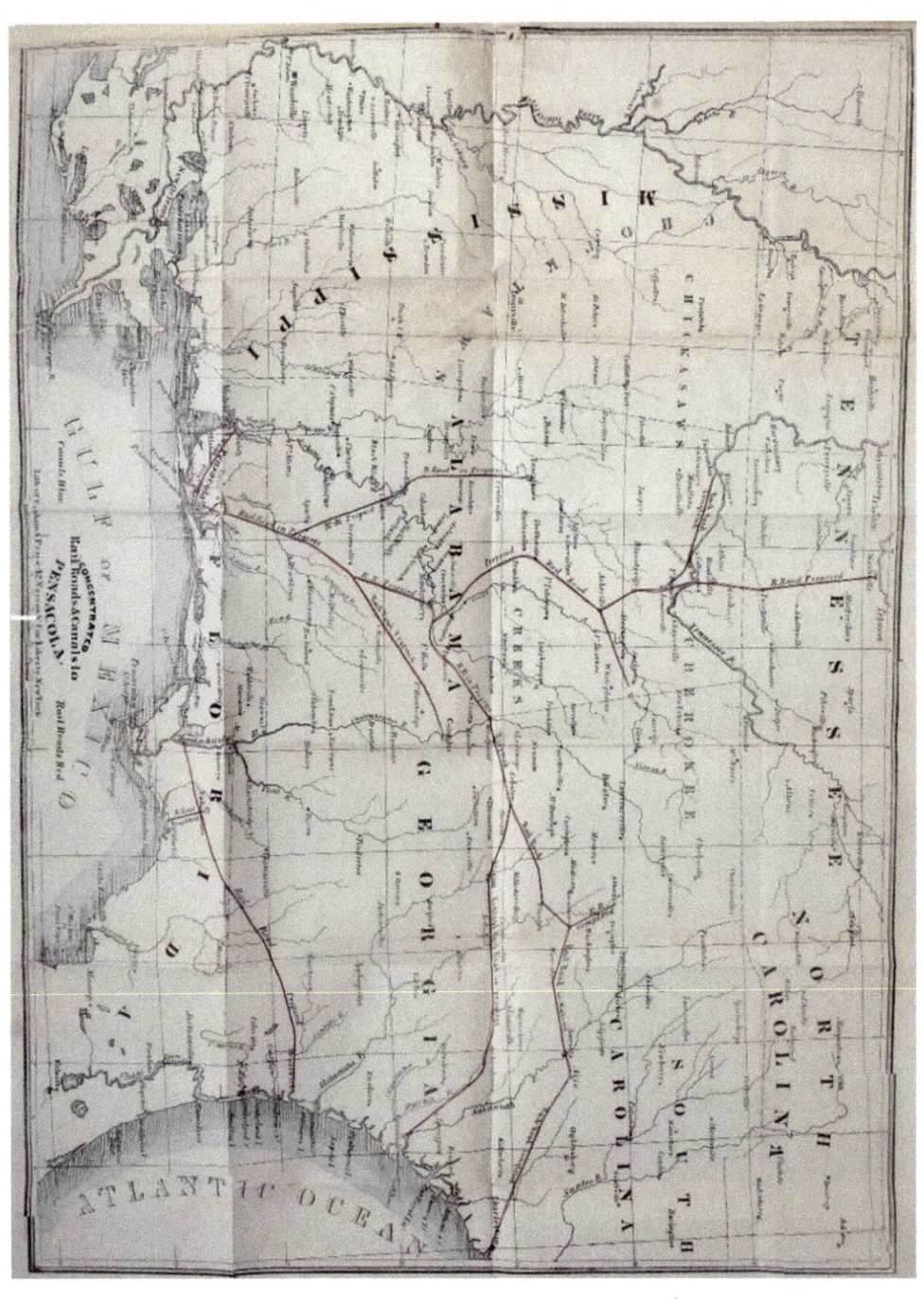

# Chapter Seven

## Restructuring and Financing Plan

**BUS Parties, With Plan**

The Philadelphia and New York investors in the Pensacola transactions were neither passive nor docile. They were sophisticated bankers and financiers with extensive involvements in railroads and other internal improvements. They came with a plan. An integrated restructuring and financing plan for the Bank of Pensacola that also encompassed the Pensacola Railroad and the Pensacola land development initiative.[1]

The restructuring portion entailed acquisition of a controlling shareholder position by the Philadelphia and New York investors in each of the Bank of Pensacola and the Pensacola real estate endeavor. The financing portion entailed (a) acquisition by the Bank of Pensacola of stock in the Pensacola Railroad, (b) issuance of bonds by the bank to obtain the funds necessary to acquire the railroad stock, (c) the guarantee of those bonds by the Territory of Florida, and (d) purchase of the guaranteed bonds by the Philadelphia and New York financiers.

To give effect to the restructuring and financing plan, the Legislative Council of the Territory of Florida enacted the 1835 Act on February 13, 1835. It was approved by Territorial governor John Henry Eaton the next day.[A] First, the authorized capital of the Bank of Pensacola was increased to $2.5 million, allowing issuance of 23,000

---

[A] Eaton was a Tennessee lawyer, born in North Carolina, who served Andrew Jackson in the Creek Wars and War of 1812, including at the Battle of New Orleans. Eaton served in the Tennessee House of Representatives in 1815 and 1816. In 1818 he was elected to the U.S. Senate, although he was 28 years old (below the constitutionally mandated minimum age of 30). In 1829 Eaton resigned his Senate seat to join Jackson's cabinet as Secretary of War. He and his exceptionally attractive, gregarious, and outspoken wife, Margaret O'Neale (sometimes O'Neal or O'Neil) Timberlake Eaton, were the subject of the Petticoat Affair in which Washington society wives refused to socialize with the Eatons because they married before the end of the mourning period after the death of Peggy's first husband. Vicious rumors were spread about Peggy's promiscuity while working at her father's boardinghouse and tavern, where John Eaton first met Peggy O'Neale. Eaton resigned as Secretary of War and was appointed governor of the Territory of Florida (and two years later as U.S. Minister to Spain).

additional shares. Second, the bank was authorized to purchase the Pensacola Railroad stock. Third, the bank was authorized to issue, and deliver to the Florida Territory, $500,000 principal amount of 6% bonds due January 1, 1860 (1835~1860), with interest payable semi-annually. Fourth, the Territory was directed to endorse and guarantee the 1835~1860 bonds and return them to the Bank of Pensacola to allow the bank to sell the bonds. Fifth, the use of bond sale proceeds was restricted to construction of the Pensacola Railroad and, to the extent of 33%, a retention for bank operations. Sixth, the bank was required to execute and deliver to the Territory an indenture mortgaging all the bank's property and assets, expressly including its stock in the Pensacola Railroad. Seventh, Bank of Pensacola stockholders were made "individually and personally liable for the redemption of said bonds." No provisions required the Pensacola Railroad to mortgage its property. It then owned no property. The Pensacola Railroad was merely an idea.[2]

Figure 5: Bank of Pensacola Bond, 1835

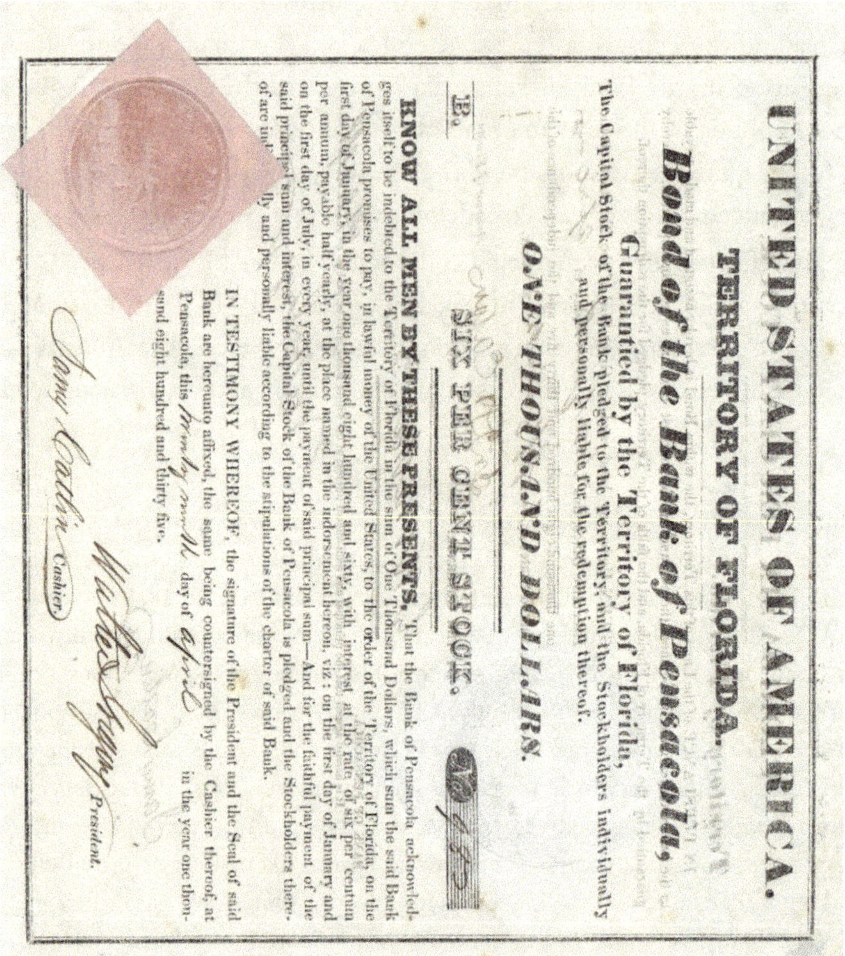

UNITED STATES OF AMERICA.

TERRITORY OF FLORIDA.

Bond of the Bank of Pensacola,

Guarantied by the Territory of Florida,

The Capital Stock of the Bank pledged to the Territory; and the Stockholders individually and personally liable for the redemption thereof.

ONE THOUSAND DOLLARS.

B. SIX PER CENT STOCK.

KNOW ALL MEN BY THESE PRESENTS, That the Bank of Pensacola acknowledges itself to be indebted to the Territory of Florida in the sum of One Thousand Dollars, which sum the said Bank of Pensacola promises to pay, in lawful money of the United States, to the order of the Territory of Florida, on the first day of January, in the year one thousand eight hundred and sixty, with interest at the rate of six per centum per annum, payable half yearly, at the place named in the indorsement hereon, viz: on the first day of January and on the first day of July, in every year, until the payment of said principal sum—And for the faithful payment of the said principal sum and interest, the Capital Stock of the Bank of Pensacola is pledged and the Stockholders thereof are ind[illegible]lly and personally liable according to the stipulations of the charter of said Bank.

IN TESTIMONY WHEREOF, the signature of the President and the Seal of said Bank are hereunto affixed, the same being countersigned by the Cashier thereof, at Pensacola, this twenty ninth day of April in the year one thousand eight hundred and thirty five.

Cashier

President.

As issued, the 1835~1860 bonds were obligations of the Bank of Pensacola payable to the Territory of Florida. Each bond contained an endorsement, signed by the governor, effecting assignment of the bond to its bearer with recourse against the Territory. Each bond also contained a separate provision, signed by the bank president, regarding the location for payment of principal and interest. The endorsement contained a blank space for the payment location that was to be filled in separately for each bond.

Figure 5 shows the face of a Bank of Pensacola bond. The payment location was important when the Territory later repudiated its guarantee of the bonds. For rights pertaining to bonds sold in London, see Chapter Twelve, including Figures 24 and 25. The governor's endorsement and payment location were on the reverse side of the bond: Figure 23.[3]

Eight days after passage of the 1835 Act, on February 21, the subscription books of the Bank of Pensacola were opened. Walter Gregory acquired all 23,000 additional shares without payment of any amount. The subscription books were closed on that same date. Gregory held those 23,000 shares until December 14, 1835.[4]

At some time between 1833 and January 1, 1835, Dudley S. Gregory of Jersey City (Walter Gregory's brother) became the second largest shareholder in the Bank of Pensacola, holding 289 shares. Concurrently, Henry Yates and Archibald McIntyre, each of New York and each a partner of Yates & McIntyre, became shareholders, holding 145 and 144 shares, respectively. Dudley Gregory was the superintendent of Yates & McIntyre, although Dudley formed his own firm in 1835 (D. S. Gregory and Company), which worked closely with Yates & McIntyre.[B] None of Dudley Gregory, Henry Yates, and Archibald McIntyre was a shareholder in the Bank of Pensacola by January 1, 1840.[5]

On April 29, 1835, the Bank of Pensacola issued $500,000 of 1835~1860 bonds to the Florida Territory. The bonds were endorsed by Governor Eaton, guaranteed by the Florida Territory, and returned to the Bank of Pensacola. On December 2, the endorsed bonds were sold by the Bank of Pensacola to William H. Chase, as agent for Thomas Biddle, Elihu Chauncey, and Samuel Jaudon, who were financial agents of the Pensacola Association. The Pensacola Association was comprised of Thomas A. Biddle, Elihu Chauncey, Samuel Jaudon, Charles A. Davis, S. V. S. Wilder, Morris Robinson, Walter Gregory, and William H. Chase. The Pensacola Association, through the BUS and Samuel Jaudon, Thomas Biddle & Company, and

---

[B] See Chapter Eleven regarding Dudley S. Gregory and his associates and successors in business, including Walter Gregory and other brothers.

others, made offshore sales of bonds to, among others, Hope and Company of Amsterdam (with Edward M. Forestall of New Orleans as U.S. agent), Gowan & Marx of London (with Henry J. Williams of Philadelphia as U.S. agent), S. Waymouth, Overend, Gurney and Company, John Alliard, Thomson Hankey and Company, William Tritton, H. L. Thomas, Coutts and Company, Ewart, Taylor and Company, and Grayson and Company.[6]

The Bank of Pensacola received $100,000 cash from the bond sale. The remaining purchase price was payable by the Pensacola Association from November 2, 1836 to December 31, 1838 based upon miles of road completed by the Pensacola Railroad ($100,000 after each ten miles).

Bond issuance proceeds were held by the Bank of Pensacola. The Pensacola Railroad, while entitled to two-thirds of the proceeds, orally agreed to take only so much as it needed from time to time upon completion of each ten miles of road, the balance remaining with the bank. Of the initial $100,000, $18,662.50 was disbursed to the railroad. Those funds were expended for a route survey by Major James D. Graham of the United States Topographical Engineers, who later became chief engineer of the Pensacola Railroad. See Map 3. It is unclear whether further issuance proceeds were expended for the purchase of iron for rails or whether funds for iron derived from loans, stock, or other sources.[7]

On December 14, 1835, Walter Gregory transferred 13,000 of the additional 23,000 bank shares to the Pensacola Association. The remaining 10,000 went to seventeen other individuals.[8] On December 15, 1836, the 1,750 shares in the Bank of Pensacola originally issued to Gregory in 1831 were merged into the 1835 subscription and installments paid on those original shares were refunded. The increase in paid-in capital was approximately $60,000, of which $37,000 was paid in endorsed promissory notes, callable at the discretion of the board of directors of the Bank of Pensacola.

During 1835, the Bank of Pensacola purchased 14,920 Pensacola Railroad shares for $332,840.33, leaving the remaining 80 as director qualifying shares. How payment for that purchase was made is unknown. The remainder of the purchase price, up to $500,000, was payable on the demand of the railroad directors, with an oral agreement between those directors and the bank that the unpaid price would be called as needed by the railroad. Between July 1837 and December 31, 1839, the Bank of Pensacola loaned to the Pensacola Railroad an amount which, with accrued interest as of March 21, 1840, totaled $259,173.33 (with interest accruing). The loans were due on December 31, 1839, were unpaid as of that date, and were protested as in default on April 2, 1840. The loans were not secured by any railroad assets. The total Bank of Pensacola investment in the Pensacola Railroad as of

March 21, 1840 was thus $592,013.66. No rail was laid by the Pensacola Railroad, ever.[9]

Map 3: Graham Map of Proposed Railroad

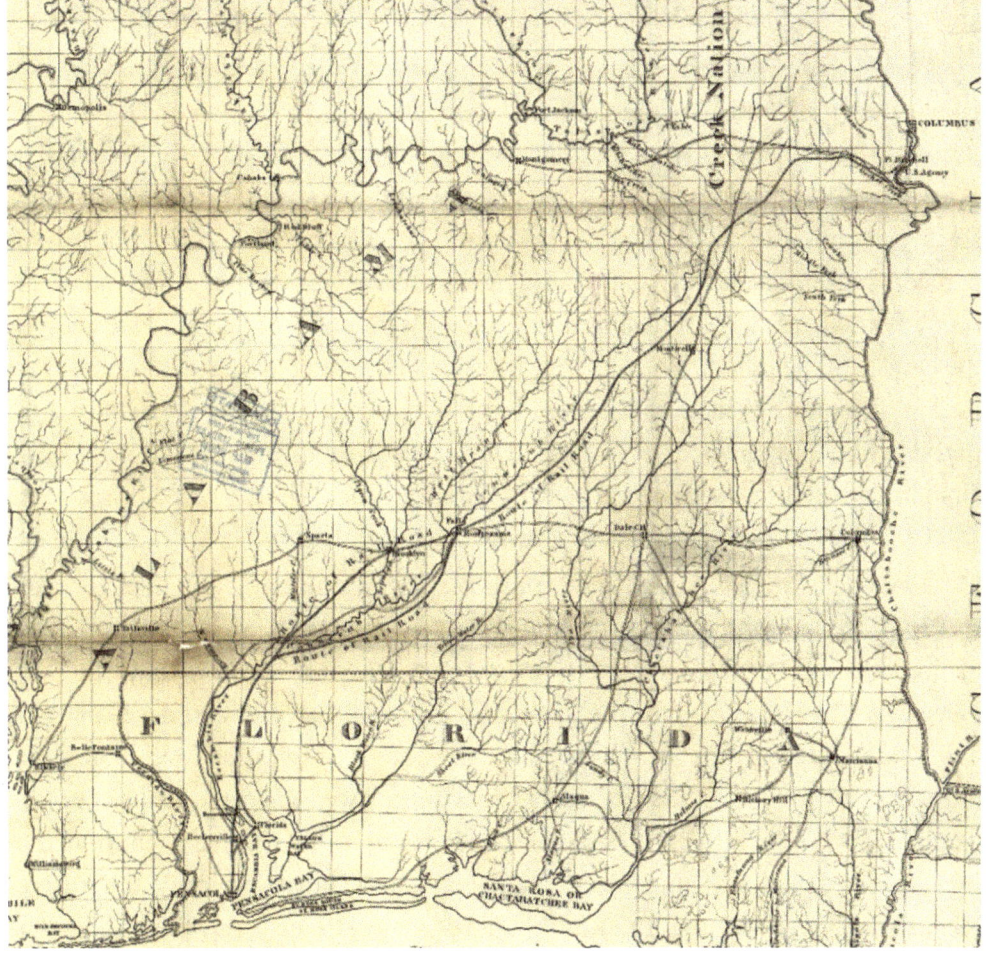

The Bank of Pensacola financial statements as of March 21, 1840 indicated a separate (non-bond) obligation to the BUS of $107,746.72. Intriguingly, that obligation was $84,303.35 at year-end 1837, and had been paid down to $64,531.88 as of January 1, 1839. As of 1841, when liquidation of the BUS commenced, the BUS held $110,469.25 of Bank of Pensacola loan obligations and $90,149.31 of Pensacola Railroad loan obligations.[10]

### Land Matters

The Pensacola Land Company was formed on December 8, 1835 to effectuate the "New City" real estate development project. William H. Chase and Walter Gregory transferred to Chase, as trustee for Pensacola Land, real estate properties and interests in and near Pensacola (including some public lands) that had been acquired by Chase, Gregory, Chase's wife, Cameron, and other agents. Nine of the twelve shares were distributed to Chase, Gregory, Cameron, Blount, Catlin, William L. Booth, and Joseph M. White. The three remaining shares were divided, in halves, among Thomas Biddle, Chauncey, Jaudon, Davis, Wilder, and Robinson.[11]

This Pensacola Land arrangement was modified in 1837 and again in 1838. On January 13, 1837, Chase, Gregory, Cameron, Blount, Booth, James D. Graham, Jackson Morton, Henry Hyer, Charles Le Baron, Biddle, Chauncey, Jaudon, Davis, Wilder, and Robinson executed articles of association for an unincorporated joint stock company that succeeded to the rights of Pensacola Land. That entity was named the "Pensacola City Company". A trust deed was executed that same day whereby the lands were transferred to Chase, Davis, and Robinson, as trustees for the benefit of the others. The property transfers were complex. Property titles were held in the name of Chase, as trustee. The properties had to be transferred to a third party before any transfer to Chase, Davis, and Robinson, as Pensacola City Company trustees. The third party was Walter Gregory. The articles of association and trust deed were filed with the Escambia County Clerk.[12]

A new entity, also named the "Pensacola City Company", was then formally incorporated in Florida on February 11, 1838 to take over the rights and properties of both Pensacola Land and the unincorporated joint stock company (the first Pensacola City Company) for the "confirmation of said articles and deed" of 1837. The shareholders in the Pensacola City Company (corporation) were the same individuals who formed the Pensacola City Company (unincorporated joint stock company) in 1837. Both entities named the Pensacola City Company continued to exist, and at some time Samuel Jaudon and Nathaniel Thurston became the trustees for each. Thereafter, the trustees changed many times over the years. The Philadelphia and New York investors eventually took complete control through the trustee positions, which came to be held by Jaudon, Davis, and Robinson, each being related to, and at some time an officer of, the BUS.[13]

### Diverging Interests

Walter Gregory resigned as a director of the Bank of Pensacola on January 9, 1838 and as president on February 2. William B. Rochester became president but died in June of 1838. He was succeeded by Henry Hyer, who served until March 25, 1839.[C]

---

[C] Henry Hyer was a founder and shareholder in the Union Bank, the Bank of Pensacola, and the Pensacola Railroad. Hyer was no longer a shareholder in the Bank of Pensacola by 1840.

Thomas Blount became president on March 27, 1839 and served through 1842. Henry Yates disposed of his shares in the Bank of Pensacola between January 1 and April 29 of 1835. Dudley S. Gregory and Archibald McIntyre disposed of their shares in the bank before January 1, 1840, likely at the same time Walter resigned. The interests of the parties were diverging.[14]

### Endnotes: Chapter Seven

[1] Description of the restructuring and financing plan is primarily from the BoP Commissioner's Report, except as noted. It includes, at 457-60, the original subscribers on May 16, 1833, the stockholders at January 1 of 1835 and 1840, and share distributions after the passage of the 1835 Act.

[2] The "1835 Act" is FL Law (1835) Ch. 843: for the capital increase to $2.5 million, § 1; for authorization to purchase Pensacola Railroad stock, § 3; for the bond issuance authorization (including an additional $10,000 of bonds for each completed mile), § 4; for issuance of additional bonds for railroad construction, § 6; for Territorial endorsement of the bonds, § 4; for use of bond sale proceeds, §§ 5 and 8 (the latter providing for use of not more than 33% for bank operations and restricting bank dividends until full payment of the bonds); for the indenture, § 7; and for shareholder personal liability, § 8. See the BoP Indenture from the Bank of Pensacola to the Territory of Florida.

For the Petticoat Affair or Eaton-imbroglio, Remini (1981), especially at 203-16, Marszalek (1996), Wood (1997), Latner (1977), Dahl (1974), Eaton (1932), Pollack (1931), and Clark (1942). For Eaton, Appleton's Biographies (1888), at 294. Eaton's biography of Andrew Jackson is Eaton (1824).

[3] A copy of the bond, endorsement, and provisions regarding payment of principal and interest is in BoP Commissioner's Report, at 456.

[4] BoP Commissioner's Report, at 439, and Floridian (1840, August 1).

[5] See Chapter Eleven.

[6] For the bond issuance and sale, BoP Bond Sale Contract (1835), providing a first offer of subsequently issued bonds to the Pensacola Association through William H. Chase, as agent, to be sold in the U.S. or Europe at a commission not exceeding 2.5%. For the Pensacola Association and bond sales, FL Gov. (1842), at 11 and 38-52 (the latter relating to defaults of the Bank of Pensacola and the Florida Territory), and Veenendaal (1996), at 11. The governor's message was presented to the Florida Legislative Council on January 6, 1842.

Jaudon was a significant owner of P&R stock during this period. Chauncey was the P&R president and a large shareholder. For Jaudon's holdings (combined with those of Cowperthwaite and Andrews), BUS Investigation (1841), at 17. Jaudon introduced Colonel John G. Gamble, president of the Union Bank, to Hope & Co., to whom Gamble sold bank shares. Gamble also had contracts with Prime, Ward & King, J. L. & S. Joseph, and Thomas Biddle for sales of Florida bonds and obligations to the BUS. See McGrane (1933), at 676, McGrane (1935), at 10-1 and 228-44 (which includes interactions with Hope & Co. in connection with the Florida repudiation), FL Bank Comm. Rep. (1840), and Schene (1975).

[7] Gregory & Catlin Bond Letter (March 12, 1836).

[8] See endnote 13 of Chapter Eleven.

[9] For purchase of Pensacola Railroad shares, BoP Indenture. For payment of the remaining stock purchase price, BoP Commissioner's Report, at 447-48, and *Statements of the Bank of Pensacola*, including *State of the Bank of Pensacola, April 29, 1835*, at 447-54. See BoP Commissioner's Report, at 440, for loans to the Pensacola Railroad, and 442, for the total investment.

[10] BoP Financials (December 1837), at 451-52, and BoP Financials (1839), at 453. The obligation was $82,541.34 as of June 30, 1838, pursuant to the BoP Financials (1838), at 452. For amounts owed to the BUS, BUS Investigation (1841), at 33.

[11] For formation of Pensacola Land, *McGuire v. Blount* Certiorari (1903), at 22, 37, 38, 50, 66-7, 319-34, and 370, *McGuire v. Blount* Plaintiff Brief (1903), at 53-4, Dodd (1931), at 233, 235, 237, 238, 239, and 240, and the 1837 Indenture, at 319 and 238, Schedule A, referencing the December 8, 1835 Pensacola Land articles of agreement and describing share allocations as of that date. Chase, Blount, Booth, Gregory, Cameron, and White each owned one-ninth, and Davis, Biddle, Wilder, Robinson, Chauncey, and Jaudon each owned one-eighteenth. For the real estate transactions, Dodd (1931), at 235, 1837 Indenture, especially at 319-28, and Riley-Taylor (2013), at 13-6.

[12] During this period both Chases, Walter Gregory, Catlin, Anderson, and Strong, among others, actively sought to integrate Pensacola with Mobile, including by obtaining a directive that the U.S. Post Master General establish a steamboat mail route. See Mail Route Petition (1837). For the use of trusts to hold property for unincorporated joint stock companies in this period, Morley (2016).

[13] For formal incorporation of the Pensacola City Company, FL Law (1838) No. 60 (the 1837-1838 events are in the recital). For the continuing existence of both the unincorporated joint stock company and the corporation, Pensacola City Company Indenture (May 13, 1870), at 337. For changes in trustees and the many deeds and indentures for land transfers, *McGuire v. Blount* Certiorari (1903).

[14] For Gregory's resignation as president, Emancipator (1842, July 28). For Rochester, Hyer, and Blount as presidents, BoP Financials (1839) and Emancipator (1842, July 28). For Hyer and the Union Bank, FL Law (1833) Ch. 697, at § 2, and Abbey (1937). For shareholdings of Dudley S. Gregory, Yates, and McIntyre, BoP Commissioner's Report, at 458 and 460 and endnote 13, Chapter Eleven.

In the realm of curiosities, Buckingham (1842), at 515, recites the following regarding a Columbus, Georgia "Singular Bank Note":

> The town was suffering, it was said, under a pressure of pecuniary difficulties, such as had never been before experienced since it was built, partly owing to

wild speculations of men who meant honorably, but imprudently ventured beyond their reach, partly from the fraudulent and swindling transactions of others of dishonest origin and purpose, and partly from the reckless dissipation of many, who, in desperation of their circumstances, resorted to the race-course or lotteries, or the gaming-table, to recover themselves, and thus lost their all. As a singular, yet melancholy relic of some such wrecked and ruined individual as this class alone could furnish, there came into my possession, received among the change for a payment made at the hotel, a note of the bank of Pensacola for ten dollars, lettered A. No. 107, dated Nov. 1, 1838, and signed by Walter Gregory, president, and James Calten [stet], cashier, on the back of which, as an indorsement, was written the following remarkable sentence in clear and legible hand—

"Here goes the last of an ample fortune, spent in debauchery and every sort of vice. So now farewell dissipation—farewell to courtezan—to the gaming-table—to wine—to sleepless nights and haggard days. Farewell, farewell. Reform! reform! I *will* reform.—Spent in a brothel!"

This note had been thus in general circulation probably for some months, as it was evidently much soiled by use, since this sentence had been written on it. My first impulse was to tear it up or commit it to the flames, and thus prevent its further proclamation of infamy and crime; but, considering that it might possibly have been the writer's wish and intention that this melancholy confession should operate as a warning to others—believing at least that by passing through many hands, it might by accident recall some guilty possessor of it from a similar career—I thought it best to let it continue in circulation, with the change of its thus doing good; though I doubt whether any similar record of confession and repentance could be found in open circulation as money, in any other country on the globe.

Walter Gregory had resigned as president and director approximately eleven months prior to the date of the note bearing his purported signature. And James Catlin was the cashier, not James Calten.

# Chapter Eight

## Control

Through savvy use of trust vehicles after a reorganization and restructuring, the Pensacola Association and friends took control of the Bank of Pensacola and the New City real estate project. Locks & Canals involvement with the Pensacola transaction was influenced by assessments of and relationships with six of the eight individuals comprising the Pensacola Association and a few intimates of those six. The six were Thomas A. Biddle, Elihu Chauncey, Samuel Jaudon, Charles A. Davis, Sampson Vryling Stoddard Wilder, and Morris Robinson. Walter Gregory and William H. Chase were the other two. Friends of the BUS were also Bank of Pensacola shareholders. These included William Gibbs McNeil, Henry Steele,[A] and W. L. Booth & Sons of New York, each well known to L&C and Patrick Tracy Jackson.[1]

In 1835 (after implementation of the reorganization and restructuring plan) and as of January 1, 1840, the stock of the Bank of Pensacola was held in both direct ownership and trust arrangements. These holdings are summarized in Table 1. Presciently, William H. Chase sold his personal shares not controlled by a trustee to his brother George before the post-1837 crash.[2]

Discernable from Table 1 is control of the Bank of Pensacola by a group of individuals with close ties to the BUS: the Pensacola Association and friends. All funds infused between 1835 and 1840, excepting only $50, came from that group. The Pensacola Association, formed in connection with the 1835 reorganization, was comprised of all eight shareholders for whom shares were held in trust.[3]

There were two trusts. Each was administered by Thomas A. Biddle, Elihu Chauncey, and Samuel Jaudon, as trustees. Seven shareholders were beneficiaries of one, and one shareholder (Walter Gregory) was the beneficiary of the second. Walter Gregory also held 916 shares outside the trusts. The trust arrangements ensured that Biddle, Chauncey, and Jaudon controlled most of Gregory's shares. Gregory's direct shareholdings allowed compliance with ownership requirements under Florida law. More importantly, both the direct and beneficial holdings of

---

[A] Steele's wife was a sister of the wife of Charles Howard (the Baltimore & Susquehanna president); each was a daughter of Francis Scott Key.

Gregory were structured to allow the Pensacola Association to dilute Gregory's voting power by virtue of the graduated allocations of votes.[4]

Table 1: Share Holdings in Bank of Pensacola

| Owner of Record | Beneficiary | Shares (1/1835) | Shares (2/1835) | Shares (1/1840) |
|---|---|---|---|---|
| Thomas A. Biddle, Elihu Chauncey, and Samuel Jaudon, as trustees | Walter Gregory | -- | 1,625 | 1,625 |
| Thomas A. Biddle, Elihu Chauncey, and Samuel Jaudon: trustees for the Pensacola Association members | William H. Chase | -- | 1,625 | 1,625 |
| | Thomas Biddle | -- | 1,625 | 1,625 |
| | Samuel Jaudon | -- | 1,625 | 1,625 |
| | Elihu Chauncey | -- | 1,625 | 1,625 |
| | Morris Robinson | -- | 1,625 | 1,625 |
| | S. V. S. Wilder | -- | 1,625 | 1,625 |
| | Charles A. Davis | -- | 1,625 | 1,625 |
| | Total | -- | 11,375 | 11,375 |
| Walter Gregory (OH/FL) | | 621 | 916 | 916 |
| William H. Chase (FL) | | 0 | 917 | 0 |
| George E. Chase (FL) | | 0 | 0 | 1,167 |
| Dudley S. Gregory (NJ/NY) | | 289 | 289 | 0 |
| Henry Yates (NY) | | 145 | 0 | 0 |
| Archibald McIntyre (NY) | | 144 | 0 | 0 |
| William L. Booth (NY) | | 100 | 400 | 400 |
| William Gibbs McNeil (NY) | | 0 | 300 | 300 |
| Charles A. Davis (NY) | | 0 | 0 | 850 |
| Henry Steele (NY/NJ) | | 0 | 0 | 753 |
| William H. Chase, as trustee | ? | -- | 850 | 850 |
| Others | | 701 | 6,617 | 4,602 |
| Bank of Pensacola | | 0 | 0 | 1,912 |
| Territory of Florida | | 0 | 0 | 250 |
| Total: All Shares | | 1,750 | 23,000 | 25,000 |
| Amount Paid (cash, $)[B] | | | | 69,115 |
| Amount Paid (notes, $) | | | | 41,335 |
| Unpaid shares | | | | 4,332 |

Three individuals, acting as trustees, controlled 13,000 shares (of the 25,000 authorized), which included 1,625 shares owned beneficially by Gregory. Likely the

---

[B] Cash payments were from the Pensacola Association ($65,000), Henry Steele ($3,765), and two Pensacola shareholders ($25 each).

trustees were entitled to exercise considerable (probably absolute) discretion in voting those shares. Davis, McNeil, Steele, and Booth held 1,500 shares outside the trusts and likely voted in the same pattern as the 13,000 shares held in trusts.[5]

The BUS "friends" (Davis, McNeil, Steele, and Booth) were critical to BUS control of the Bank of Pensacola because of graduated voting restrictions in the law establishing the bank. Votes were: (a) for one share and not less than two shares, one vote; (b) for every two shares not exceeding ten, one vote; (c) for every four shares above ten and not exceeding thirty, one vote; (d) for every six shares above thirty and not exceeding sixty, one vote; (e) for every eight shares above sixty and not exceeding one hundred, one vote; and (f) no person, partnership, or body politic was entitled to more than thirty votes.[6]

By 1840, the holdings of George E. Chase, the Bank of Pensacola, and the Territory of Florida increased. William H. Chase exited from his direct non-trust Bank of Pensacola share holdings by 1840 and held 850 shares in trust.

## Endnotes: Chapter Eight

[1] For Bank of Pensacola shareholders, BoP Commissioner's Report, at 460. For the wives of Henry Steele and Charles Howard, *Francis Scott Key's Last Child: Mrs. Charles Howard Passos* [stet] *Away at Her Cottage in Oakland*, No. 6,759 THE WASHINGTON POST (September 10, 1897), at 7.

[2] Data in Table 1 is from the BoP Commissioner's Report, at 458 and 460, and may not disclose all beneficial ownership relationships. For share sales, Walby (2014), at 31, stating that Chase, Walter Gregory, and Catlin sold their shares before the crash, which is supported by the BoP Commissioner's Report. Chase and Gregory may have sold beneficial interests that were subject to the trust arrangements; that has not been determined. For share issuances, BoP Commissioner's Report, at 439-40. For holdings of Gregory and other investors, Dewey (1910), at 32.

[3] The BoP Financials (July 1837) contain six debit entries: capital stock ($500,125), total bills in circulation ($85,516), "Amounts to the act. of [Pensacola] Rail Road and other Depositers" [stet] ($118,919.42), "Bank of U.S. agency account and other Banks" ($180,681.84), and profits ($27,023.93). At that time, $332,840.19 had been paid by the Bank of Pensacola in respect of Pensacola Railroad stock. The March 21, 1840 financial statements also show (a) obligations to the BUS of $107,746.72 and, to the BUS New York Branch, $2,013.35, and (b) the outstanding bonds in the amount of $500,000 (BoP Commissioner's Report, at 463-64).

[4] For Gregory's share ownership, Dewey (1910), at 32.

[5] The trust agreements were not located. Thus, exact voting cannot be determined.

[6] FL Law (1831), § 6, ¶ I.

Figure 6: Nicholas Biddle, 1843

## Chapter Nine

### Pensacola Association and Friends

**Guardians**

Direct access to southern cotton was alluring to Locks & Canals as well as the Bank of the United States. Enough for L&C to contemplate a naked and unprotected sale of rolling stock to opportunistic promoters in the distant wilds of the Territory of Florida. To ensure that access, the financial arrangements for the different, though interrelated, Pensacola transactions, and the Floridians, had to be managed and controlled.

No Boston Associates being involved, for adequate control L&C was forced to rely on the Pensacola Association and its friends. Most of those men were well known Whig stalwarts closely aligned with the BUS and Nicholas Biddle (in sharp contrast to the Jacksonian bent of the Floridians). Many had roles in other transactions in which L&C and Patrick Tracy Jackson were involved. Control was maintained by the Pensacola Association and friends through the trust ownership arrangements and graduated voting restrictions. Reassuringly, from the L&C perspective, the involvements of Biddle, the BUS, and some Pensacola Association members was an extension of their aggressive efforts to control cotton pricing and internal improvements. As further comfort, most of the debt was guaranteed by the Territory of Florida. These factors, and L&C's desire to keep the machine shop working, obscured (or diverted critical analysis of) realities that foretold disaster.[1]

The Pensacola Association and friends were comprised of three groups. The core group consisted of Thomas A. Biddle, Elihu Chauncey, and Samuel Jaudon. These three functioned as the trustees that controlled the voting stock of the bank, the land ventures, and, indirectly, the railroad.[2]

The second group was comprised of Pensacola Association members that were not trustees: Charles A. Davis, S. V. S. Wilder, and Morris Robinson. Each was a long-time intimate of Nicholas Biddle and the BUS in trading, cotton, internal improvements, and other financial matters.

William Gibbs McNeil, Henry Steele, and William L. Booth constituted the third group. None was a member of the Pensacola Association. Each had long involvements with and was a dependable ally of Nicholas Biddle and the BUS. These men were critical to managerial control because they voted in harmony with the Pensacola Association members that served as trustees holding the other shares.

From Patrick Tracy Jackson's perspective in 1845 as he reconsidered the Pensacola transactions, the critical questions related to whether reliance on these men and their arrangements regarding the Pensacola endeavors was appropriate and prudent?

Figure 7: Bank of the United States

## Thomas A. Biddle

One of the most extensive brokerage businesses in Philadelphia was Thomas Biddle & Company, which acted for Stephen Girard, among many others. Its London correspondent was Thomson Hankey & Co. which played a significant role in the early affairs of the Philadelphia & Reading, succeeding Gowan & Marx.

Biddle was a prominent and well-respected Philadelphia banker, financier, investor, broker, and merchant. He and his brokerage were instrumental in placing loans for the P&R, directly and through Hankey & Co. Biddle privately placed loans for many small U.S. railroads, including those in Virginia and Pennsylvania. Biddle sold bonds on behalf of the Union Bank of Florida in 1834, taking some for his own account. The other selling agents for the Union Bank were Prime, Ward & King, J.

D. Beers & Co., and J. L. & S. Joseph, each of New York. Biddle invested in and provided financing for internal improvements undertakings, especially railroad and canal companies, although he had interests in diverse enterprises, including coal and whaling companies.[3]

Figure 8: Thomas A. Biddle

Thomas A. Biddle was a member of the P&R board of managers at various times, including in 1834-1835, as a founding member, and in 1838-1839. He declined election in 1837 and the position was filled by Samuel Jaudon. Biddle was intimately involved in the Little Schuylkill Navigation, Rail Road and Coal Company. He was instrumental in causing the Little Schuylkill to commission Moncure Robinson to survey its route. Both Biddle and the Little Schuylkill played prominent roles in the P&R's development. Robinson, while chief engineer of the P&R, worked with Patrick Tracy Jackson on the specifications of the engines built under the Engines Contract. Biddle also arranged the engagement of Samuel Bradford as treasurer of the Little Schuylkill and was instrumental in Bradford becoming treasurer of the P&R. Biddle was a founding shareholder in the Lycoming Coal Company in 1833, together with Elihu Chauncey and Patrick Tracy Jackson.[4]

Thomas A. Biddle was an early member, together with his distant relative, Nicholas Biddle, of the Pennsylvania Improvement Society, established in 1824 to promote roads, canals, railroads, and other improvements. Many of his investments in internal improvements were made together with Nicholas Biddle and the BUS. That rendered him subject to inquiries in the investigation of the BUS in 1832, with the minority report taking pains to note that Thomas Biddle engaged in no culpable conduct in either his discounting or borrowing transactions with the BUS. Thomas Biddle later became U.S. Consul in Singapore.[5]

**Elihu Chauncey**

Elihu Chauncey was a banker, investor, lawyer, newspaper editor (THE UNITED STATES GAZETTE, an influential federalist paper, with Enos Bronson), and intimate of the Pennsylvania political, financial, and merchant elites.[6] He was born in New Haven on January 15, 1779, the second son of Charles and Abigail (Darling) Chauncey. His father was a judge in New Haven. Elihu died in Philadelphia on April 8, 1847. The Chaunceys were a wealthy merchant and intellectual family. Elihu descended directly from Charles Chauncey, the second president of Harvard College. He moved to Philadelphia in 1796 upon completing his schooling at Yale College and was admitted to the bar in 1800. In his early years in Philadelphia he resided at Mrs. Smith's boarding house, as did the later-prominent lawyers Horace Binney and Charles Chauncey, the latter being Elihu's older brother.[7]

Soon after moving to Philadelphia, Elihu Chauncey became active in banking. He remained active in banking, as well as railroading, throughout his life. He was a director of the Bank of Pennsylvania for many years. He was a director of the BUS in 1816. On June 1, 1838, he was appointed to the committee of delegates of associated Philadelphia banks that coordinated with banks in other states regarding the resumption of specie payments. Chauncey was for many years a member of the City Councils of Philadelphia and was actively involved in negotiating financings for the Commonwealth of Pennsylvania.[8]

Elihu Chauncey's business involvements were many, broad, and deep. He was a director of the Marine Insurance Company, The Pennsylvania Company for Insurances on Lives and Granting Annuities, the West-Chester Rail-Road Company (as one of the largest shareholders), and, from and after the Civil War, the Richmond, Fredericksburg and Potomac Railroad Company. Chauncey was an incorporator and founding shareholder of the Lebanon Valley Railroad Company in 1836 (together with Thomas and Edward Biddle) and The Richmond and Ohio Railroad Company in 1846 (with Moncure Robinson and Benjamin Etting of Philadelphia). Elihu Chauncey was a stockholder, with Thomas A. Biddle, and on the committee to investigate the transactions of the directors, of the Delaware & Raritan and the Camden & Amboy. He was a stockholder in the Bald Eagle and Spring Creek Navigation Company (with Thomas A. Biddle), the Union Canal Company of Pennsylvania, the North Branch Canal Company, and, with Patrick Tracy Jackson, Lycoming Coal Company. Chauncey was a founder of the Preston Retreat to provide obstetrics services for indigent married women of good character, together with other prominent Philadelphians, including Nicholas Biddle, Joseph Cowperthwaite, Charles Chauncey, Frederick Fraley, and Caleb Cope. Chauncey was a land speculator in Wisconsin in the 1830s, together with Thomas A. Biddle and Edward R. Biddle. Chauncey was also a member of the Welsh Club of Philadelphia.[9]

Elihu Chauncey's involvements with the P&R and the Little Schuylkill were well known to Jackson. Chauncey was a major investor in the P&R and was elected its president at the first meeting of stockholders on November 22, 1834. He served as president until January 10, 1842, when he retired immediately upon completion of the P&R's first run from Mount Carbon to Philadelphia. Through the P&R, he worked intimately with Edward R. Biddle, Thomas A. Biddle, Samuel Jaudon, Ashbel Green Jaudon, William McKee, John A. Brown, Moncure Robinson, and a litany of other railroad investors and managers, as well as Jackson and L&C. Both Biddles, both Jaudons, McKee, and Brown all served on the P&R board of managers during Chauncey's tenure as president. Shortly after his election as president, Chauncey was instrumental in hiring Moncure Robinson as the P&R's chief engineer.[A] Chauncey handled financing matters and worked closely with Robinson. Robinson handled operational matters (assisted by his cousin, Wirt Robinson) and provided significant assistance in obtaining financing in the P&R's early years.[10]

Elihu Chauncey was an early investor in the Little Schuylkill, together with Thomas A. Biddle, Thomas Sergeant, Joseph Cowperthwaite, and Edward R. Biddle. The Little Schuylkill was promoted by, among others, Frederick List, who had moved to Reading, and Stephen Girard of Philadelphia, a founding investor. The Little Schuylkill played a decisive role in the P&R's early development. As a condition to the P&R's ability to operate, critical route rights of the Little Schuylkill

---

[A] Moncure Robinson was introduced to Elihu by Elihu's brother, Nathan, who met Robinson during European travels and became a close friend.

were relinquished to the P&R in its formative years. The Little Schuylkill was eventually (in 1868) leased as an entirety by the P&R.[11]

Figure 9: Samuel Jaudon

**Samuel Jaudon**

After Nicholas Biddle, Samuel Jaudon was the most powerful officer of the Philadelphia incarnation of the Bank of the United States. His most important roles were principal cashier and London agent. He became cashier in 1832 after serving as assistant cashier (1826-1828) and cashier (1828-1832) of the New Orleans branch.[B] His responsibilities included placing securities and loans with European investors and financiers on behalf of U.S. railroad, canal, and internal improvements companies and the speculative ventures of Nicholas Biddle and the BUS, including in cotton and securities trading. His foreign placements included other assets as well. For example, Chauncey handled European sales of land holdings of his friend, Daniel Webster. Jaudon served as a BUS director. He also served as the trustee in the liquidation of the BUS.

Jaudon was paid handsomely as BUS cashier: $7,000 per annum. After November 8, 1837, when he assumed the London agent role, he was paid $28,000 annually (the amount formerly paid to Baring, Brothers & Company). His supplemented his income with agency commissions of $335,937.39.[12]

Samuel Jaudon's mandate as BUS agent

> was to devote himself exclusively to the business of the Bank, to negotiate an uncovered credit in England, to provide for the then existing debt in Europe, to receive its funds, to pay its bills and dividends, to effect sales of stocks, and generally to protect the interests of the Bank and the "country at large."[13]

Notwithstanding the mandate to act exclusively as BUS agent, Jaudon supplemented his income by acting as agent for the P&R and Morrison, Sons & Co., and others.

Samuel Jaudon, an intimate of Nicholas Biddle, was a banker, broker, director, manager, and investor, including in internal improvements and coal companies. He served as a director of many entities in which he had an interest. He served on boards of directors as a BUS representative where the BUS had an interest in an entity. For example, while in the employ of the BUS, Jaudon served as a member of the P&R board from its inception until October 11, 1837, when he was appointed BUS general agent in London. Jaudon also served as the London agent of the P&R with respect to critical financing and iron rail supply matters from 1839 to 1841. His brother and co-investor, Ashbel Green Jaudon, served on the P&R board from October 5, 1837 until January 14, 1839 and then again from January 11, 1841 to

---

[B] The position of "cashier" was especially powerful in the BUS structure under Nicholas Biddle. There were cashiers at the parent and each branch, all appointed by the parent board of directors. Biddle characterized cashiers as "confidential officers". They represented the interests of the parent and implemented, and were held responsible for implementing, parent board policies at both the parent and the branches. The cashier was the general manager of the bank. "Much tact was necessary for the position, since the cashier of the branch was more than an employee of the office in question. He was the local confidential officer of the parent board and as such was entitled even to give his opinion on the election of directors and the qualifications and conduct of branch presidents."

September 1, 1841. In later years, Samuel Jaudon had investments in companies such as the Ocean Steam Navigation Company in New York and The Lake Huron Silver and Copper Mining Company.[14]

Samuel Jaudon, Nicholas Biddle, John Andrews, and others were arrested on a bench warrant for conspiracy to commit frauds allegedly perpetrated by the BUS. They were released after obtaining *habeas corpus* rulings. Jaudon was also active in various societies in Pennsylvania, such as the Young Men's Colonization Society of Pennsylvania.[15]

Samuel, born in 1796, was one of nine children of Daniel and Anna McNeil Jaudon. Through their marriages, two siblings (Charles Bancker and Ashbel Green) played influential roles in Samuel's life. Charles Bancker Jaudon married Mary Taylor Bainbridge, and Ashbel Green Jaudon married Lucy Ann Bainbridge. Mary and Lucy were daughters of Commodore William Bainbridge.[16]

Figure 10: William Bainbridge, circa 1814

Noteworthy familial dealings involving Mary and Lucy relate to a later and more unfortunate period when Samuel Jaudon was engaged in speculative transactions in Pennsylvania coal fields. At that time Samuel was the trustee of trusts established by Commodore Bainbridge for Mary, Lucy, and their two other sisters. Because of Samuel's activities, Mary sued Samuel in a case that made its way to the U.S. Supreme Court as *Duncan v. Jaudon*.[17]

Terms of the Bainbridge trusts required the two original trustees to invest in stocks of the U.S. or its states. Earnings were paid to the Commodore's daughters during their lives, with the corpus of the trust passing to their children. When Mary and the other sisters determined the payments to be less than desired, the original trustees were discharged in 1865 and Samuel Jaudon was appointed trustee. Lucy was then a widow, Charles Bancker having died on February 7, 1864.

Samuel, with the consent of the sisters, sold the 5% Pennsylvania state stock held by Mary's trust and invested the proceeds in stock of the Delaware & Raritan, which was yielding 10% annually, was stable, and was considered a "blue chip" stock. Mary received 117 shares of Delaware & Raritan stock. The stock certificates bore identical legends (except as to the number of shares). One stated that "S. Jaudon, trustee for Mrs. Mary T.B. Jaudon, is entitled to seventy shares in the capital stock of the Delaware and Raritan Canal Company.... Transferable on the books of the Company, on surrender of this certificate only by him or his legal representative."[18]

In 1865 Samuel was dealing in speculative stocks of companies working Pennsylvania's Broad Top coal and iron region. He took a two-year revolving loan facility from the National City Bank of New York, securing the loan with forty-seven Delaware & Raritan shares. Samuel executed a power of attorney allowing the bank to sell the stock upon a loan default. That power of attorney was executed by "S. Jaudon, trustee for Mrs. M. T. B. Jaudon". Ten separate loans were made and repaid under the facility, with the stock returned to Samuel upon each payment and redelivered to the bank upon each new loan. In 1867 the loans came due, Samuel was unable to pay, the bank was unwilling to renew the facility, and the bank sold the forty-seven shares.

Shortly thereafter, in 1867, Samuel Jaudon took a 90-day loan from the New York firm of Duncan, Sherman and Company, with whom Jaudon had a long relationship. Duncan-Sherman was a U.S. special friend of George Peabody and Company of London. To secure the loan, Samuel pledged the remaining seventy shares of Mary's Delaware & Raritan stock, providing a power of attorney identical to that previously used in the National City Bank loan. Jaudon defaulted on repayment of this loan and Duncan-Sherman sold the seventy shares. Although valued at approximately $20,000, the shares were sold for $7,729.88 and a residual amount of $969.24 was paid to Samuel Jaudon.[19]

Mary was unaware of the two loans and related share pledges. It was established that, in taking these loans, Samuel Jaudon acted for his personal benefit to purchase Broad Top stock. The Broad Top stock was registered in Jaudon's name, personally and not as trustee. After learning of the stock foreclosure sales, Mary sued Samuel, National City Bank, and Duncan-Sherman (and other suits were filed). Samuel was then insolvent.

The circuit court ordered each of National City Bank and Duncan-Sherman to account to Mary for the value of the shares (forty-seven and seventy, respectively) and all dividends and other proceeds that would have been earned had the stock not been sold. The basis of the ruling was that the banks knew or should have known (by actual or constructive notice) that Jaudon, without authorization, was applying the loan proceeds to his personal use. Among the relevant factors was the statement on stock certificates that Samuel was a trustee for Mary.

The U.S. Supreme Court affirmed the circuit court holding in Mary's favor, characterizing Samuel Jaudon's actions as a "gross" and "flagrant breach of trust, without either justification or excuse" and a breach of his fiduciary duties, and characterizing the actions of National City Bank as "gross negligence". It is unclear whether Mary was paid by Samuel. It is unlikely given his financial position at the time. No information is available regarding the other sisters.

Samuel Jaudon died insolvent on May 1, 1874, ten months after the Supreme Court's ruling in *Duncan v. Jaudon*. Samuel, Marguerite (Samuel's wife), Ashbel Green, Lucy, Charles Bancker, and Mary all reside together, in whatever state of harmony or disharmony, in the Jaudon Vault, Mount Vernon Cemetery, Philadelphia.

**Charles Augustus Davis**

Charles Augustus Davis was a principal, with Sidney Brooks, of the New York merchant firm of Davis & Brooks. The firm specialized in the Mediterranean trade, especially fruits, wines, and iron.

Davis was a close friend of Nicholas Biddle, a director of the BUS, and a director of the State Bank of New York. He was a member of the Friends of Domestic Industry where he served on committees with Patrick Tracy Jackson and worked with other Boston Associates, including Warren Dutton, Abbott Lawrence, William Appleton, William Lawrence, Israel Thorndike, and Amos Binney. Press criticism of Whig internal improvement policy in 1842 identified Charles A. Davis, Morris Robinson, and others, such as Daniel Webster, Governor William H. Seward, J. S. &

L. Joseph, and the Grand Island company ("probably Webster and White's speculation"), as borrowers from the Life and Trust Company of Baltimore upon the "bursting up of [this] humbug institution".[20]

In 1836 Davis was a trustee of the Apalachicola Land Company, had direct involvements with the Floridians in the Pensacola Railroad venture, and was an active promoter of the Pensacola Railroad.[21]

Figure 11: James DePeyster Ogden & Charles Augustus Davis

Care of New York City's Gramercy Park, upon its formation, was reposed in Charles A. Davis as one of the original trustees under the December 17, 1831 land grant of Samuel B. Ruggles and Mary R. Ruggles. The grant conveyed forty-two lots between 20th and 21st streets for, as the deed states,

> the formation and establishment of an ornamental private Square or Park with carriage-ways and footwalks at the south-eastern and north-western ends thereof for the use, benefit and enjoyment of the owners and occupants of sixty-six surrounding lots of land belonging to the said Samuel B. Ruggles and with a view to enhance the value thereof....[22]

78 | Lost in Florida

Figure 12: *Cider Making*, William Sidney Mount, 1840-1841

Charles A. Davis, a copyist of the Seba Smith series, was the author of fictional and satirical Major Jack Downing letters. Possibly, the letters were created as part of a broader pro-Whig, anti-Jackson campaign. In any case, they increased his access within elite New York political and literary circles.

Davis was a patron of the painter William Sidney Mount. Davis commissioned Mount's painting of *The Rabbit Trappers* (also known as *Boys Trapping* or *Catching*

*Rabbits*) in 1839 for $250. Davis next commissioned *Cider Making* (1841) by Mount, also for $250, to celebrate the Whig victory over the Jacksonians in 1840: the Whig slogan was "Log Cabin and Hard Cider".[23]

The slogan was a bit ironic. It derived from a Democratic characterization of Harrison. The Whigs positioned Harrison as a poor, humble farmer: the "Ploughman Candidate for President". In fact, Harrison was an Ohio senator and former Indiana territorial governor descended from a Virginia plantation owner who signed the Declaration of Independence. Democrats mocked "Old Granny" Harrison: he should be given a barrel of hard cider so he could sit for his remaining days in his log cabin and study moral philosophy.

Whigs seized the moment, designating Harrison the Log Cabin Candidate and campaigning in horse drawn log cabins mounted on wheels. President Van Buren's regal ways were lampooned, including by Davy Crockett. Van Buren was characterized as "Sweet Sandy Whiskers" by representative Charles Ogle of Pennsylvania in a congressional speech.

*Cider Making* probably hung in the home of Charles A. Davis prior to April 1841, when it was exhibited at the National Academy of Design's Sixteenth Exhibition. Davis, a member of the American Art-Union, once owned the portrait of George Washington by Adolph Ulrich Wertmüller. Davis also opened his home to the poet F. G. Halleck and other Knickerbocker writers.[24]

Despite the winding up of the Pensacola Railroad, and despite different political orientations, Davis remained involved with the Floridians as they pursued revival of the railroad. For example, an 1844 revival committee was comprised of William H. Chase, Hanson Kelly, Henry Hyer, Thomas M. Blount, Dillon Jordan (chairman), and others. The final resolution passed at the committee meeting was in tribute to Davis, as well as the other New York and Philadelphia villains.[25]

> *Resolved*, That in consideration of the interest manifested by certain gentlemen of New York and Philadelphia on the construction of this Rail Road, that the meeting express its gratitude by three cheers for those gentlemen in general and to Charles Augustus Davis, of New York, in particular.
>
> Whereupon, three hearty cheers were rendered.

## Sampson Vryling Stoddard Wilder

During a period of residence in Paris, Sampson Vryling Stoddard Wilder undertook to advocate a position of the Prime Minister of France, the Duc de Broglie, to President Andrew Jackson. The French demanded an apology from President Jackson for statements made during his first inaugural address. Without the apology, France felt itself unable to make an agreed settlement payment to the U.S. of $25 million. Wilder prevailed with Jackson and the payment was made.[26]

Figure 13: Sampson Vryling Stoddard Wilder, circa 1808

The representation of the Duc de Broglie and French interests exemplified the depth and breadth of Wilder's contacts with French governmental, merchant, and financial communities. As a merchant and international financier, his ties to the New York and New Jersey merchant and financial communities were equally deep and broad.

Wilder was the New York correspondent of the French firm of Hottinguer & Company of Paris and Havre, a leading seller of securities of U.S. states. He was courted by Nicholas Biddle and became involved with the BUS as its New York agent, working closely with Samuel Jaudon. John Tappan, a life-long friend and member of many of the same societies as Wilder, wrote scathingly of Wilder's involvements with Biddle.

> In the seductions of Nicholas Biddle ... I date his [Wilder's] ruin.... In the misfortune of Mr. Wilder, the utmost that enmity or envy could charge him with was, and has ever been, in my opinion, a want of judgment in putting trust in so large a schemer as Mr. Biddle has proved after his failure to have been.

Wilder died impecunious in Boston on March 3, 1865.[27]

Figure 14: Sampson Vryling Stoddard Wilder

Wilder was born on May 20, 1780 in Lancaster, Massachusetts to Levi Wilder and Sarah Stoddard. His great-grandfather was a minister in Chelmsford and his great-uncle was a minister in Northampton. Wilder's mercantile activities included Southern cotton trading and his investments were in banks, coal, iron, and real estate, among other industries.

Wilder was a principal participant in the efforts of Nicholas Biddle to control the supply and pricing of cotton. As part of that effort, Wilder authored and distributed an 1839 circular on cotton. The circular suggested that American cotton sales be concentrated in one Liverpool house and be consigned and sold, in their entirety, through Humphreys & Biddle. Humphreys & Biddle, whose principals were Mays Humphreys, a BUS director, and Nicholas Biddle's son, Edward, was formed in 1837. It was established in connection with the plan of Nicholas Biddle, drawing on the Philadelphia firm of Bevans & Humphreys, to support and control Southern cotton production and pricing in England and Amsterdam. Humphreys & Biddle circumvented sales by, and sale practices of, Baring Brothers and Company in London. The activities of the Pensacola Association were an extension of the endeavor to control Southern cotton.[28]

Wilder was a devoted evangelical Calvinist. He was deeply involved in religious, temperance, educational, and social movements. He was a founder and the first president of the American Tract Society. He was an early and active member of the American Peace Society, together with John Tappan and Lewis Tappan. Wilder presided at the annual meetings of the American Peace Society from 1831 to 1837 and declined its presidency in 1837. Wilder instigated the founding of La Société des Amis de la Morale Chŕetien et de la Paix in 1821 in France. He was also a prominent member of the American Temperance Society,[C] the American Education Society, and the Prison Discipline Society.[29]

From 1841, Wilder was unable to fund the American Tract Society and other projects in which he had long been involved. He resigned as an officer of each. Wilder then served a period in debtor's prison. The American Tract Society ascribed the prison term to the actions of "rum-dealing creditors" that Wilder so often assailed in his role with the temperance societies.[30]

### Morris Robinson

Morris Robinson was born in Nova Scotia, his family having fled from Virginia because of their loyalist beliefs during the revolutionary war with England.

---

[C] Wilder and Charles A. Davis must have avoided discussions of temperance. Wilder did indulge in a pinch of snuff now and then, asserting he did so on his physician's advice.

Following an apprenticeship in his uncle's St. John counting house, Robinson moved to New York in 1810. In 1812 he became cashier of the Orange County Bank in Goshen, where he remained until he became cashier of the New York Branch of the BUS in 1819. Robinson worked as cashier in the BUS branch until 1836. He became a trusted friend and ally of Nicholas Biddle. Robinson became president of the New York incarnation of "the Pennsylvania Monster" in 1838 and served on the board of directors.

Figure 15: Morris Robinson

By 1839 Robinson represented the American Exchange Bank in London. Soon thereafter he became a vice president of the American Life Insurance and Trust Company of Baltimore, remaining there until it ceased operations in 1842.

In 1842, Morris Robinson and Alfred Pell founded The Mutual Life Insurance Company of New York. Robinson was the first president, with an annual salary of $1,500 per year, which became $4,000 by 1848. From 1843 to 1847, he transformed the U.S. life insurance business, particularly regarding principles of mutuality and person-to-person marketing, which he introduced.[31]

## William Gibbs McNeill

William Gibbs McNeill, a West Point graduate, was not a member of the Pensacola Association but maintained extensive contacts with its members and their associates. McNeil had considerable experience in the railroad and canal industries, including as an engineer and surveyor. Examples include the Chesapeake and Ohio Canal and the Baltimore & Ohio railroad. McNeil was engaged to construct the Boston & Providence (which he completed) while Patrick Tracy Jackson was a director. Thereafter, McNeil was retained by Jackson as a consultant for the Boston & Lowell with the mandate to survey its route. Upon completion of his survey report, the Boston & Lowell board retained McNeil as both agent and engineer.

William Gibbs McNeil was a close friend of George Washington Whistler who had worked with Jackson at both L&C and the Boston & Lowell. He had been an engineer of the Western Railroad with Whistler. McNeil's sister, Anna, was Whistler's wife.[32]

Figure 16: William Gibbs McNeill

## Other BUS Relationships

A few more interrelationships among the different principals of the Bank of Pensacola and the Pensacola Railroad endeavors played through the analysis. The most important related to the BUS.

In 1833 and 1841, Nicholas Biddle and Samuel Jaudon were members of the BUS board of directors. Horace Binney and Thomas Cadwalader, legal counsel to Nicholas Biddle, were also directors, as was John A. Brown, a member of the P&R board of managers. William Appleton was president and Abbot Lawrence and Charles Chauncey were directors of the Boston Branch of the BUS.[D] Roswell L. Colt, another close friend of Nicholas Biddle, was a director of the BUS Baltimore Branch.[33]

Philip Hone's diary sheds light on some interrelationships of these people, direct and indirect.[E] During the 1830s and early 1840s Charles A. Davis and his wife, individually and together, dined with Hone and various luminaries, including Daniel Webster, Washington Irving, James Monroe, John Quincy Adams, James Kent, and Peter A. Jay. Hone dined and sailed with William Sturgis, John Bryant, and other Boston Associates. Hone also dined with Abbot Lawrence and his wife during the tariff conventions and before Lawrence was elected to Congress. Hone attended the opening of the Boston & Providence and was shown about Boston by William Appleton. The inauguration of Martin Van Buren brought Hone together with Daniel Webster, Abbot Lawrence, and James Kent, although Morris Robinson was unable to attend due to troubles in Wall Street.[34]

The Philadelphia and Boston investors cooperated in civic and humanitarian initiatives as well. Upon the 1835 New York fire, Elihu Chauncey, Thomas Biddle, and Samuel Jaudon called meetings of the Philadelphia citizenry to assist the "New

---

[D] William Appleton and Abbot Lawrence were investors in L&C and other Lowell and Waltham ventures, and each was a shareholder in the Lowell Machine Shop, which purchased most assets of the L&C machine shop.

[E] Philip Hone was a founding commissioner, prominent shareholder, the first president, and a director of The President, Managers and Company of the Delaware and Hudson Canal Company. He remained a director until his death on May 5, 1851. Honesdale, Pennsylvania was named after him. He was the mayor of the City of New York in 1826-1827. Hone acquired his wealth in the auction business and was a successful merchant and arts patron. He was the founder of the Mercantile Library Association. The site of his New York home, at 235 Broadway, was purchased by F. W. Woolworth as the site for the Woolworth Building. Hone was buried at St. Mark's Church in the Bowery. His diary was kept from 1826.

York sufferers". A Committee of Fifty was organized by Nicholas Biddle and Samuel Jaudon, among others. Patrick Tracy Jackson, William Sturgis, Henry Lee, William Appleton, John A. Lowell, William Lawrence, Amos Lawrence, Thomas H. Perkins, and Samuel Appleton spearheaded the response in Boston.[35]

### George's Creek Coal & Iron

Events involving George's Creek Coal and Iron Company provide a flavor of interrelationships among individuals involved in the Pensacola Railroad transactions. And a flavor of what those interrelationships begat. Of course, the full flavor was not perceptible until years after Patrick Tracy Jackson's reassessment in December of 1845.

Nicholas Biddle's wife was a cousin of Roswell L. Colt's wife, Peggy Oliver, the daughter of Robert Oliver of Baltimore. The lands of Robert Oliver and Peggy's brother, Charles, became part of the capital of George's Creek Coal & Iron soon after its incorporation in 1835. It was originally incorporated as George's Creek Mining Company by John H. Alexander and Philip T. Tyson but changed its name in June of 1836. By the first shareholders meeting on March 4, 1837, its shareholders included Charles A. Davis, Morris Robinson, S. V. S. Wilder, Roswell L. Colt, William S. Wetmore,[F] Joseph L. Joseph, Samuel Joseph, Philip Hone, Isaac Lawrence

---

[F] Wetmore was a New York merchant and financier, a principal of Alsop & Wetmore (his first firm), Wetmore & Wetmore, Wetmore & Co., Alsop, Wetmore & Cryder, Wetmore, Cryder & Co., and, in Canton, Wetmore & Co., and a director of many railroads. Wetmore had close relationships with Morrison, Cryder & Co. of London. He and John Cryder, a president of the P&R, were partners. Wetmore was engaged in opium, silk, and tea trades in Canton, living in Canton and Macao in the 1830s. He was the first to import gutta percha into the U.S., in 1847. In international finance, Wetmore was a secret partner of George Peabody. He later invested in steamship travel between the U.S. and England and ran mail ships between New York and Liverpool for the U.S. Navy in 1849.

Wetmore was a delegate to the Internal Improvement Convention of New York State. He was a trustee of P&R bond financings. He was a director of the Phoenix Coal Mining Company, the Dauphin & Susquehanna Coal Co., and the Central Railroad Company of New Jersey. He was a member of the stockholders investigating committee of the Delaware, Lackawanna and Western Rail-Road Co. Wetmore was a trustee of the General Mutual Insurance Company and the Atlantic Mutual Insurance Company, an agent of the North American Fire Insurance Company, and a manager of the Life Saving Benevolent Association (for saving shipwrecked mariners and passengers off Long Island). Wetmore was a member and auditor of the Morrison Education Society, which (president of the New York Branch of the BUS), the lawyers John Duer and Samuel Ruggles, and American Life and Trust Company. Davis and Wilder held some shares as agent for other investors, which likely included foreign investors to which Jaudon or others had made sales.[36]

George's Creek C&I issued additional shares to Morris Robinson, then cashier of the BUS New York Branch. The shares were registered in two accounts, one designated "Morris Robinson, New York" (354 shares, in his personal capacity) and the other "Morris Robinson, Agent" (350 shares). Of the personal shares, Robinson assigned 331 to others, leaving 23 in Robinson's name. Of the "Agent" account shares, 250 were acquired from John H. Alexander, president of George's Creek C&I, on December 26, 1837, and 100 were acquired from John Duer, vice president of American Life & Trust, on September 8, 1838.

On September 14, 1838 George's Creek C&I re-issued 250 shares to John H. Alexander. That left Robinson holding 100 shares, acquired from Duer, in the Agent account. There was evidence that Duer had acquired those shares as security for a $1,500 loan by American Life & Trust to James Watson Webb. That loan was paid, in whole or in part, on September 7, 1838. There was also evidence that the BUS may have made a loan to Webb of $3,090, with the 100 shares becoming collateral for the BUS loan. Robinson died in 1849, with the 23 and 100 shares still in the respective personal and Agent accounts.[37]

No dividends were issued on the George's Creek C&I stock prior to Robinson's death. Commencing in 1864, dividends were issued regularly, including a 100% stock dividend in 1903.

Letters of administration on Morris Robinson's personal estate were issued to Malcolm V. Tyson in 1909. Tyson was unable to locate stock certificates for the 23 and 100 shares and filed a notice of loss or destruction. George's Creek C&I refused to reissue shares to Tyson, asserting there was no proof that Robinson continued to hold the shares at his death, that Tyson was not an appropriate administrator, and, with respect to the 100 shares, that those shares were held as agent and thus not part of Robinson's personal estate. Tyson sued for reissuance of the certificates plus all dividends on those shares from and after the death of Robinson.

The Maryland court of appeals, in *Tyson v. George's Creek C&I* (1911), upheld a lower court decision mandating reissuance of the 23 personal shares to the

---

was devoted to the education of Canton's Chinese population. He was a Member of the Council of the University of the City of New York and of the Green-Wood Cemetery of New York and a donor to the New York Historical Society.

administrator, with unpaid dividends, and determined the administrator was not entitled to reissuance of the 100 shares held as agent because those were not part of Robinson's estate and had not become a part of that estate by operation of law.

Comes then the case of *Peabody v. George's Creek C&I* (1913), addressing claims to the 100 shares held in agency. Relatives of George Peabody, as trustees of his estate, claimed George acquired the 100 shares from the BUS through Samuel Jaudon, as trustee, for $100,000 on June 25, 1867, as approved by a Pennsylvania court on December 31, 1866. Jaudon had acquired the BUS assets under the BUS Assignment (September 1841) on May 21, 1855. That assignment related to one of three trusts established in connection with liquidation of the BUS. All property under the three assignments reverted to the BUS after full payment of specified debts. <sup>G</sup>

After tracing through the transactions, the Maryland appellate court determined that Peabody *et al.* had no right to the 100 shares or dividends on those shares. The holding was based upon factual evidence that the records showed no sale of the note evidencing the $3,090 BUS loan or sale of the 100 shares out of the three BUS liquidation trusts and that neither the note nor the shares were listed in the schedules of BUS assets sold by Jaudon to Peabody. That determination was made despite the listing of the loan in the BUS Assignment (June 1841): the Webb loan was listed, but no mention was made of the 100 shares as collateral for the loan. And despite the listing of the loan and note in the November 16, 1855 report of the liquidation trustees indicating their possession of the unpaid note in 1855 when the remaining BUS assets passed into the hands of Samuel Jaudon. George's Creek C&I

---

G   Three liquidation trusts were created pursuant to the BUS Assignment (May 1841), the BUS Assignment (June 1841), and the BUS Assignment (September 1841). Jaudon was the liquidation trustee under all three assignments. The BUS Assignment (September 1841) was for BUS obligations to "sundry persons and bodies corporate, in diverse sums of money … from various causes". It was made to compensate for judgments against the BUS, claims brought against Charles H. Phelps and his estate "by reason of any suretyship, engagement or responsibility of any kind whatsoever", including on behalf of the BUS, other sureties of the BUS, and any BUS creditors other than those addressed in the other two assignments. A September 6, 1841 indenture modified the September 4 assignment to exclude property provided as security or in payment or indemnity in Europe. This trust actively settled claims for many years, as described in the BUS Auditors Report (1853). The trust corpus was $659,981.02 as of July 25, 1853.

The BUS Assignment (June 1841) was in respect of BUS obligations to depositors and holders of BUS notes, other than banks referenced in the BUS Assignment (May 1841).

had not recorded any change in ownership of the 100 shares since 1838. Morris Robinson, as agent, remained the registered owner. The shares vanished.[38]

**Conclusions and Questions**

After a ride in reflection and reconsideration, Patrick Tracy Jackson concluded that L&C's principal errors in assessing the Pensacola Railroad transaction fell into three categories. One pertained to L&C's assumptions regarding the Pensacola Association and friends. The second pertained to inadequate knowledge of the Florida parties. The third related to the transactional structure used in the rolling stock sale. The extent of degradation in the economy was not foreseeable.

Relying on the Pensacola Association and friends as the primary source of protection and transactional integrity was not entirely imprudent. These were knowledgeable, sophisticated, capable men. As a general matter, their interests were aligned with those of L&C. While not imprudent, the reliance was misconceived, inappropriately premised, and inadequately secured. An assumption that L&C protection would derive from management of the Floridians to the benefit of the Pensacola Association was faulty, in numerous respects. No assurances were obtained from these guardians that L&C interests would be protected. No arrangements were made to ensure L&C protection. All L&C benefits were derivative, incidental, and secondary to the objectives of the Pensacola Association and the BUS.

The inescapable conclusion was that the transactional structure for the sale of rolling stock to the Pensacola Railroad was inadequate to protect L&C upon a railroad default, especially when accompanied by the degradation of the economy. So inadequate that L&C losses could not be mitigated. That set of errors was remediable. And, flowing from Jackson's discussions with Horace Binney in 1845, had been remedied in significant part for subsequent transactions.

What of L&C's assessment of the Floridians?

**Endnotes: Chapter Nine**

[1] For summaries of the involvements of the BUS and Nicholas Biddle in the London cotton markets, redirection of cotton trading through Humphreys & Biddle, and replacement of Baring Brothers and Company in BUS London cotton trading and financing, Smith (1953), at 195-98, Buck (1925), at 30-97, Sumner (1896), at 296-308, Geller (1916), at 38-42, Govan (1940), McHenry (1863), at 31-3, and BUS Investigations Report (1841), at 18-20 and 61-2. See also, Watkins (1908), at 103-04.

[2] For the BUS Pennsylvania charter, PA Law (1836) Pamphlet.

[3] For the Union Bank, Schene (1975), at 69, and Abbey (1937), at 212.

4   For Lycoming Coal Company, PA Law (1833) No. 132, § 3, and MA Law (1833) Ch. XXV.

5   For Thomas Biddle, including internal improvements involvements, Chandler (1954), at 252-53, Cochran (1982), at 333-34, Hare (1909-1914), at 4, 10, 12, 14, and 40 (including a picture at 40), Shelling (1938), at 177, Osborne (1921), at 248-49, Breck (1843), at 64, (Little Schuylkill), PA Law (1828) No. 47 (Pennsylvania and Ohio Canal Company), PA Law (1833) No. 132 and MA Law (1833) Ch. XXV (Lycoming Coal), PA Law (1819) Chap. CLX (Union Canal Company), VA Public Works Report (1839), at 316-17, (securities of James River and Kanawha Company), Bald Eagle & Spring Creek Ann. Rep. (1836) (Biddle elected chairman), PA Law (1832) No. 229 (Portsmouth and Lancaster Rail Road Company and Williamsport and Elmira Rail Road Company), Schene (1975), at 69 (initial stock sale of Union Bank), PA Law (1837) No. 69 (Wallenpaupack Improvement Company), FCC Stockholders (1837), at 462 (stockholder in Franklin Rail-Road Company in 1837), PA Law (1839) No. 159 ("West Branch" Franklin Rail-Road Company), Martin & Sinclair (1974), at 28-9 (Wilmington whaling), Meredith (1934), at 162 (financial merchandizing), and Wealthy Philadelphians (1846), at 7. For the Pennsylvania Improvement Society, Carlson (1964), at 297-99. For BUS involvements, Breck (1979), at 88. For involvements in the BUS investigations, Minority Report (1832), especially at 7-8, and U.S. House Bank Report (1838). For Biddle as Singapore consul, Sodhy (1965), including at 14, 18, and 21, and Ahmat (1965), at 256.

6   THE UNITED STATES GAZETTE was a continuation of the GAZETTE OF THE UNITED STATES. The first Bronson-Chauncey issue with the new title was published on February 20, 1804 (volume 25, number 3546, continuing the numbering). The last Bronson-Chauncey issue was published on March 9, 1805. Bronson continued as publisher thereafter, until the last issue on March 7, 1818 (volume 53, number 6821). The paper then merged with THE TRUE AMERICAN to form THE UNION, published by Bronson and Thomas Smith. Upon Smith's death in 1819, the paper was published by William Henry Sanford. Brigham (1847), at 957 and 958, and Scharf & Wescott III (1884), at 1968-70. For Bronson, Chauncey, and THE UNITED STATES GAZETTE, Konkle (1933).

7   A short biography of Elihu Chauncy is Dexter (1911-V), at 186-87. Elihu married Henrietta Teackle of Accomac County, Virginia. They had three daughters. Henrietta died in Philadelphia on March 2, 1832. A short biography of Charles Chauncey is Dexter (V), at 8-9.

8   For Elihu Chauncey and the BUS, US House BUS Report (1832), at 285. For Mrs. Smith's boarding house, Binney (1903), at 44-5. For Chauncey, associated banks of Philadelphia, and specie payments, Financial Register (1838, June 6). For Chauncey and the Bank of Pennsylvania, M'Elroy (1839), at 305, 316, and 320. For a short biography of James Kent, Dexter (1911-IV), at 189-94.

A "permanent loan" of $600,000 was made by Pennsylvania to Chauncey, as disclosed in PA HJ (1851), at 158. Its interest rate of 2.58% contrasts with other loans made under the same authorization, stated as "Loan per act of 5th April, 1834". Those

⁹ For Chauncey and the insurance companies, M'Elroy (1839), at 305, 316, and 320. For Chauncey and the Richmond and Ohio Railroad, VA Law (1846) Ch. 113, and for the RF&P, RF&P AR (1865) and RF&P AR (1872). For the Delaware & Raritan and the Camden & Amboy, Hazard's Register (1832, January 27). For the Lebanon Railway, PA Law (1836) No. 123. For Chauncey and Bald Eagle & Spring Creek Navigation, PA SJ (1836-1837). For Chauncey and canal companies, PA SJ (1836-37). For the Preston Retreat, PA Law (1836) No. 198. For Chauncey's ownership of 4,450 Wisconsin acres, Gates (1969), at 309, footnote 10. For the Welsh Club, Scharf & Westcott II (1884), at 1468.

acts pertained to internal improvements and the Bank for Savings. The loan was for a 'voluntary proposal'. The date of the loan is not stated, nor is the purpose.

¹⁰ For Chauncey and the P&R, Hare (1909-1914), at 18-9. Short biographies of Moncure Robinson are ASCE (1892), at 84-90, Osborne (1921), Fisher (1940), Fisher (1962), and Holton (1989), at 40-7. A sketch of his professional work is Stapleton (1991), at 294-96.

¹¹ The Little Schuylkill was formed on February 20, 1826 pursuant to PA Law (1826) Ch. XI. It was authorized to build a railroad on April 14, 1828 and its name was changed on April 23, 1829, when it was authorized to extend its line to Reading. See PA Law (1829) No. 76. The Little Schuylkill was allowed to acquire certain coal-bearing lands pursuant to PA Law (1826) Ch. CIX. For promotion of the Little Schuylkill by List, Bell (1942), at 38 (footnote 38). For commissioning of Robinson's survey, Holton (1989), at 39. For the 1838 leasing of the Little Schuylkill as an entirety by The Philadelphia and Reading Railway Company (P&R successor) in 1897, see Hare (1909-1914), at 220 and 242-43.

¹² BUS Investigation (1841), at 12-4, specifying salary and commissions and discussing "large sums for expenses" and debts of Jaudon, Cowperthwaite (cashier), and Andrews (first assistant cashier) to the BUS, at 12-20.

¹³ BUS Investigation (1841), at 12.

¹⁴ For Jaudon's P&R involvement, Hare (1909-1914), at 11. For his Ocean Steam Navigation involvement, NY Law (1846) Ch. 145. For his Lake Huron Silver & Copper Mining involvement, Canada Law (1847) Ch. LXXII. For Ashbel Green Jaudon, Hare (1909-1914) 11, 17, and 18. For Jaudon as agent for Morrison Sons, *Union Bank v. Call* (1854), at 7. Ashbel Green Jaudon was a Philadelphia (later New Orleans) merchant and banker. His primary firms were Whitall, Jaudon & Co., Jaudon & Mason, Manufacturers, and A.G. Jaudon & Sons, Bankers. For Nicholas Biddle's appointment of Jaudon as a BUS director in 1841, by way of proxies, Niles' Register (1841, January 16).

¹⁵ For BUS cashiers and footnote B, Redlich (1968), at 113-16. For Jaudon's positions, appointment as BUS general agent, and the quotation, BUS Investigation (1841), at 12-4 (the quotation is at 12). For Jaudon becoming cashier in 1832, Niles' Register (1832, September 15) and Redlich (1968), at 115. For Jaudon's European securities placements, examples include Hidy (1939), Macesich (1960), at 414, Gregory (1983), Govan (1940), Hammond (1947), Hamilton (1957), and Hidy (1946). For sales of Webster's lands, Wiltse (1973), at 67-9, including footnote 22. Jaudon and his second wife, the daughter

of senator Hugh Lawson White of Tennessee (the "lady"), were unofficial hosts of Webster and his family during their 1839 London visit. For the bench warrant and *habeas corpus* actions, *Biddle v. Morris* (1842) and *Jaudon v. Wertheym* (1842), and see Benton (1854), at 471 *et seq*. For a Jacksonian perspective and grand jury presentment, PDR (1842). For the Young Men's Colonization Society, YMCSP (1836), at 127, and Tyson (1834). Among other notables, Josiah White was listed as a Vice President.

[16] For Jaudon's family history, Jaudon Family (1890), at 10, 13-6, 20, and 21.

[17] Unless otherwise noted, the facts and holdings involving are from the Supreme Court case, *Duncan v. Jaudon* (1873), and the more detailed circuit court opinion, *Jaudon v. National City Bank* (1871).

[18] For Bainbridge, Harris (1837). For Ashbel Green's death, Jaudon Family (1890), at 20. For the Duncan-Sherman and George Peabody releationship, Hidy (1939), at 304-06, and Hidy (1941), at 56, the latter discussing other relationships between London and U.S. firms.

[19] The valuation is from Legal Opinion (1871).

[20] For Davis, his companies, and Mediterranean trade, Scoville-Barrett (1862-1866), Volume I, at 84-5, and Wilson & Fiske (1889), at 93-4. For Davis and Nicholas Biddle, Harvey (1977), at 13. For the BUS, Biddle, and the State Bank of New York, Harvey (1977), at 12, Schlesinger (1945), at 214, and, for examples of the Davis-Biddle interactions, Gatell (1966), especially at 23, including footnote 15. For committee involvements, DIP (1831), at 6, 15, 40, and 41. For criticism of borrowings from Baltimore Life and Trust Company, Weekly Globe (1842, August 27), at 608.

[21] For Davis as trustee, *Davis v. Garr* (1851), *Wright v. Delafield & Curtis* (1857), and *Apalachicola Land & Development v. McRae* (1923).

[22] Pine (1921), at 5, with excerpts from the deed to Davis *et al.* as trustees.

[23] Mount, Cowdrey & Williams (1944). For the $250s payment to Mount, Mount – Suffolk Museum (1968), at 19 and 17, respectively. For the Major Jack Downing letters, Davis (1834) and Davis (1835).

[24] For the Washington portrait, Feld (1967), at 297. For Halleck and Knickerbocker writers, Wilson & Fiske (1889), at 94.

[25] Pensacola Gazette (1844, December 7).

[26] For the intercession on behalf of the Duc de Broglie, PSA (1871), at 94. For the founding of La Société des Amis de la Morale Chŕetien et de la Paix, PSAH (1907), at 16, and Davis (1978), at 94.

[27] For Wilder, Hottinguer & Company, and the BUS, *Rockwell v. Wilder* (1842), Nolte (1854), at 426-27 and 440, Barrett (1864), at 317-18, ATS (1865), at 72, Govan (1940), at 304-06 (Biddle and the BUS), Govan (1959), including at 319-25, 340-41, 344-46, and 370-1, Wilkins (1989), and, for the London cotton ventures, the sources cited in endnote 1 of this Chapter. For the quotation, ATS (1865), at 317, from a Tappan letter. For Wilder's death, NY Observer (1865, March 9).

[28] For Wilder, Wilder (1865), ATS (1865), and Wilson & Fiske (1889), Volume VI, at 507. For Wilder's great grandfather, ATS (1865), at 16.

[29] For the founding of the American Tract Society and Wilder as president, Twaddell (1946), with the presidency at 120, and Thompson (1941). For the pinch of snuff, Wilder letter to Tappan, September 16, 1834, reprinted in ATS (1865), at 306-08. The exchange quoted in the letter moved Wilder to forego snuff, whereupon he gifted the snuff box to Tappan. For Wilder and the American Peace Society, PSAH (1907), at 16, PSAM (1837), at 17 and 18, and PSA (1844). For the American Temperance Society, ATS (1830), at 10 (Wilder chaired the third annual meeting). For the American Education Society, AES AR (1828). For the American Prison Society, an example is PDS (1836), at 61. Alexis de Tocqueville and Guy de Beaumont were corresponding members. Regarding the benevolence societies, Griffin (1957), Cutler (1972), and Heale (1976).

Wilder was a friend of Samuel F. B. Morse, as well as the Tappans. Morse conceived of the JOURNAL OF COMMERCE. It was published by the Tappans in 1827 (and merged with THE COMMERCIAL BULLETIN in 1893), was transmitted over electric telegraph, and has been continuously published ever since. Howe (2007), at 1. It carried economic and religious news (the brothers were "notorious for their Christian principles"). It was sold to David Hale in 1829. Wyatt-Brown (1966) discusses business affairs of the Tappans, including credit rating concepts developed by Lewis, an abolitionist, peace advocate, and anti-credit, hard-money believer who desired to ensure that granting credit would be based upon more honest, reliable information. Lewis formed the Mercantile Agency, which became Dun & Bradstreet Company. See Lauer (2008) and Madison (1974).

[30] For the ascription to the rum-dealing creditors, ATS (1865), at 323-28.

[31] For Robinson, the BUS, and Biddle, Scoville-Barrett (1862-1866), Volume 1 at 373, and Volume 2, at 50 and 260, Harvey (1977), at 13, Gatell (1964), at 44 and 49, Stalson (1942), at 98, 113, 115, 127, 128 (a picture follows page 128), 131, 133, 204, 242-43, 265, and 360, Clough (1946), at 17 (picture), 18, 30, 33, 34, 109, and 113, Weaver (1833), at 165, Philadelphia (1824), at 77, NY Commercial Information (1823), at 138, and MONY (2021). For the Robinson presidency, New Yorker (1838), including the quoted language, Financial Register (1838, October 17), Niles' Register (1836, June 11), at 251, and Niles' Register (1838, July 14), at 205. For Robinson's life insurance involvements, Stalson (1942), especially at 98, 112-59, 201, 205, 242-43, 254, and 265, Depew (1895), at 93-6, and Buley (1959), at 12.

[32] For McNeil at the Boston & Providence, Kennedy (1951-1), at 65. For his hiring at the Boston & Lowell, Kennedy (1951-2), at 87. For McNeill at the Western Railroad, Fisher (1947) and Kennedy (1951-3), at 191-92. For the marriage of Anna McNeil and George Washington Whistler, Fisher (1947), at 87.

[33] For BUS officers, Register of Officers (1833), at 165-69. For Cadwalader, Lindsey (1996), at 36-7. For Colt, Harvey (1977), especially at 13.

[34] For Hone, Hone (1889), with biographical information at iii-ix, Hone (1927), with biographical information at vi-xx, Kriedman (1965), Landon (1956), Lowenthal (1997), including at 14, 16, 23, and 102-06, Hemstreet (1900), D&H (1925), especially at 8-61,

but interspersed throughout, D&H History (1906), at 1 (charter) and various minutes, and Hone (1828). Hone (1889), 5, 6, 8, 12, 17, 23, 28, 30, 34, 38, 41, 53, 54, 55, 61, 72, 73, 74, 82, 96, 106, 116, 124, 131, 132, 133, 134, 140, 141, 144, 149, 157, 158, 160, 165, 187, 190, 194, 198, 205, 207, 209, 210, 237, 248, 249, 250, 288, 293, 313, 335, 354, 356, and 381, among others. For Kent, Dorfman (1961). For the Woolworth Building, Bruce (1913), discussing Hone's home, with a map.

[35] For the Philadelphia response, Hazard's Register (1835, December 26), and for the Boston response, Boston Courier (1835, December 28).

[36] For George's Creek Mining incorporation and name change, MD Law (1835) Ch. 328 and MD Law (1836) Ch. 382, respectively. For George's Creek C&I and investors, Harvey (1977), at 9 and 12-3. For Wetmore, Hidy (1939), at 188-90, Hamilton (1957), at 586-90, *Russell v. Wetmore* (1845), House of Commons Return (1840), at 4 (opium trade), Bishop (1868), at 198 (gutta percha), Wilson (1852), at 41 of Appendix – Societies (Phoenix Coal Mining), D&S Coal AR (1852), at 1 (Dauphin & Susquehanna Coal), CNJ Stock Offering (1854), CNJ Annual Report (1860) and Poor (1860), at 389 (Jersey Central), DL&W AR (1857), at 66-7 (Delaware, Lackawanna & Western investigating committee), F&L Insurance (1854) (Fire & Life Insurance), Merchants' Magazine (1849, June) (Life Saving Benevolent Association), MES AR (1837) and MES AR (1842) (Morrison Education Society), Mail Indenture (1849) (mail ships), Green-Wood Cemetery (1844), at 5 and 16, NY Law (1842) Ch. 217 (Atlantic Mutual), UCNY Catalogue (1844), at 2, and UCNY Faculty Circular (1851), at 2 (University of the City of New York), and Wilson's NYC Directory (1864), at 96 (Wetmore & Cryder in 1864). A family presentation is Wetmore (1861), at 354-60. For Wetmore's estate in Newport, Veeder (1970) and Ames (1970).

[37] Facts are primarily from *Tyson v. George's Creek C&I* (1911). The BUS loan of $3,090 is described in *Peabody v. George's Creek C&I* (1913), at 662-63.

[38] *Peabody v. George's Creek C&I* (1913), at 663-70.

# Part IV

## Pensacola People

Figure 17: Fort Pickens and Fort McRee

## Chapter Ten

### William H. Chase

Conclusions regarding Locks & Canal's assessments of the Pensacola people were harsher. The assessments were incomplete and inadequate. They seemed desultory, although that was not characteristic of directors or officers that made the assessments. Reliance on the assessments was imprudent. Despite all efforts at neutrality in his reassessment, those sequiturs dogged Patrick Tracy Jackson.

William Henry Chase was born in Buckfield, Maine (then part of Massachusetts) in 1798 and died in Pensacola on February 8, 1870. He was an 1816 graduate of West Point Military Academy. After entering the U.S. Army Corps of Engineers, his first posting was Brooklyn, New York. In 1816-1817 he was posted near Lake Champlain as a surveyor. The following year he was posted to Fort Niagara making repairs. In 1819 he was posted to Fort Pike, Louisiana, where he remained until 1828, when he was posted to Pensacola.[1]

While in Louisiana, Chase met and in 1824 married Anne Paul Matthews of West Feliciana Parish, leading to his integration into Louisiana society. Anne's grandfather, George Matthews, was a former Georgia governor and U.S. congressman who was implicated in the Yazoo land scandal. Anne's father, also George Matthews, was a judge in the Mississippi Territory. As a wedding gift, Anne's father gave the newlyweds one of his plantations, in Lecomte, Louisiana on the Red River, which became known as "Chaseland". William and Anne also made use of the Matthews plantation at St. Francisville, Louisiana as well as the flatlands bestride the Mississippi River outside St. Francisville near the cotton transshipment port of Bayou Sara. Chase lived in grand style in Pensacola as well. In later years, his mansion became the Continental Hotel.[2]

Throughout his involvements with the Bank of Pensacola and the Pensacola Railroad and until his resignation in 1856, Chase was an army engineer. His duties included building Forts Pickens, Barrancas, and McRee, among other forts and facilities in the Gulf of Mexico. Chase promoted the forts as a defensive bulwark across the Gulf.

In support of his official responsibilities, but not unmindful of personal opportunities, Chase used his position as dispenser of federal largess to establish a Pensacola industry to make bricks for his forts, breaking the monopoly held by Mobile, Alabama. Supplying bricks expanded to supplying labor and other materials, and Chase was quick to develop those capabilities in Pensacola for use in building forts and other government-funded projects throughout the Gulf.[A] Chase immersed himself in construction details, including the composition of bricks, which led to Chase obtaining a patent for mastic cements. Under Chase's direction, the construction of Fort McRee, and possibly other forts, circumvented the Elijah Mix competitive bid process for masonry brick and embankment construction.[3]

In 1825, while a captain, Chase extended his activities beyond projects for which he had construction responsibilities. He served as the investigating officer concerning fraudulent claims of snag-removal by the Superintendent of Western River Improvements of the Army Corps of Engineers (John Bruce) and the supervising officer (Samuel Babcock). Babcock was suspended, as was Bruce's contract. Chase also served as a member of the U.S. Treasury Department commission to resolve disputes regarding the architectural design and construction of the New Orleans Custom's House.[4]

Chase was a committed southern slaveholder. He introduced the system for leasing slaves for military fort construction in Pensacola and Key West. He sought to arrange contracts with slave holders for "FOUR HUNDRED BLACK LABOURERS for which a liberal price will be paid" for construction of the Pensacola Railroad (and for two hundred white laborers at $20 per month per person plus $30 per month to anyone bringing thirty laborers). Chase was aggressive in litigating slave related claims. He prevailed in a suit against New Orleans for $600, the value of a slave that fled while in the city's custody working on a chain gang. The award was overturned on appeal. Another suit involved Chase as an endorser on a note for the sale of ten slaves. In later years, after emancipation in Mississippi and when Chinese laborers were being used, Chase opined that renewal of the African slave trade was preferable to Chinese contract labor.[5]

---

[A] One observer ventured that the means used by Chase "might today have earned him the severest of censure, if not actually a private room in the nearest federal house of correction. But in those days, the distinctions among military, government, and private interests were blurred at best, and their relations were often more informal, homey, and personal."

Chase's involvements with the Army Corps of Engineers did not dissuade him from suing the U.S. for service-related matters. In an 1856 suit, Chase was awarded a credit of $812.50, $130 as reimbursement for hire of a fishing smack to convey him to Havana from Key West, and $150 as reimbursement of a surgeon's bill, and was denied a $50 reimbursement to a boat captain for docking a vessel. He lost his 1859 suit for double rations in the amount of $1,129.60 for the period from July 1, 1851 to February 15, 1856.

Figure 18: William H. Chase

Chase used his Army Corps of Engineers position to infuse cash into the Pensacola economy. It is estimated that Chase, with Jasper Strong and Fred Underhill, injected $1,850,000 into Pensacola for the construction of Forts Pickens, Barrancas, and McRee. His advocacy of naval and military development and the Pensacola Railroad was intended to bring millions more into Pensacola, and he aspired to reap the benefits through the Pensacola Land Company, the Pensacola Railroad, the Bank of Pensacola, and other ventures. The bank allowed Chase to receive, dispense, and otherwise control government largess for military construction and revenues from his brick, labor, materials supply, and other ventures, rather than relying on New Orleans banks. However, Chase did not neglect involvements elsewhere in the Gulf of Mexico. In addition to building forts across the Gulf, he became one of the largest landowners in Rapides Parish, Louisiana.[6]

Both predating and postdating the Pensacola Railroad, Chase strove to build a railroad west from Florida to tap into cotton and lumber production of Alabama and Georgia. Two months after chartering of the Pensacola Railroad (AF&G), a second railroad was chartered out of Pensacola. On February 14, 1835, the Pensacola and Perdido Rail Road Company was chartered to connect Pensacola Bay to Perdido Bay. It ran 5-5/8$^{ths}$ miles from Pensacola to the Florida lumber town of Millview. Its purpose was exploitation of lumber resources along the Perdido River. Pensacola & Perdido stockholders included William H. Chase, Walter Gregory, John A. Cameron, Jasper Strong, Hanson Kelly, and Robert Mitchell. Together with Strong, Chase sought to build a canal from the Perdido River to the Grand Lagoon. Some years later, in 1856, after serving for fifteen days as the military superintendent of West Point, Chase resigned from the army (driven out by a series of postings designed to achieve that result) to become president of the ill-fated Alabama and Georgia Railroad Company. The Alabama & Georgia was not completed until 1861 and was never used. It was destroyed by Confederate troops effecting their scorched earth policy.[7]

William H. Chase was an advocate of secession of the Cotton States from the Union. He wrote letters to New York and London newspapers explaining the logic of secession. His arguments were based on free trade principles, especially for agricultural production of the south and west. He envisioned the Cotton States as an independent nation free of tariffs and duties that he believed were imposed to maintain the supremacy of Northern shipping, manufacturing, mining, and internal improvements interests as well as standing armies and navies. Chase berated the maintenance of "enormous standing armies and formidable navies; and, especially, of the locust like followers, retainers and suppliers of these armed forces." That was rather brazen given his career-long position in the army and extensive efforts to capitalize on government funds for military infrastructure projects that fed Chase's personal businesses.[8]

He envisioned the new nation having no armies or navies, defended by England and France because of their interests in obtaining the new nation's agricultural production. He averred that Cuba, Mexico, and some northern states would join the new Cotton States, or at least emulate its free trade policies. He posited that western states would supply the soldiers to resist the north upon secession because of their interests in free trade for their agricultural production.

William H. Chase entered the Civil War as a colonel of the army assembled by Florida to secure Pensacola. He was subsequently commissioned major-general by Governor Madison S. Perry. In January 1861 Chase designed a post-secession flag (thirteen red and white stripes and a blue field with a lone white star) which was ordered flown throughout Florida.[9]

**Endnotes: Chapter Ten**

[1] For Chase, Walby (2014), including, for his land acquisitions, at 31 *et seq*. For Chase at West Point, Select Committee Report (1837), at 48, and West Point Reminiscences (1880), at 4.

[2] For the Louisiana land holdings, Louisiana Landholders (1988). For the Continental Hotel, Clubbs (1959), at 383-84. For Bayou Sara, Bayou Sara (2019).

[3] For an overview of Chase's activities in Pensacola and the Gulf, Burnett (1988), at 179-83 (the footnote A quotation is at 179). For Chase's construction responsibilities, Smith (2009), at 133-54, and Doherty (1959), at 345. For the Pensacola forts, Weaver (2018), especially at 57-8. For his brick, mastic, and patent involvements, Ellsworth (1974) and Patent List (1874), at 101. For circumvention of competitive bidding, Shallat (2008), at 9, Coleman (1988), at 26 and 32, and Calhoun Report (1827).

[4] For the Bruce-Babcock investigation, Manders & Rentfro (2011), at 20. For Chase's investigations, including lighthouse visibility in the Dry Tortugas: Dean (1998), at 80. For the Treasury Department dispute resolution commission, Patrick (1979), at 180 *et seq*. and see also Pearce (2000).

[5] For slave and white labor for the Pensacola Railroad, Pensacola Gazette (1837, April 15), Pensacola Gazette (1837, April 22), Pensacola Gazette (1837, May 6), Pensacola Gazette (1837, May 13), Pensacola Gazette (1837, May 20), and Pensacola Gazette (1837, May 27). See also American Slavery (1839), at 136, containing an abridgement of the May 27 advertisement. For the naming of Fort McRee, Totten Letter. For Chase as slaveholder, Karp (2011), including at 295-97, Smith (2008), at 500, 506, 511, and 524, Dibble (1974), at 31-60, and Pearce (1980), at 36-42 and 67-71. For comments regarding Chinese labor, Wong (1996), at 34, citing Cohen (1984), at 57. Involvements of Chase with slave matters are *Chase v. New Orleans* (1836) and *Hereford v. Chase* (1841). For military leasing of slave construction labor, Hulse (2010) and Karp (2011). While of no known direct relevance to Chase, consider Brown (1995-2) in respect of race relations in Territorial Florida.

[6] For the estimated cash infusion into Pensacola, Walby (2014), at 13, citing no source. Fort Pickens, on Santa Rosa Island, was the largest Pensacola fort, and to Chase's consternation, was under Union control throughout the Civil War. For Union control of Fort Pickens, Weaver (2018), at 68.

[7] For the Pensacola & Perdido and its shareholders, FL Law (1835) Ch. 825. For the Perdido River canal, FL Law (1853) Ch. 504, No. 25. For attempts to build a railway connecting Pensacola Bay and the Alabama interior, De Bow (1854), at 567-72. For Chase's 1849 efforts to build a railway between Montgomery and Pensacola, Chase (1849). The Alabama & Florida was sold to A. E. Maxwell on August 7, 1872 and

profitably resold by him to the Louisville and Nashville Railroad Company on December 10, 1872: Walby (2014), at 56. The military duties and stations of Chase are included in documents in *Chase v. United States* (1860). For litigation regarding rations, *Chase v. United State* (1856) and *Chase v. United States* (1859).

8 The quotation is from Chase (1860), at 4 of the second letter (*"Secession of the Cotton States" – Number 2*), to THE OBSERVER. For Chase's writings to the New York press in support of secession, Chase (1860).

9 For Chase during the Civil War, Dibble (1971), at 232 and 236, and Yonge (1959), at 357, and, with respect to the flag, Jarvis (1994), at 1053-54.

## Chapter Eleven

### Walter Gregory

Benjamin and Abigail Starr Gregory were prominent wealthy residents of Albany, New York. Benjamin, an innkeeper in Redding, Connecticut, moved to Albany in 1808. His uncle, Matthew, owned and operated the acclaimed Tontine Coffee House so favored by politicians and dignitaries and, in 1806, built the Eagle Tavern, which quickly achieved equivalent patronage and acclaim. Benjamin achieved financial success as an accountant and real estate investor. He provided his family an affluent life and connections to the commercial, social, and political elite of Albany.[1]

Walter Gregory, born on January 28, 1803, was one of nine children of Benjamin and Abigail. He married Angeline M. Vanderheyden on October 31, 1821 and seems to have lived in Albany and Boston in the early years of their marriage. Walter found his way to Florida in 1831 in connection with formation of the Bank of Pensacola, his acquisition of 1,705 bank shares, and his election as bank president. Angeline died on April 18, 1834. Two years later, on April 6, 1836, Walter married Amanda Caroline Kelly, a daughter of Hanson Kelly,[A] in Pensacola.[2]

In addition to involvements with the Bank of Pensacola and the Pensacola Railroad, including directorships at each, Walter Gregory was a founder and shareholder in the Florida Insurance and Banking Company of St. Augustine and Southern Life and Trust Company. Other shareholders and directors of Florida Insurance & Banking included William H. Chase, Jasper Strong, John A. Cameron, Walker Anderson, and Henry Hyer. Shareholders and directors of Southern Life & Trust included Chase, Hyer, and Florida governor Richard Keith Call. Gregory was a founder of the College of Pensacola in 1834, together with Chase, Hyer, Kelly, Cameron, Anderson, Blount and others.[3]

Throughout his time in Pensacola, Gregory maintained a residence in Cincinnati, where he conducted a publishing business[B] and was active in community affairs. He was a founding proprietor of the Glendale Association in

---

[A] Hanson Kelly was a Pensacola lumber mill owner who became a shareholder in and director of the Bank of Pensacola and a shareholder in the Pensacola Railroad and Union Bank. Kelly was appointed by the board of directors to wind up the Bank of Pensacola in 1842. Kelly served as Pensacola Port Warden from 1843 to 1845.

[B] Possibly related, in significant part, to printing lottery tickets.

1851. That association was established by wealthy Cincinnatians as a locale for country homes "sufficiently removed from the city to be safe from the encroachments of manufactures and commerce". The homes were to be perpetuated "in the hands of responsible and desirable persons".[4]

Walter and his wealthy brother, Dudley S. Gregory, provided financial support for their sister Clara and her husband, the painter George Catlin, who married on May 10, 1828 in Albany. In 1833, at Walter's expense, Clara and George resided for six months in the Pearl Street House, the newest and most luxurious hotel in Cincinnati. George Catlin was then preparing for a post-Pittsburgh showing. Walter, through publishing and pocketbook, supported Catlin's exhibitions, such as the one-man show entitled *The Indian Gallery*. Walter is said to have reframed more than one hundred of Catlin's paintings. To ensure his appropriate presentation, Walter purchased Catlin a new suit from Cincinnati's best tailor for $51.[C] Some years after Clara's death in London on July 28, 1845, at age 37, George Catlin surrendered to bankruptcy. Dudley removed three children of George and Clara to his care in Jersey City. Walter adopted one of Clara's children, Elizabeth Wing.[5]

Supporting George Catlin suited Walter and Amanda well as they strove to promote the arts in Cincinnati, a pursuit that occupied much of their philanthropic activity. Walter, a founder of the Spring Grove Cemetery, contributed Cincinnati artist Nathaniel F. Baker's statute of *Egeria at the Fountain* to the cemetery in 1856, where it was placed on an island in the cemetery's lake. See Figure 19. Walter commissioned *Bo Peep*, a painting by Lilly Martin Spencer in 1846. Amanda loaned various works to the Ladies Fine Art Association upon its opening in 1854. These included *Mother and Child* by Lilly Martin Spencer and *Venus and Cupid* by Thomas Buchanan Read, both Cincinnati artists, and *Diana with Dog and Bow*, *Nursing Mother and Children*, and *Landscape with Cattle*. Walter was a stockholder in the Cincinnati Astronomical Society and had minor involvements with the launch the Cincinnati-Covington suspension bridge. He was a dependable contributor to the American Colonization Society.[6]

The Catlin connection extended beyond George, to his father and siblings. George's father, Putnam, persuaded son James to relocate to Pensacola. Through the urging of Walter and Dudley Gregory, the latter having become the largest

---

[C] Support for Catlin waned over the years. For example, Dudley declined to assist Catlin in approaching the Smithsonian, Astor Library, and Boston Free Library for the purchase of his paintings. Henry Steele, a friend of Francis Catlin, George's brother, then introduced the Catlin brothers to Ezra Cornell, the president and principal owner of American Photo-Lithographic Company at Cornell's fledgling university in Ithaca.

shareholder in the Bank of Pensacola, James became cashier of the bank. James, at his father's urging, assisted two other siblings in relocating to Pensacola: Richard and Francis. Financed by Dudley, the Catlin brothers purchased large blocks of land in Alabama. Walter owned property and held property mortgages in Pensacola.[7]

Figure 19: Egeria at the Fountain

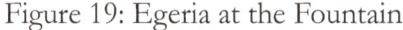

In 1837, Walter and Amanda began liquidating their Pensacola properties in anticipation of permanent residency in Cincinnati. On August 1, 1837 they sold their lot-and-a-half adjoining the Tivoli house on the east side of the Hospital Lot on Pensacola Bay.[8]

Eight days after reelection to the board of directors of the Bank of Pensacola on January 1, 1838, Walter resigned the directorship. He resigned as president on February 2. Concurrently, he advertised the sale of his assets. On February 17 he offered to sell a custom-built one-horse carriage that had only just been delivered, with harnesses, noting they would be sold at public auction if not otherwise sold. Walter and Amanda relocated to Cincinnati but retained relationships with Pensacola and the Kelly family. Another daughter of Hanson Kelly, Susan, was married to Robert Good of Philadelphia at the home of Walter and Amanda in Cincinnati.[9]

Walter Gregory was at times characterized as a "banker" in his more visible Cincinnati listings, such as Amanda's loan of paintings to the Ladies Fine Art Association. In Cincinnati, Walter became known also as a publisher, promoter of the arts, and philanthropist. To the bitter end, and not as a matter of preference or choice, Walter retained his shares in the Pensacola Railroad.[10]

Walter Gregory died in New York on September 21, 1857, age 54. The funeral was at the home of his brother, Dudley, in Jersey City. Walter Gregory was buried at Spring Lake Cemetery in Cincinnati.[11]

### Endnotes: Chapter Eleven

[1] For Benjamin Pitt Gregory and Abigail Starr Gregory, Gregory (1938), at 189, Gregory (1938), at 128-29, and Sanford (1911), at 320. For the Eagle Tavern, Worth (1866), at 82 (a picture follows 82), and Lathrop (1937), at 257-58.

[2] BoP Commissioner's Report, at 438, indicates that Gregory came from Boston, and notes his share ownership, as does Dewey (1910), at 32. Gregory may have been living in Boston in 1831. For Walter Gregory, Gregory (1938), at 189, and Sanford (1911), at 320. For Gregory's marriages, Gregory (1938), at 189, and Pensacola Gazette (1836, April 9-1). For the founders of the College of Pensacola, FL Law (1834) Ch. 774. For Hanson Kelly, Eisterhold (1973), at 268, Hildreth (1959), at 400, and FL LCJ (1843), at 72, 78-9, 185, and appendix 19.

[3] For incorporation of Florida Insurance & Banking, FL Law (1836) Ch. 973, § 1. For incorporation of Southern Life & Trust, FL Law (1835) Ch. 826. Gregory, Chase, Hyer, and Call were founders. Governor Duval was the largest stockholder in the Union Bank: Walby (2014), at 25.

[4] Maxwell (1870), at 76-7.

⁵ For Gregory in Cincinnati, BoP Commissioner's Report, at 460 (a schedule of BoP shareholders at January 1, 1840), Eisler (2013) (including the 1833 Cincinnati stay and suit of clothes), at 168-69, Haberly (1948), at 81-2, Pensacola Gazette (1839, November 23) (the Kelly-Good wedding), and citations in the next endnote. For Dudley Gregory's declining to assist George Catlin and Steele's introduction, Dippie (1990), at 374-75.

⁶ For *Egeria at the Fountain*, Ford & Ford (1881), at 378, and Spring Grove Cemetery (1862), at 88. Breidenbach (2001) considers art patronage and class identity in Cincinnati between 1828 and 1872 and, at 293, notes Amanda Gregory's loan of pictures. For *Bo Peep*, Spencer (1973), at 95-6, with a copy at 95, Figure 71. For Gregory as a Cincinnati Astronomical Society stockholder, Cincinnati Astronomical Society (1844), at 43. For the American Colonization Society, ACS (1849) and ACS (1850).

⁷ For Walter Gregory's Pensacola mortgage, Walby (2014), at 23-4. See also Ellsworth (1976). Walby (2014), at 23-4. For George Catlin, Roehm (1966), Balch (1918), Hauptman & Hamell (2003), Hight (1990), Bennett (1994), Dippie (1990), Dippie (1994), McCracken (1959), and Dysart (1982) at 40. For Clara Bartlett Gregory Catlin, Gregory (1938), at 124, and Sanford (1911), at 321. For George Catlin, Eisler (2013), Haberly (1948), and Sterling (1998).

⁸ For sale of Walter and Amanda's Pensacola property, Ellsworth (1976).

⁹ For Walter's January 1, 1838 reelection as director, Pensacola Gazette (1838, February 17), with the carriage and harnesses sale notice following. For Walter Gregory, Gregory (1938), at 189, and Sanford (1911), at 320. For Gregory's resignation as bank president, Emancipator (1842, July 28). For the wedding of Sara Kelly and Robert Good, Pensacola Gazette (1839, November 23).

¹⁰ Breidenbach (2001), at 379.

¹¹ For the death announcement, NY Herald (1857, September 22) and see the Walter Gregory obelisk in Figure 20.

Figure 20: Walter Gregory Monument, Spring Grove Cemetery

# Chapter Twelve

## Family Business

**Gregory Family Cottage Business**

While he had wealth from his father and his own business ventures, Walter Gregory had an additional, more lucrative source of income that derived from his brother, Dudley Sanford Gregory. That source was something of a cottage industry for the Gregory siblings, including brothers James and Benjamin.[A]

Dudley S. Gregory was born in Albany on February 5, 1800. After working as an errand boy for his uncle Matthew at the Eagle Tavern in Albany, Dudley served as a clerk in the office of the comptroller of the State of New York for fourteen years under Archibald McIntyre. He was promoted to chief clerk of the canal division, with responsibility for Erie Canal matters.

Dudley worked in New York City until 1832, when he begam managing the Jersey City office of Yates & McIntyre. He moved to Jersey City permanently in 1834, where he remained for the rest of his life. In 1838, he became the first mayor, serving until 1840, and then again from 1858 to 1860. Dudley also served in the U.S. House of Representatives from 1847 to 1849. Dudley enhanced his wealth through involvements with railroads, banks, Jersey City real estate investments, and other endeavors, including involvements with Archibald McIntyre (after whom Dudley named his thirteenth child (of fourteen)). Dudley was a principal investor in the Darcy House, one of Jersey City's first major hotels and the residence of his son-in-law, George Catlin.[1]

Dudley was a director for many years of the United New Jersey Railroad and Transportation Company, which became part of the United New Jersey Railroad and Canal Company with the Delaware & Raritan (which owned The Philadelphia and Trenton Railroad) and the Camden & Amboy. The three railroads were leased to the Pennsylvania Railroad in 1877. Dudley Gregory was also a long-time director of the Erie Railway and held directorships in more than nineteen railroads, including the Lehigh Valley Railroad. In 1864 Dudley purchased and became president of the Adirondack Steel (Manufacturing) Company. He was active in

---

[A] Most of Walter Gregory's involvements arose after his 1838 resignation from the Bank of Pensacola. The extent of his involvements prior to that resignation are unknown.

Democratic Whig politics. He was active in the American Bible Society and the American Tract Society, led the construction of Temperance Hall for meetings of the local chapter of the Washington Temperance and Benevolent Society. He was involved in the American Colonization Society, serving as vice president, from 1871 until his death from stomach cancer on December 15, 1875. Indicative of his lifestyle, Dudley Gregory's home became the post office of Jersey City.

Through familial connections in Albany and his work with Archibald McIntyre, Dudley was well acquainted with John Barentse Yates and Yates & McIntyre of New York City, which managed lotteries. In addition to other states, the firm controlled lotteries in New York, New Jersey, Pennsylvania, Rhode Island, Delaware, North Carolina, South Carolina, Maryland, Virginia, and the District of Columbia. Dudley worked as superintendent of lotteries for Yates & McIntyre from 1826 to 1836.

Figure 21: Dudley S. Gregory

Henry Yates, John's brother, joined Yates & McIntyre in 1826. Henry became a partner while still treasurer of Union College, which was a lottery client of Yates & McIntyre. Although Henry moved to New York City, his partnership with Yates & McIntyre was unknown to Union College until 1832. For six years, Henry Yates continued to draw a Union College salary as well as income from Yates & McIntyre.[2]

Dudley Gregory, Archibald McIntyre, and Henry Yates each acquired stock in the Bank of Pensacola by January 1, 1835. Each disposed of all shares by January 1, 1840. Yates disposed of his shares between January 1 and April 29 of 1835. Gregory and McIntyre probably disposed of their shares in early 1838 when Walter Gregory resigned his positions as a director and the president of the bank.[3]

Archibald McIntyre was born in Scotland and came to the U.S. in his youth. After working as a teacher and in a conveyancing office, he ventured into mercantile businesses and politics. He was a member of the New York Assembly from 1798 to 1804, served as deputy secretary of state from 1801 to 1806, was state comptroller from 1806 to 1821, and a state senator in 1823. As comptroller, McIntyre oversaw all lotteries in New York.

The Yates brothers were from a prominent Schenectady family. Each was educated as a lawyer and engaged in a wide array of businesses. Henry, as Union College treasurer, became involved with lotteries in 1814 when the college awarded management of their lottery to Yates & McIntyre. John established numerous businesses in Chittenango, New York. Another Yates brother, Joseph, was the first mayor of Schenectady after its incorporation, a state senator, a judge of the New York supreme court (supported, at that time, by DeWitt Clinton), and, from 1823 to 1825, governor of New York.[4]

In 1832, Archibald McIntyre and John Yates retired. The partners of Yates & McIntyre were then Henry Yates, James B. McIntyre (son of Archibald), and John Ely. John Yates moved to Chittenango, where he died in 1836. Dudley Gregory continued as superintendent of lotteries for the firm until 1836, when he became mayor of Jersey City.

During his time with Yates & McIntyre, Dudley Gregory accumulated significant wealth. By 1835, overlapping with his time at Yates & McIntyre, Dudley formed his own lottery management company in New York. D. S. Gregory & Co managed lotteries in Maryland, New Jersey, South Carolina, Delaware, and Missouri, among others. James B. McIntyre retired in 1841 whereupon many Yates & McIntyre franchises were taken up by D. S. Gregory & Co. and J. G. Gregory & Co., in which James Gregory, a brother of Walter and Dudley, was a partner. Dudley continued to manage lottery programs until at least 1842, running two lottery drawings daily.[5]

From and for a period after 1835, Yates & McIntyre and D. S. Gregory & Co. took joint interests in lottery management franchises. For example, the lottery benefiting Delaware College was sold by the lottery commissioners to the two companies for $100,000 on April 13, 1835. Yates & McIntyre purchased one-fifteenth of the rights for $6,666.66 for the period from the purchase date to December 31, 1835. D. S. Gregory & Co. purchased fourteen-fifteenths for $73,333.34 for the period from January 1, 1836 to February 10, 1845. The management companies were entitled to reimburse themselves for all expenses of conducting the lotteries before paying any amounts over to Delaware College and the State of Delaware.[6]

Dudley well and truly mastered the uncertainties and risks inherent in lotteries. Desiring to concentrate on more mainstream activities like railroading, real estate, and banking, Dudley assigned some lottery management rights to his brothers, James and Walter. By way of example, after managing the New Jersey lottery, Dudley assigned the rights to J. G. Gregory on June 10, 1841. J. G. Gregory & Co. was then comprised of James Gregory and Daniel McIntyre. Other lotteries were assigned to Walter, mostly in 1841 and 1842.

In some instances, the assignments were worked through the chain of brothers. A Delaware lottery was an example. Dudley managed the lottery from 1837 to 1841, paying the state a total of $8,000. He then assigned management rights to J. G. Gregory & Co., which managed the lottery from 1841 until 1847, paying the state $7,875 in total. Next came an assignment to brother Benjamin Gregory and John W. Maury, who paid the state a total of approximately $6,000 by 1851, when Maury was challenged for inappropriately taking the net proceeds (Benjamin having died).[7]

D. S. Gregory & Co., J. G. Gregory & Co., Walter Gregory, and Benjamin Gregory conducted lotteries for states, municipalities, hospitals, schools, and myriad other entities. Among the management principles applied by Dudley, and subsequently his brothers, the contracts required specified periodic payments to recipients. That contravened some state laws providing that the recipient receive the net proceeds of the lottery after deductions for a management fee and the expenses of conducting the lottery. Litigation resulted.[B]

From March 28, 1838 to 1844, D. S. Gregory & Co., joined from 1841 to 1844 by J. G. Gregory & Co., conducted a lottery to raise $100,000 for The Society for Useful Manufactures, of which Roswell L. Colt was governor. Semi-annual payments of $6,750 were made to the Society prior to December 1844, and semi-

---

[B] In the case involving the Delaware lottery, one defendant (a partner of Benjamin Gregory) refused to allow discovery regarding disposition of lottery proceeds exceeding the payment to the state. He argued that discovery would subject him to civil and, possibly, criminal penalties. The court in *State v. Maury* (1851) did not reach that issue (although it made its views known) because the case turned on a jurisdictional issue.

annual payments of $4,062.50 were made from December 1844 until June 1848. Three lotteries were run each week, with over nine hundred conducted in five years. No accounting for profits to the Gregory firms was made to the Society. The two firms paid a total of $67,500 to the Society up to 1845. The amount paid to the two Gregory firms on that contract was between $100,00 and $200,000.[8]

Missouri officials assailed lotteries managed by Walter Gregory, employing an array of tactics as anti-lottery sentiment spread. Walter responded creatively. In 1845 Walter held the Missouri drawing in Windsor, Canada. In later years, Missouri officials brought criminal actions against Walter's agents in Missouri for selling lottery tickets.[9]

An 1833 Missouri law, as amended, sanctioned the use of lotteries to raise $15,000 for a macadamized rode in New Franklin (originally, it funded a railroad). In 1849 Walter Gregory obtained the exclusive franchise to manage and conduct these lotteries. He was to pay the town of New Franklin $250 in January and June of each year. The contract allowed Gregory to cancel if there were legislative or official interference with his franchise. Police interference occurred, during which Gregory made no payments. The issue in *State v. McWilliams* (1879) was whether the contract was still in force at a particular time. Determination of that question focused on payment flows interrupted by official interference. The Missouri court ruled that the contract had been abandoned, referencing another Missouri case that involved brother Dudley: *Gregory v. Hawthorn* (1845).[10]

*Gregory v. Hawthorn* (1845) involved a December 28, 1835 franchise held by Dudley S. Gregory for lotteries to finance a hospital for the Sisters of Charity in St. Louis. That agreement was assigned to brother Walter on August 23, 1841. In December of 1842, the Missouri legislature made it illegal to sell lottery tickets in Missouri. Hawthorn, Walter's agent, was indicted on a criminal charge for selling tickets. The Missouri supreme court determined the 1842 law to be an impairment of Gregory's contract in contravention of the United States Constitution.[11]

Walter Gregory also used out-of-state sales to evade laws of jurisdictions that prohibited lottery ticket sales, such as Delaware and Kentucky.[c] Pursuant to an agreement under Delaware law, Gregory sold lottery tickets to his agent, Jameson,

---

[c] Walter Gregory entered into a series of lottery franchise agreements with Kentucky, including an 1849 contract allowing him, as sole lottery manager and conductor, to pay $1,000 annually to the Commonwealth and retain the remaining proceeds. That contract gave rise to *Gregory's Executrix v. Shelby County* (1859), where the Kentucky court upheld the right of a franchise holder to realize vested interests in the franchise despite the impermissibility of the lump sum payment to the Commonwealth.

on a "purchase or return" basis. To secure the purchase price of the tickets, Gregory took promissory notes from Jameson. The notes were secured by mortgages from Jameson, including a senior mortgage and two junior mortgages. Jameson was permitted to appoint sub-agents. He appointed sub-agents in Ohio despite Ohio's prohibition of lottery ticket sales. Gregory having died, his executrix pursued foreclosure on the mortgages when Jameson defaulted on the notes. The lower courts allowed foreclosure on the senior mortgage but denied foreclosure on the two junior mortgages on the grounds that ticket sales to Jameson (by virtue of ticket sales to Jameson's agents) violated Ohio law. The appellate court ruled that Gregory's executrix could foreclose on all three mortgages even if Walter Gregory knew the lottery tickets would be sold by Jameson and his agents in Ohio. Gregory made his sale to Jameson in Delaware, where sale of lottery tickets was permissible.[12]

As anti-lottery sentiment increased, Walter Gregory and other lottery managers were subjected to taxation of their franchises. In 1841, Walter acquired the Kentucky lottery franchise for a city school in the town of Frankfurt. An 1847 law allowed the city of Lexington to impose taxes on lottery franchises and, in 1848, a licensing fee was imposed on lottery agents, including one of Gregory's agents. Gregory's agent contested the fee as an impermissible tax. The Kentucky court of appeals upheld the right of the city to impose the fee as a tax.[13]

**Expanding Opportunities**

The accumulation of considerable wealth was not the only benefit of conducting a lottery management business. Frequently, lottery management expanded into private banking, brokerage of debt and equity instruments, and other types of financial intermediation. Lottery managers took a range of currencies, bank notes, promissory notes, bills, bank shares, and other securities in payment for tickets. Lottery managers at times lent money to ticket purchasers and brokers that sold tickets to the ultimate purchasers. As security for the loans, lottery managers took mortgages on the property of both brokers and ticket purchasers. Foreclosures on those mortgages led to lottery managers acquiring significant property holdings.

Examples of lottery sellers evolving into bankers, brokers, and financial intermediaries included S. & M. Allen, E. W. Clark & Company, Jay Cooke and Company, John Thompson, and Jacob I. Cohen, Jr. and Brothers. And, less spectacularly, Walter Gregory.[14]

Solomon Allen of Albany began selling lottery tickets in 1808, to supplement his printing business. He established S. Allen's Lottery and Exchange Office to sell lottery tickets and other goods, including slates, pencils, writing and wrapping paper, sealing wax, gun powder, and thread. In 1812 he withdrew from printing to concentrate on S. Allen's Lottery and Exchange. In 1815 he opened a New York office and formed a partnership with his brother, Moses, under the name "Allen's Truly Lucky Office". By 1816 the brothers expanded to Philadelphia and Baltimore under the name S. & M. Allen & Co. Pittsburgh was added in 1818, Washington and Richmond in 1819, Charleston in 1820, and Fayetteville and Savannah in 1821. By 1827 Providence, Boston, Portland, and Lynchburg had offices. The brothers then began selling their lottery businesses. They concentrated on buying, selling, and collecting drafts and debt obligations throughout the U.S. and England.[15]

Enoch W. Clark was a relative of the Allen brothers that learned the lottery business at S. & M. Allen & Co. and established E. W. Clark & Company in Philadelphia. Jay Cooke learned the financing business at E. W. Clark & Company. He formed Jay Cooke and Company as an investment house, to great success during the Civil War. John Thompson began his career selling lottery tickets. He moved to a Wall Street brokerage business in 1833. Subsequently, Thompson founded the First National Bank of New York and Chase National Bank.[16]

Jacob I. Cohen and his brothers began as a Baltimore lottery seller under the name Cohen's Lottery and Exchange Office, which was founded in 1812. They became the most prominent lottery manager in Baltimore and expanded throughout the east coast. In 1830 Jacob Cohen and his brothers established J. I. Cohen Jr. & Brothers Banking House, which survived the Panic of 1837 and acted as a financier to the Baltimore & Susquehanna. Jacob Cohen also became prominent as a director of the Baltimore & Ohio, a director, and later president, of the Baltimore and Port Deposit Railroad Company, and a director of the Wilmington and Susquehanna Railroad Company. The latter two railroads merged into the Philadelphia, Wilmington & Baltimore. Jacob Cohen and Solomon Etting became the first Jews to hold public elected office in Maryland.[17]

P. T. Barnum became a seller of lottery tickets on 10% commission during his teenage years, around 1828. Barnum also sold a variety of other goods, including fruit, oysters, confectionary, and toys. Barnum sought out Dudley S. Gregory of Yates & McIntyre to open a Pittsburgh office. Dudley dissuaded Barnum from Pittsburgh, offering him the Tennessee agency instead. Barnum rejected that offer and decided to purchase tickets directly from lottery managers, which afforded him 25-30% of sales proceeds. Barnum opened offices throughout Connecticut, selling tickets through sub-agents at the rate of $2,000 per day.[18]

Dudley Gregory used his wealth primarily to expand his interests in the transportation industry, although he did not neglect other opportunities, such as banking and real estate speculation. He was a founder of The Provident Bank in

Jersey City, which continues in existence to the present. Together with William Booth, John Murray Forbes, Thomas Dewey, and other wealthy individuals, Gregory was an incorporator and founder of Freedman's Savings and Trust Company in 1865. In the transportation sector, Dudley and other prominent Jersey City residents established the first permanent night ferry between Jersey City and New York City in 1835. Dudley operated passenger ferries between those two cities for many years. In recognition of his contributions, a ferryboat was named the *Dudley S. Gregory*. While Dudley's investments in railroads were many, diverse, and profitable, one of his less successful investments was in the Pensacola Railroad.[19]

### Endnotes: Chapter Twelve

[1] For Dudley S. Gregory, Gregory (1938), at 187, Sanford (1911), at 319, Mott (1900), NJCU (undated), Railway Times (1861, February 23) (Erie Railway), Business Wire (2014) (Provident Bank), NY Times (1874, December 9) (obituary), NY Times (1874, December 12) (funeral), NY Times (1875, January 22) (will of over $1 million), African Repository (1875) (death notice), Democratic Whig Convention (1839), and *Gregory v. NYLE&Western* (1885) (Gregory's executor's suit for an accounting of oil revenues of the Buffalo, Bradford and Pittsburg Railroad Company; Gregory owned 564 shares at his death). For Gregory's home as the Jersey City post office, Muirheid (1909), at 12.

At some time before 1869, Dudley Gregory became a significant shareholder in, and a member of the board of directors of, the New Jersey Railroad and Transportation Company. He remained in that position until at least 1877, and probably thereafter. The United New Jersey Railroad and Canal Company was an April 6, 1872 consolidation of New Jersey RR & Transportation with the Delaware & Raritan and the Camden & Amboy. Through United NJ RR & Canal, and its predecessor joint association, the three railroads were jointly managed and paid dividends to each member on an equalized basis. In 1877, to provide a land route between the Pennsylvania anthracite coal regions and New York City and Philadelphia, the Pennsylvania Railroad leased all the properties of each of the three railroad companies and the Philadelphia & Trenton. The lease was hotly contested over the years. Although the Pennsylvania Railroad lost an appellate decision regarding the lease, the lease continued in effect and the four entities became the core of the "United Railways of New Jersey Division" of the Pennsylvania Railroad. See McMillen (2022-5), at Chapter Twenty, endnote 7. For Dudley Gregory on the board, URR&C AR (1869), at 24, and Sackett (1895), at 12.

[2] Ezell (1960), at 86. See Doyle (1841) for discussion of lotteries during the period in which the Gregory brothers operated, including their operations and those of Yates & McIntyre. For a history of gambling laws in the U.S., including the onslaught against lotteries, Cornell Law (1977). For a history of lotteries in New York, Ross (1906). For a survey of lotteries in colonial America, Heeney (1910).

[3] For Yates, compare lists of Bank of Pensacola shareholders in the BoP Commissioner's Report: (a) as of January 1, 1835, certified by James Catlin, at 459; and (b) as of April 29, 1835, certified by Walter Gregory and James Catlin, at 445-46. As noted at 459, Catlin certified that a distribution of bank shares was made by the directors on December 14, 1835: no shares were distributed to Dudley S. Gregory or Henry Yates.

[4] For Joseph C. Yates, see Jenkins (1852), at 319-45.

[5] Ezell (1960), at 86 and other sources cited subsequently in this Chapter. See Aitkin (1953) and Doyle (1841), at 29, for retirements of Yates and McIntyre and the Gregory brothers as successors, and, at 30, for twice daily lotteries. For biographical information on John B. Yates, Smith (1899), at 178 and 317-465, and Lanman (1862). For biographical information on Archibald McIntyre, Sprague (1858), especially at 17 *et seq.* (not mentioning his lottery business), Roberts (1897), at 17-27 (a picture follows 14), Jenkins (1846), at 215-22, 240, and 263, and Dougherty (1915), at 83-4.

[6] *State v. Platt* (1844).

[7] For the Delaware lotteries by the three brothers, *State v. Maury* (1851).

[8] For D. S. Gregory & Co., *State v. Platt* (1844) and NJ AG Report (1845), with the assignment to J. G. Gregory & Co. at 25-6, the number of lotteries run and the realization at 28-31, the Society payment of $67,500 at 42, the management contract with Dudley at 43 *et seq.*, and the assignment by Dudley to James G. Gregory and Daniel McIntyre at 49.

[9] Ezell (1960), at 134. See, also, *State v. Morrow* (1857), another unsuccessful attack on Walter Gregory's Missouri franchise.

[10] *State ex rel. AG v. Miller* (1876) also addressed Walter Gregory's New Franklin franchise, finding that a franchise extension in 1849 was without consideration and thus invalid, although the concurring opinion differed on this point, and a dissenting opinion was filed. That appellate court ruling was overruled in *State ex rel. AG v. Miller* (1877), which held Gregory's contract to be valid.

[11] See also *State v. Miller* (1872), a Missouri criminal prosecution that was overturned based on *State v. Hawthorn* (1845).

[12] *Jameson v. Gregory's Executrix* (1863). See also *M'Intyre v. Parks* (1841) (Archibald M'Intyre on behalf of John B. Yates to foreclose a Massachusetts mortgage securing notes given for the purchase of lottery tickets from New York and sold in Massachusetts, New Hampshire, and Maine) and *Sortwell v. Hughes* (1852) (liquor sales in New Hampshire).

[13] *Wendover v. Lexington* (1854). An example of a well-known anti-lottery tract is Tyson (1833).

[14] Silas C. Herring, famous for Herring Safe's, worked in the lottery business to amass capital for the safe business. Holloway (1889), at 420-24.

[15] Ezell (1960), at 83-4.

[16] For E. W. Clark, Sylla (1976) and Clark, Dodge (1945). For Jay Cooke, Larson (1936), at 61-2 and 53-63, Minnigerode (1927), at 51-82, and Holloway (1889), at 390-406.

[17] Ezell (1960), at 83-4, MD Archives (JIC), and Wiernik (1912), at 122-27. Lottery operations of the Cohen brothers gave rise to the constitutional law case of *Cohens v. Virginia* (1821), establishing jurisdiction of the U.S. supreme court to review a criminal conviction of Maryland citizens in Virginia. The Cohen brothers were convicted of violating a Virginia law prohibiting lottery ticket sales. The ruling held that the federal statute authorizing sales in the District of Columbia did not conflict with the Virginia law.

[18] Ezell (160), at 84.

[19] For Provident Bank, Business Wire (2014) and for Freedman's Savings and Trust Company, US Law (1865) Ch. XCII. For the night ferry, Jersey City (1909), at 7. For the *Dudley S. Gregory*, The Armitage Brearley (1877). For Gregory's real estate speculation, see *Associates of Jersey v. Davison* (1860), *Van Keuren v. McLaughlin* (1868), and *Southmayd v. McLaughlin* (1873).

# PART V

## DISINTEGRATION

Figure 22: Richard Keith Call

# Chapter Thirteen

## Call to Arms

### Defaults

For Patrick Tracy Jackson, the tale of the Pensacola Railroad, subsumed in the saga of the Bank of Pensacola, was one of defaults. Every party, save Locks & Canals, defaulted. There were construction defaults. There were defaults under the rolling stock sale agreement between the Pensacola Railroad and Locks & Canals. There were bank loan defaults and bond defaults. The Territory of Florida defaulted on its guarantee of the Bank of Pensacola bonds that funded the Pensacola Railroad. Territorial defaults emphasized that the excursion to Florida exposed L&C to risks beyond those customarily encountered in rolling stock sales. L&C was caught in a confluence of political currents that included Jacksonian politics and the move of Florida from territorial status to statehood.

With the onset of the Panic of 1837, the minimalist construction efforts of the Pensacola Railroad were suspended. Construction never resumed. The Bank of Pensacola, ensnared in the maelstrom of the Panic and related bank closures, ceased operations on June 5, 1838 to protect its specie reserve (probably unexpended funds from sales of Bank of Pensacola bonds).

The Bank of Pensacola defaulted in paying its bonds on July 1, 1839. Jaudon, Chauncey, Wilder, and Thomas Biddle paid the defaulted amount ($15,000 and likely the obligation shown on the June 8, 1841 Bank of Pensacola financial statements as $15,283.75). The bank also defaulted on January 1 and July 1, 1840 interest payments and on all payments thereafter. The BUS, through Jaudon as London agent, paid the January and July interest, in the amount of $30,000. Given Bank of Pensacola accounting practices, all or some of the three interest payments ($15,283.75 plus $30,000) may have been included in the Bank of Pensacola's $110,964.25 obligation to the BUS as of June 8, 1841.[1]

Holders of the Bank of Pensacola 1835~1860 bonds sought relief from the Territory of Florida. Many were European investors whose interests derived from the Pensacola Association by way of the BUS and the London house of Gowan & Marx. The entire 1835~1860 issue was sold to the Pensacola Association by the Bank of Pensacola. The BUS acquired the bonds from the Pensacola Association. The BUS, with assistance of Thomas Biddle & Company, sold interests in the bonds to European investors through Gowan & Marx.[2]

### Call to Contortions

Richard Keith Call was a man apart, from both party and public, as he began his second term as governor of the Territory of Florida on March 19, 1841. Though a protégé of Andrew Jackson, Call assumed the governorship as a Whig, appointed by President William Henry Harrison.[A] Bitterness toward Martin Van Buren induced his switch to the minority Whig party. Van Buren removed Call from his first term as Territorial governor on December 2, 1839, replacing him with Robert Raymond Reid. Call was outspokenly critical of Van Buren for his tepid interest in the Florida War and of Joel R. Poinsett, then Secretary of the War Department, for the conduct of the Florida War. The feud with Poinsett resurrected issues relating to Call's behavior during his first term as governor, while commander of the army, in not coming to the aid of General Leigh Read at the Withlacoochee River. That event elicited anger from President Jackson, and Call's removal from command of the army. Call regarded both dismissals as insults. He regarded Poinsett's inquiries for information as an insulting censure for misconduct. Sullen and indignant, Call refused to communicate directly with Poinsett or Jackson, even as Jackson attempted to mediate the matter.[3]

Despite being patriotic, conscientious, and devoted to Florida, Call had little popular support due to his mercurial and violent temperament, rash outspokenness, proclivity to duels, confrontations (verbal and physical), tantrums, imperialistic tendencies, pride, delicate ego, petulance, bitterness regarding adverse outcomes, and sullen retreat from criticism into a state of defensive remove. All of which were seized upon by the many enemies he had made by 1841.

Call's 1842 gubernatorial message to the Territorial legislature addressed the circumstances of the Bank of Pensacola, Southern Life & Trust, and Union Bank. The Bank of Pensacola and Southern Life & Trust had defaulted on their bond payments, which were guaranteed by the Territory. The Territory was issuer and

---

[A] Andrew Jackson appointed Call to his first term as governor on May 16, 1836. Call was an ardent supporter of Jackson, having served in Jackson's initial campaigns against the Seminoles. Call successfully cultivated the relationship for years. He followed Jackson to Florida in 1821 when Jackson became provisional governor. Call was married at Jackson's Hermitage in 1824. Call remained in Florida after Jackson returned to the Hermitage. Call became a Pensacola lawyer and, upon Jackson's suggestion, was appointed brigadier-general of the West Florida militia. He served on the Pensacola Municipal Board and as a delegate to the Florida Legislative Council and the federal Congress. In 1825 he moved to Tallahassee where he was appointed receiver of public moneys for Middle Florida land matters. He then became a successful land speculator.

primary obligor on bonds sold by the Union Bank, which were secured by mortgages on the bank's real and personal property. To the date of Call's address, the Territory had not made payment on its guarantees or its bonds.[4]

Call's central assertion was based on the Bank of Pensacola charter. He opined that the charter required interest and principal on its bonds to be paid in Philadelphia. European holders expected payment in London, which Call concluded to be a charter violation.[B] He reasoned that the BUS had entered into a separate agreement with European holders when it sold them bonds, thereby becoming the obligor to those holders. As for bondholder remedies, Call's position was that, before seeking payment from the Territory, the holders (the Pensacola Association, the BUS, and the European holders) had to pursue remedies against (a) the Bank of Pensacola, (b) in the case of the foreign bondholders, the sellers of the bonds to those foreign holders (the sellers being Pensacola Association members and the BUS), and (c) individual Bank of Pensacola shareholders (being mostly Pensacola Association members). All of which justified the Territory in not honoring its bond guarantee.

In considering Call's assertions, a review of the bond-related documents is instructive. Five documents are critical to the analysis: (i) the Bank of Pensacola charter; (ii) the Bank of Pensacola bond; (iii) the bond endorsement of the Florida Territory, (iv) the BoP Bond Sale Contract (1835), which was the agreement between the Bank of Pensacola and the Pensacola Associates for the sale of the endorsed bonds; and (v) the London Bond Agreement, being the document affording foreign bondholders rights in and to the bonds and rights to payments of interest on and the principal amount of the bonds.[C]

The 1835 Act established the Bank of Pensacola charter. Section 4 authorized the bank to issue bonds and pay principal and interest "at such place or places within the United States or this Territory [of Florida] as may be deemed most expedient; and said bonds to be payable after the first day of January, 1860….". The 1835 Act and the charter support Call's assertion that principal and interest were required to be paid in the United States and that payment in London was not authorized. The 1835 Act and the charter did not require payment in Philadelphia.[5]

---

[B] European holders included Hope and Company, Gowan & Marx, S. Waymouth, Overend, Gurney and Company, John Alliard, Thomson Hankey & Company, William Tritton, H. L. Thomas, Coutts & Company, Ewart, Taylor & Company, and Grayson & Company.

[C] The distinction between an interest in the bond (and thus ownership of the bond) and an interest in payments in respect of the bonds was important.

Each 1835~1860 bond was an obligation of the Bank of Pensacola to the Florida Territory. See Figure 5 (in Chapter Seven). The bond recited the personal liability of Bank of Pensacola shareholders and the pledge of Pensacola Railroad stock to secure the bond. The bond did not specify a payment location for either principal or interest.

---

Figure 23: Endorsement of Bank of Pensacola Bond

FLORIDA SIX PER CENT. STOCK, *Territory of Florida*

In pursuance of the laws of this Territory, the within bond is hereby assigned and made payable to bearer hereof; and the payment thereof, and the interest thereon, as within stipulated, is hereby guarantied [stet] by the Territory of Florida, and the faith of the Territory pledged for the redemption thereof.

Given under my and hand, and the great seal of the Territory, at the Executive Office, this ___ day of _____ one thousand eight hundred and thirty-five, and the independence of the United States the _____ year.

    By the Governor:     _____ *Governor of Florida.*
                              _____ *Secretary.*

BANK OF PENSACOLA:
    It is hereby agreed that the principal and semi-annual interest of the within bond shall be paid at _____.
                              _____ *President.*

---

The Territory's bond endorsement is replicated in Figure 23. The form of the endorsement was set forth, verbatim, in Section 4 of the 1835 Act. The endorsement assigned the bond, as guaranteed by the Territory, to its bearer. The endorsement did not specify a payment location for either principal or interest. Beneath the endorsement on each bond was a one-line agreement of the Bank of Pensacola, signed by its president, specifying that principal and interest would be paid at a specific location. The location was left blank, to be filled in for each bond. The location was not limited to the United States, Philadelphia, a place in the Florida Territory, or any other jurisdiction.

Figure 24: London Bond Agreement

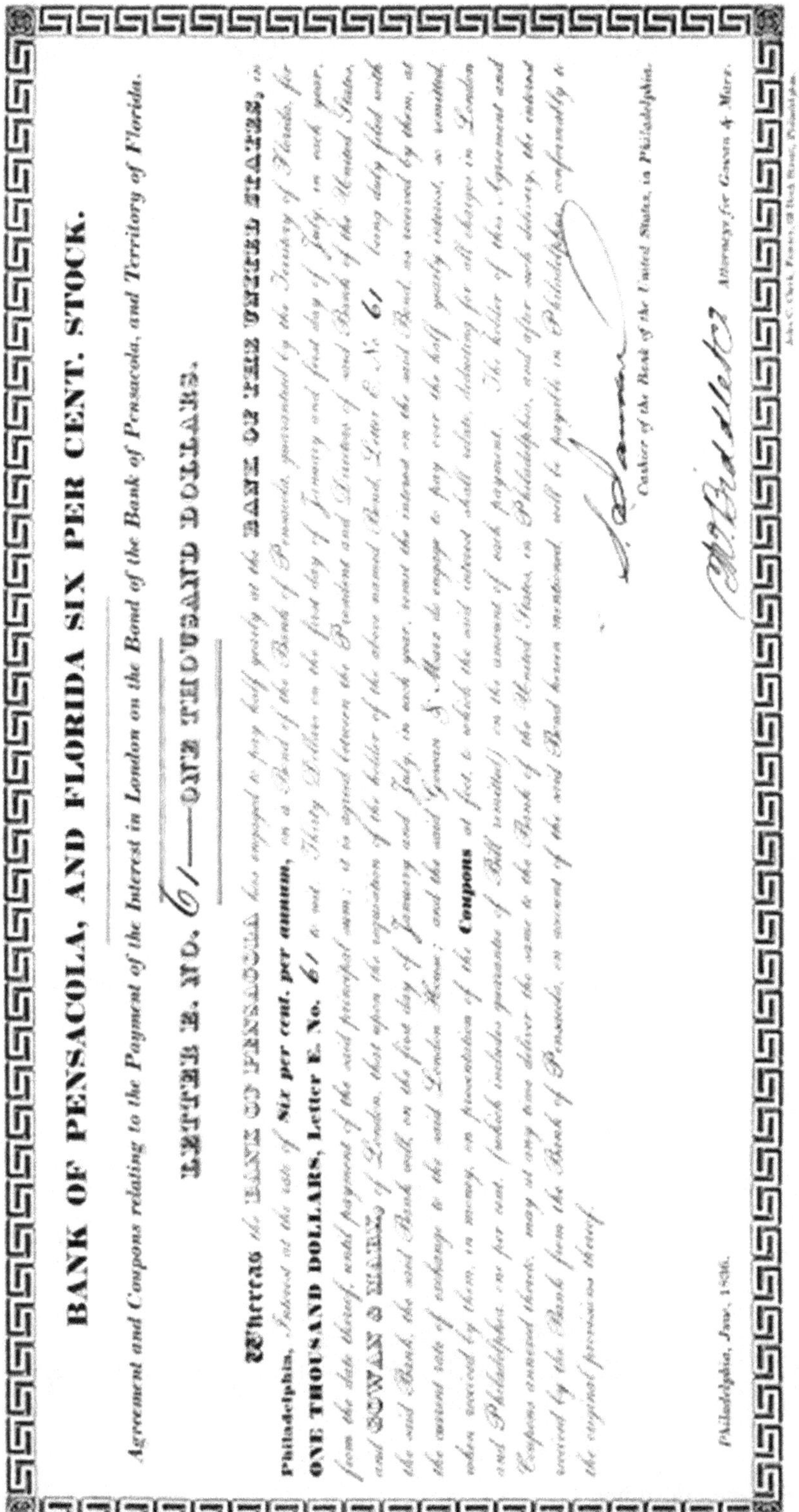

Figure 25: Text of London Bond Agreement

**BANK OF PENSACOLA, AND FLORIDA SIX PER CENT. STOCK.**

Agreement and Coupons relating to the Payment of the Interest in London on the Bond of the Bank of Pensacola, and Territory of Florida

LETTER E. NO. 61 – ONE THOUSAND DOLLARS

**Whereas** the BANK OF PENSACOLA has agreed to pay half yearly at the BANK OF THE UNITED STATES, in **Philadelphia**, Interest at the rate of **Six per cent. per annum**, on a Bond of the Bank of Pensacola guaranteed by the territory of Florida for **ONE THOUSAND DOLLARS, Letter E. No. 61** to wit: Thirty Dollars on the first day of January and the first day of July in each year, from the date hereof, until payment of the principal sum; it is agreed between the President and Directors of the Bank of the United States and Gowan & Marx of London, that upon the requisition of the holder of the above named Bond, Letter E No. 61 being duly filed with the Bank, the said Bank will, on the first day of January and July in each year, remit the interest on the Bond received by them, at the current rate of exchange to the said London House; and the said Gowan & Marx do engage to pay over the half yearly interest, as remitted, when received by them, in money, in presentation of the **Coupons** at full, to which the said interest shall relate, deducting for all charges in London and Philadelphia, one per cent. (which includes guarantee of Bill remitted) on the amount of such payment. The holder of this Agreement and Coupons annexed thereto, may at any time deliver the same to the Bank of the United States, in Philadelphia, and after such delivery, the interest received by the Bank from the Bank of Pensacola, an amount of the said Bond herein mentioned, will be payable in Philadelphia conformably to the original provisions thereof.

/s/ S. Jaudon
Cashier of the Bank of the United States in Philadelphia
/s/ T. W. Biddle & Co.
Attorneys for Gowan & Marx

Philadelphia, June, 1836

The BoP Bond Sale Contract (1835) governed sale of the bonds (as endorsed and assigned by the Territory) to the Pensacola Association. It was executed on behalf of the Bank of Pensacola by Walter Gregory, president, and James Catlin, cashier. It was executed by William H. Chase, as agent for the financial agents of the Pensacola Association (Thomas Biddle, Samuel Jaudon, and Elihu Chauncey).

The BoP Bond Sale Contract (1835) recited, with slight modification, the language of the 1835 Act stipulating that payment of principal and interest be made within the United States or the Territory of Florida. The operative language then stipulated that:[6]

> the interest on said bonds, at the rate of six per cent. per annum, shall be paid semi-annually, in Philadelphia, at the Bank of Pennsylvania, or at such other bank as may hereafter be agreed upon. The said bonds, when they become due and payable, shall be paid at Philadelphia…. And it is further agreed by the parties contracting, that the future payments shall be made in Pensacola, or New Orleans, or in Philadelphia, at the option of the parties of the second part [the Pensacola Association], upon their giving notice to the bank, of one month at least before the said payments shall become due and payable, of the place of payment, whenever New Orleans or Philadelphia shall be selected as the place of payment.

In answers to interrogatories of the investigating commissioner in 1840 (see Chapter Fifteen), James Catlin characterized the sale contract with some distortion (emphasis added): "interest on said bonds shall be paid in Philadelphia, at the Bank of Pennsylvania, or such other bank *in Philadelphia* as maybe designated afterwards by the purchasers of said bonds in Europe." Despite Catlin's characterization, the reference to "such other bank as may hereafter be agreed upon" was not geographically limited in the BoP Bond Sale Contract (1835). [7]

Call's assertion that the bonds were payable in Philadelphia was correct, in part. The initial place of payment of bonds when due at maturity was the Bank of Pennsylvania in Philadelphia. However, the Pensacola Association had the option of changing the place of payment to New Orleans or Pensacola. There was no indication that London was a permissible payment location for interest or principal.

The London Bond Agreement (Figure 24, with text in Figure 25), governed the sale in England of interests in the bonds. The agreement was between the BUS and each London investor holding that document. It provided for sale of *an interest in the bonds* through the London house of Gowan & Marx. Interest coupons (not here shown) were attached to the London Bond Agreement.

The London Bond Agreement stated that interest was payable in Philadelphia. The BUS, over the signature of Samuel Jaudon, agreed with the counterparty that interest received by the BUS would be remitted to Gowan & Marx in London.

Thomas Biddle & Co., as attorneys for Gowan & Marx, agreed with the counterparty that Gowan & Marx would remit that interest to the counterparty. The counterparty was also provided the option of presenting the London Bond Agreement, with coupons attached, to the BUS for payment of interest in Philadelphia.

The London Bond Agreement was not itself a Bank of Pensacola bond. It was a BUS agreement to pay interest received by the BUS on the Bank of Pensacola bonds (if and when received) either to Gowan & Marx for payment to the counterparty in London or directly to the counterparty in Philadelphia. The London Bond Agreement did not address payment of principal on the bonds. As noted in the BoP Bond Sale Contract (1835), principal was payable in Philadelphia.

Governor Call was well versed on the niceties of the relevant legal requirements, contracts, and enforcement procedures.[8] The Bank of Pensacola bonds were not assigned and transferred to London holders. As Call asserted, those holders had a contractual claim against the BUS. That claim would likely be unsuccessful. The BUS agreed to pay to the London investors only so much as the BUS received from the Bank of Pensacola. Which was zero, absent an action by the BUS as a bondholder against the Bank of Pensacola and the Territory of Florida.

All such niceties aside, however, it is indisputable that the Bank of Pensacola defaulted on its obligation to pay the bonds, and the Territory of Florida defaulted on its payment obligation under its guarantee. Neither the bank nor the Territory paid the bondholders, in Philadelphia or elsewhere. The BUS, and other bond holders (but not holders of interests in the bonds pursuant to the London Bond Agreement), had direct claims against the Bank of Pensacola and the Territory of Florida for defaults. No amount of rhetorical gymnastics regarding contractual privity and remedial procedures could detract from that fundamental conclusion.

Call argued that, procedurally, a claim could not be made against the Territory until the bondholders had exhausted all recourse against each of the Bank of the Pensacola and its individual shareholders, especially members of the Pensacola Association. The basis for exhaustion of remedies against the shareholders was that the shareholders were personally liable for the bond indebtedness.[D]

---

[D] Call presented a range of other related arguments.

    The bonds were issued under the charter for the exclusive use and benefit of the stockholders of the bank. They are their property. The Territory had no interest whatsoever in them, and became the endorser merely to promote private enterprize, [stet] for the construction of a Railroad, which, had it been

Although present in the initial authorizing legislation, shareholder personal liability was eliminated by Territorial act on February 10, 1838, which was signed by Governor Richard Keith Call. The governor argued in 1842 (though not at signing in 1838) that elimination of personal liability was invalid because the act was passed after issuance of the bonds. He argued that the bonds passed into the hands of the original bondholders, as bona fide purchasers for value, containing the personal liability provision. Unmentioned was the fact that the bona fide purchaser was the Pensacola Association, the largest shareholder in the Bank of Pensacola and the sole purchaser of the bonds. Or that the bona fide holder was fully aware of, had no objection to, and consented to elimination of personal liability.[E]

On March 2, 1840, a Florida law was passed reinstating the individual and personal liability of shareholders. Call cited, among other things, the $30,000 payment by the BUS to the London investors for defaulted interest payments as evidence that the BUS had accepted responsibility for bond payments to foreign holders.[9]

Call acknowledged that all shares in the Bank of Pensacola were pledged to the Territory of Florida under the charter provisions and that there was an argument that the Territory should thus be considered responsible for the bond interest. His consideration of this complexity was brief, dismissive, and a bit contrived given the reverence with which he described the charter provisions in other respects and the importance of the bond pledge to the structure. "However plausible this argument may be, this hypothecation could never have been considered any thing more than a nominal security." Rather disingenuously and unrealistically, given the nature of a mortgage or pledge, Call argued that a stock pledge to the Territory that did not grant the Territory control over the funds and capital of the Bank of Pensacola left

---

completed, would have been the property of the stockholders of the Bank. They are rendered liable by the charter of the Bank. They had the use and management of the funds produced by the sale of the bonds, and should be held responsible for their mismanagement. Another reason ... is, that most of the stockholders are non-residents, and would not participate in the general loss which our citizens would sustain, if this debt were discharged by the Territory.

[E] Call stated that "The Territory had an unquestionable right, by legislative enactment, to release the stockholders from all responsibility to her; but she could not discharge them from their slightest obligations to the bond-holders." That statement, and the law removing personal liability, undermined the Territory's right to claim against individual shareholders. In respect of the law removing personal liability, Call also invoked the constitutional prohibition against laws impairing the obligation of contracts.

the Territory "little more than the stock without the capital, which can be considered of but small value".[10]

Call had to avoid, at all costs, any procedure in which the Florida Territory paid the bonds because the Territory had no recourse against the Bank of Pensacola or its individual shareholders.

> It is manifest, from the charter itself, as well as from all subsequent legislation of the Territory, that it never was the design of the Legislative Council to pay interest on the bonds, and then to collect the amount, as a reimbursement, from the Bank, or its individual shareholders.

Call spent much of his 1842 address asserting that the Territory was the payor of last resort, available only after all remedies had been pursued against the Bank of Pensacola and its shareholders. Call admitted that the law of 1838 repealing the individual personal liability of the shareholders, which he signed, might well bar an action by the Territory against the bank and its individual shareholders.[11]

In sum, Call's position was that the domestic bondholders should seek remedies against themselves, with the foreign bondholders left to pursue remedies against their vendors and the stockholders, that is, against the Philadelphia and New York shareholders. The BUS ceased doing business in February of 1841 and thereafter operated in a liquidation mode.

―――

The contortions regarding payment derived from the difficult position in which Governor Call found himself in early 1842. Bond repudiation was being discussed. Sensitive to adverse consequences, Call opposed repudiation. He could not disavow the Territorial obligation under its guarantee despite his refusal to honor the guarantee by payment.[12]

> But, gentlemen, after the observes of this due diligence, and proper efforts, to recover the amount which may be due from the bank and its stockholders—if the effort should prove successful, I have no hesitation in expressing to you my opinion that the Territory is bound by the highest obligations to satisfy the demand.—However convenient it may be to disavow our responsibility, in order to avoid the embarrassment of an onerous debt; however popular the argument may be, which is offered in favor of the repudiation of these bonds, I have an irresistible conviction on my own mind that we are bound by all the principles of good faith, and by the rules of common honesty, to redeem the pledges so solemnly given, whenever our responsibility may arise. The honor of the Territory has, by her Legislation, been put in pledge. That pledge must be redeemed. Our honor must be vindicated, or we leave an indelible stain on our reputation.

## Endnotes: Chapter Thirteen

1. FL Gov. (1842), with interest default payments at 9-11, and BoP Financials for June 8, 1841, FL SJ (1842), at 52 (including correspondence between the BUS and bondholders and the Florida Territory), with discussion of interest default payments at 35, and JCCB (1896), at 319. William B. Taylor, cashier of the Bank of Pensacola in 1842, identified Biddle, Jaudon, Chauncey, and Wilder as having paid the 1839 semi-annual interest in his responses to Anderson's investigative committee, Taylor Letter (June 8, 1841), at 53.

2. Examples of pleas of European holders are the letters included in FL Gov. (1842), at 38-52, regarding defaults and Territorial payment obligations.

3. For the battle of Withlacoochee and related matters, Bittle (1966), Doherty (1961), at 93-108, Martin (1943), at 339-44, Brevard (1908-1), at 9-12, and Call (1837), the last a lengthy letter of June 20, 1837 from Call that was reprinted in NILES' WEEKLY REGISTER. Poinsett explained that Call was removed as governor because Call "thought proper to assume an attitude opposed to this Department, and his continuance in office, was, therefore, deemed incompatible with the interests of the public service." Doherty (1961), at 116, quoting a letter from Poinsett to Senator William S. Fulton. For Call as *aide de camp*, Turner (2003), at 16.

   Call spent his youth in Kentucky and attended a Tennessee military academy. He built an estate in Tallahassee named "The Grove". Call was born on October 24, 1792 and died on September 14, 1862. Doherty (1961), Martin (1943), Brevard (1908-1), Brevard (1908-2), FL Department of State, and Long (1962). For call as a Unionist, Doherty (1961), Doherty (1950), Reiger (1968).

4. For Call's address, FL Gov. (1842), at 6 *et seq*. Criticizing the bank's stockholders, at 20, Call asserted the bank transferred an Apalachicola land parcel to Biddle, Jaudon, and Chauncey, violating the mandate that all bank property be mortgaged to the Territory to secure the bond guarantee.

5. For charter provision regarding location of payment, 1835 Act, § 4.

6. BoP Bond Sale Contract (1835), first paragraph of covenants, at 466-67.

7. For the Catlin testimony, response of James Catlin, Cashier, March 31, 1840, BoP Commissioner's Report, at 456-57.

8. Governor Call's address walked a politically difficult line. He had a masterly grasp of contractual rights and enforcement procedures. He was aware of the weaknesses of arguments. He used valid legal principles and practical observations that were inapplicable or neglected facts. At times, he gave full vent to parochial emotional interests.

9. For the act eliminating individual and personal liability of Bank of Pensacola stockholders, FL Law (1838) No. 38, § 2. For Call's argument that elimination of personal liability occurred after bond issuance, FL Gov. (1842), at 11-25. For reinstatement of personal liability, FL Law (1840) No. 40. Lawsuits were pursued against

the Pensacola Association. An example is that of Owen M. Avery, noticed in Pensacola Gazette (1842, March 5).

10  Fl Gov. (1842), at 14.

11  See, for example, FL Gov. (1842), at 12-3; the quotation is from 13.

12  FL Gov. (1842), at 15.

# Chapter Fourteen

## Repudiations

**Florida Judiciary Committee Report**

The challenge to Territorial support of the Bank of Pensacola, Southern Life & Trust, and the Union Bank began well before Florida repudiated its support for the bonds and obligations of these banks. The Territory's Committee of the Judiciary, through Walker Anderson, issued the FL Judiciary Committee Report (1840). It addressed (a) the authority of the Territory's Legislative Council to charter banks and pledge the faith and credit of Florida for the banks and their obligations, and (b) whether those Territorial actions were binding on the State of Florida. The report addressed the Union Bank. By implication, it also addressed the charter and Territorial guarantee of bonds of the Bank of Pensacola and Southern Life & Trust, whose circumstances were nearly identical.[A]

The report concluded that the Territory did not have authority to charter the banks or support the banks with the faith and credit of the Territory. However, the report did acknowledge that opinions had been obtained from prominent legal counsel in 1834 on the same issues. Copies of those opinions were included in the report. Those opinions addressed only the Union Bank, although nearly identical facts rendered their logic applicable to the Bank of Pensacola. Those rendering the legal opinions were James Kent, Horace Binney, Peter A. Jay, and Daniel Webster, each an eminent lawyer and jurist.[1] Each opined that the Territory had authority to charter the banks, the banks were validly chartered, the Territory had authority to provide, by law, its faith and credit support, and validly did so, and the Territorial obligations would be binding upon the State of Florida. The opinions did not

---

[A] The issues pertaining to bank chartering, the pledge of Florida's faith and credit, and enforceability against the State of Florida were identical. The method by which the faith and credit supported the banks was not. Bonds issued by the Bank of Pensacola and Southern Life & Trust were guaranteed by the Territory. Union Bank bonds were direct obligations of the Territory, bearing the official seal and governor's signature. Many Union Bank investors were members of the old "Nucleus" or Call faction. The Territorial government under Call continued to issue faith bonds to the Union Bank during the 1837 Panic, opening Call to criticism by political opponents who focused on Call's relationship with John Gamble of the Union Bank.

address provision of "faith and credit" using those words. The opinions were that contracts made under the laws that provided such support were valid and binding and could not be annulled.[2]

**Repudiation and Persistence**

On February 3, 1842, identical resolutions were adopted by the Senate and House of Representatives of the Florida Territory, each entitled "A resolution respecting the Faith Bonds and Guarantees". The resolutions stated that "the Territorial Legislature does not possess, nor was it ever invested with authority to pledge the faith of the Territory, so as to render the citizens of the Territory responsible for the debts, or engagements of any corporation chartered by said Territorial Legislature."

The resolutions were initially vetoed by Governor Call, consistent with his concerns regarding the many implications of repudiation. The resolutions were passed over his veto and constituted the formal repudiation of the Territorial guarantee of the Bank of Pensacola (and other) bonds.[3]

The repudiation was published and widely criticized. The harshest criticism focused, not on repudiation, but on the Pensacola Association, the BUS, and the bondholders. The governor's annual report singled out the BUS and Nicholas Biddle, Samuel Jaudon, Elihu Chauncey, and S. V. S. Wilder as inflicting "boundless injury upon this whole country by the[ir] management and frauds". Other commentary was directed at Morris Robinson. Even the Boston capitalist, Walter Gregory, did not escape demonization for his villainy. As of March 1842, the BUS held approximately $436,300 in obligations of the Bank of Pensacola, the Pensacola Railroad, and the Union Bank.[4]

Governor Call, in his January 5, 1843 message, observed that the BUS and the other bondholders had made no demand for overdue interest on the Bank of Pensacola bonds (including for the $30,000 paid by the BUS) since January 1842 and that it was believed that there would be "nothing available from this source [the Bank of Pensacola], to pay the principal and interest of the Bonds, to the amount of five hundred thousand dollars, endorsed by the Territory." Call also reaffirmed his position that the bondholders must pursue remedies against the Bank of Pensacola and its individual shareholders. The Bank of Pensacola was then in the process of winding-up its affairs.[5]

The silence of the Bank of Pensacola bondholders was not an indication of acceptance of loss. In December 1841, the bondholders took their pleas to the U.S. federal government, proposing that it take responsibility for payment of the bonds. Call found that argument a "gross … absurdity". After strident debate, that effort proved unavailing.[6]

Nor were the 1842 resolutions of the Florida Legislative Council the end of efforts on behalf of Florida. Florida became a state on March 3, 1845. In connection with proposals to carry Territorial resolutions to the new State, on July 3, 1845 Florida senator Broward offered a resolution stating the governor and the Territorial Legislative Council

> had no power to pledge the faith of the people of Florida in aid of any banking institutions ... [and] That the acts of said Governor and Council, authorizing the Governor of the Territory to pledge the faith of the people of Florida, in aid of the Union Bank, the Bank of Pensacola, and the Life Insurance and Trust Company, are usurpations of the rights of the people of Florida, and that said acts therefore impose no binding obligation on the people or the State of Florida; and that the bonds issued by virtue of said acts, an entirely null and void, so far as they profess to bind the people of Florida.[7]

By July 15, 1845, the Florida Committee on Banks and other Corporations delivered a report, aimed directly at Territorial guarantees of bonds issued by Bank of Pensacola and Southern Life & Trust and Territorial bonds sold by Union Bank. It was a lengthy tirade that characterized the Territory as acting beyond its powers.[8]

> But your committee is of the opinion that the people of Florida are now, for the first time, acting for themselves, and that their reputation must be established by their own future conduct, not by that of those who have assumed to speak for them, and were reckless of the result to the people or the State, so long as their own corrupt purposes were served. ... Th[e] Territorial Government, established temporarily until Florida could become a State, then undertook to grant to certain persons special privileges, rights and immunities to be extended for a long series of years, and of a very extraordinary character, and to pledge the faith and honor, and give the obligations of the people of Florida, for a large amount of money, to enable those persons to raise capital upon which to exercise these extraordinary privileges for their own benefit, and not that of the people of Florida. A law thus passed is claimed to have all the sanctity and unalterable qualities of a contract. If it was a contract, neither the state or people were parties to it. No consideration moved to them. ... If it was a contract, it was not a law, or the exercise of legislative power.

On November 18, 1845, the Florida attorney general, Joseph Branch, issued an opinion to Florida's General Assembly. His opinion was that the Bank of Pensacola was duly incorporated by the Territory, the transition from territorial status to statehood did not abrogate the bank's charter, the bank had violated its charter by abandoning its purposes and was subject to judicial forfeiture of its assets, and the bank charter should not be legislatively annulled. By that time, the Bank of Pensacola's only assets consisted of shares in the Pensacola Railroad, which were pledged in their entirety to the Territory of Florida.[9]

## Endnotes: Chapter Fourteen

[1] James Kent was a monumental and famous figure in the law during his life, and thereafter. He was born in 1763 in Doanesburg, New York, and died on December 12, 1847. He had a rich and varied life as an attorney, state legislator, trial judge, appellate judge, master in equity, chancellor in equity, statutory compiler, law professor, and juristic writer. Like his father and grandfather, he was a graduate of Yale College. He graduated in 1781, with Simeon Baldwin. He read volume 4 of Blackstone's *Commentaries* at age sixteen and determined to be a lawyer.

Kent apprenticed under Egbert Benson, a prominent Poughkeepsie lawyer and the next-door neighbor of John Jay, later Chief Justice of the U.S. Supreme Court and Governor of New York. Kent was admitted to the bar in 1785 at age twenty-one.

He became a law professor at Columbia College in 1793. His lecture notes formed the basis of his COMMENTARIES. Governor John Jay appointed Kent master in chancery in 1796 and, in 1797, as Recorder of New York City, a part-time judgeship. In 1798 Jay appointed Kent to the New York supreme court. He became chief justice in 1814. He left the court to become Chancellor of New York, a position he held until 1823. In 1824 he returned to Columbia College. For Kent, see Langbein (1993) and Dorfman (1961).

Peter Augustus Jay, born on January 24, 1776, was the son of John Jay. He was a lawyer, banker, abolitionist, reformer, and philanthropist. He died on February 20, 1843. He was president of the New York Manumission Society, the New York Public School Society, the New York Hospital, and the New York Historical Society, and a founder of the New York Bank for Savings. Jay was an author of the Penitentiary System Report (1822), an early penal rehabilitation report, and a prominent member of the Society for the Prevention of Pauperism in the City of New York. Jay also served as a long-time trustee, and eventually first vice president, of the Bank for Savings in the City of New York, which opened in 1819 to cater to the poor. While his father was a foreign minister and governor of the New York, Peter Jay served as his private secretary.

Peter Jay served as a member of the New York house of assembly, a recorder of the City of New York, and a member of the convention for amending the New York constitution. He also worked with Albert Gallatin and James Kent at the Free Trade Convention in Philadelphia and in various tariff committees. For Jay, Jay (1905), Cutler (1972), Law Reporter (1843), at 528, Bank for Savings AR (1820), at 4, PSS AR (1830), Longworth's Almanac (1834), at 46, Heale (1976), Griffin (1957), and Hone (1889), at 35, 55, and 131.

[2] FL SJ (1842), Appendix (following page 200), with the text of the legal opinions at 17 *et seq.*, and FL Judiciary Committee Report (1840). See also USMD (1842), which includes discussion of state debts and, at 524-25, discussion of the Florida debts and legal opinions of Kent, Binney, Jay, and Webster. For Call and the Union Bank, Doherty (1961), at 109-12.

³ For Florida's formal repudiation, FL Law (1842) Res. 9. For these and other state and territorial debt guarantees, English (1996), Ratchford (1941), Scott (1893), Kim & Wallis (2005) (the three Florida entities at 47 *et seq.*), Curtis (1844) (also discussing Michigan and Pennsylvania repudiations), Randolph (1931) (with Florida repudiations at 67-8), and McGrane (1935). See *How General Jackson Ruined the Bank of the United States*, 1 WEEKLY GLOBE 209 (March 12, 1842).

⁴ For publication of the repudiation and the quotation, Repudiation (1842, April 9). Regarding territorial and state debt repudiations, McGrane (1935), Florida being discussed at 232-44, Kim & Wallis (2005), at 742-44, English (1996), Ratchford (1941), Wallis, Sylla & Grinath (2004), and Grinath, Wallis & Sylla (1997). For the villainy of the Boston capitalist Walter Gregory, Ohio Statesman (1842, November 23), taken from the BALTIMORE SUN.

⁵ For Call's quoted language, FL Gov. (1843), at 12. Despite the winding-up, in 1844, two committees were formed in Pensacola to revive the Pensacola Railroad, as reported in Pensacola Gazette (1844, December 7). At least one, somewhat reconfigured (to add Walker Anderson, and others, and still including Chase, Kelly, and Hyer) was pursuing the revival effort in October of 1849: Pensacola Gazette (1849, October 20).

⁶ See, for example, referral of Bank of Pensacola bondholder claims of December 8, 1842 to the Committee on Foreign Affairs of the U.S. House of Representatives on February 6, 1843 in U.S. HJ (1842), at 319. An editorial on federal government responsibility in Boston's EMANCIPATOR AND FREE AMERICAN is Emancipator (1842, July 28). McGrane (1935), at 223-44, discusses the Florida Territorial bonds and, briefly, efforts to get the national government to assume responsibility. For Call's gross absurdity characterization, FL Gov. (1842), at 15-7 (the words are at 16).

⁷ For the quotation, FL SJ (1845), at 31.

⁸ For the quotation, FL SJ (1845), at 83.

⁹ FL AG (1845, November 18). In a December 16, 1845 letter to the Florida House of Representatives, Branch indicated he had taken no action to revoke the charters of the Bank of Pensacola, the Union Bank, or Southern Life & Trust. "Should your honorable body deem it wise and politic to order the Attorney General to institute the proper proceedings for the purpose of having the charters of those associations forfeited, and their franchises seized into the hands of the State, it will be promptly attended to." FL AG (1845, December 16).

Figure 26: Walker Anderson

## Chapter Fifteen

### Engines Enigma

Engine purchase payments by the Pensacola Railroad to Locks & Canals were in default from inception and remained continuously in default. The remedy available to L&C was legal action on the rolling stock sale agreement. That remedy was never pursued. L&C did not retain title to the engines pursuant to a conditional sale agreement. Title was conveyed to the Pensacola Railroad upon delivery of the engines. L&C had no security interest in the engines. Nor is there evidence that the Bank of Pensacola, the BUS, the Pensacola Association, or any other entity had a security interest in the engines. L&C took the only other action it could take. It did not build the other four engines, twelve passenger cars, or wheels, axles, springs, and iron work for one hundred burthen cars that were part of its Pensacola Railroad contract.[1]

The fate of the two engines built by L&C remains a mystery. Different sources provide varying, sometimes conflicting, statements. The report providing the most information is that of Walker Anderson. In his January 13, 1840 address, Florida governor Richard R. Reid called for investigation of the Bank of Pensacola, the Union Bank, and Southern Life & Trust.[A] Anderson rendered his report as Commissioner of the Bank of Pensacola.[2]

**Walker Anderson**

Walker Anderson was born in Petersburg, Virginia on July 18, 1801 and died in Pensacola on January 18, 1857. In Anderson's youth, his family moved to North Carolina, where Anderson was educated, through university. He became a lawyer, studying in Raleigh under his uncle, Judge Duncan Cameron. Anderson emigrated to Florida in 1836. Together with Thomas Blount, Anderson was a delegate prominent in drafting the State of Florida constitution in 1838. Together with William H. Chase, Walther Gregory, Henry Hyer, Hanson Kelly, and Thomas Blount, Anderson was a founder of the College of Pensacola. He served as chairman of the board of trustees of the West Florida Collegiate Institute in Pensacola. Anderson learned to play the coronet and displayed his skills as a member of the Oriental Brass Band.[3]

---

[A] Call was the third and fifth governor (March 16, 1836 to December 2, 1839 and March 19, 1841 to August 11, 1844). His 1854 bid to become governor failed. Reid was governor from December 2, 1839 to March 19, 1841.

Soon after his election to Florida's lower house in 1840, Anderson became chairman of the judiciary and banking committees. In those roles, he was a central figure in the initiation and conduct of debates regarding whether Territorial acts of incorporation of the Bank of Pensacola, Union Bank, and Southern Life & Trust could be annulled and whether the State of Florida could release itself from obligations undertaken by the Territory of Florida, including bond guarantees and payment obligations. Anderson's position, as reflected in his report, was that the Territory had no authority to create banks or authorize bond issuances and that Territorial obligations, including guarantees, were null and void.

Commencing in 1844, Anderson served as U.S. district attorney for Florida's Western District, where he was responsible for prosecution of the abolitionist Jonathan Walker for abduction of slaves. The charge was filed in connection with Walker's efforts to transport seven runaway slaves to the British West Indies. Walker was seized at sea by an American vessel, consigned to Key West, and then sent to Pensacola for trial. Walker became known as "The Man with the Branded Hand" when the U.S. government branded his right hand with the marking "S S" for slave stealer. He was the subject of John Greenleaf Whittier's 1846 poem *The Branded Hand*.

In his recounting, Walker thanked Anderson and his wife for their kindness and humanity during the prosecution and characterized Anderson as mild, considerate, and intelligent, with "the most amiable disposition of any person I ever knew in Pensacola". That assessment had long been shared by Floridians, facilitating Anderson's rapid advance in politics.[4]

In 1850 Anderson was again in the Florida house of representatives, functioning as chairman of the Judiciary Committee and the Federal Relations Committee. During that session, pursuant to legislation sponsored by Anderson, a new supreme court of Florida was created, independent of the circuit courts. Anderson was elected its chief justice on January 14, 1851, serving until his resignation in 1853.[5]

The 1850 report of the Federal Relations Committee, signed by Walker Anderson, also achieved notoriety. The report supported arguments for Florida's secession from the Union and defended the right of Southern states to resist the fugitive slave bill:[6]

> Concession by the South, for the sake of the Union, has now been made to the very verge of dishonor, and every Southern heart revolts at submission to further injustice. This is the common ground upon which all Southern men meet, and, laying aside all differences that have hitherto divided them, pledge to each other their mutual vows to recede no farther. For her love of the Union, the South may

proudly appeal to the past—for her greater love of liberty, let her now appeal to the future.

Walker Anderson's involvement with William H. Chase's efforts to build roads into Alabama's cotton lands did not cease with the demise of the Pensacola Railroad. Anderson chaired two further efforts. One was an effort to build the Montgomery and Pensacola Railroad, initiated by Anderson and Chase in 1849. The railroad was completed in 1861. The other was an 1850 initiative to build a plank road north from Pensacola, which Anderson advocated as superior to a railroad.[7]

### BoP Commissioner's Report

Walker Anderson had little involvement in the transaction between L&C and the Pensacola Railroad until the Bank of Pensacola failed to pay its bonds and Florida failed to honor its guarantee. Then, as commissioner, he rendered the BoP Commissioner's Report. That report and related responses to interrogatories regarding the Bank of Pensacola and its assets were of special interest to Patrick Tracy Jackson because they addressed—or failed to adequately address—the fate of the engines built by L&C.

The BoP Commissioner's Report of April 7, 1840 described sales and transfers of various Pensacola Railroad assets in connection with its winding-up. Portions of the report were based upon Anderson's inquiries at the customs house. The descriptions were quite specific: except regarding the locomotives. Thus, an iron shipment was made to Montgomery in 1838 to consummate a sale to the Montgomery and West Point Railroad in exchange for stock. An iron shipment was made in 1839 to Tallahassee for the use of the Tallahassee and St. Mark's Railroad Company. A shipment of iron "in October and November, 1839, [was made] to New York", with no designation of the recipient. That is followed by: "The locomotives and other machinery were shipped also to New York, in November, 1839." No recipient was specified.[8]

The statement regarding shipment of the engines to New York is supported by some information in the report and contradicted by other information in the same report, even though much of the contradictory information was provided by a single individual, William B. Taylor. Taylor was president of the Pensacola Railroad as well as a director and the president and cashier of the Bank of Pensacola.

On April 2, 1840, Taylor provided condensed financial statements of the Pensacola Railroad that made no mention of the locomotives.[9] Shortly thereafter, on April 27, Anderson posed interrogatories to Taylor, including specific inquiries regarding dispositions of Pensacola Railroad assets. Taylor answered that same day. Two answers were relevant to the engines.[10] Taylor confirmed that two engines and tenders and a steam pile-driver had been purchased by the railroad. He confirmed that, as of April 27, two engines and a steam pile-driver, with an aggregate value of $19,000, were still in the possession of the railroad. As the Pensacola Railroad never owned or possessed but two engines, it seems clear these were built by Locks & Canals. Taylor's answer obviously contradicted the assertion that the engines were sent to New York in November 1839 and omission of the engines from the April 2, 1840 Pensacola Railroad financial statements.[11]

An 1841 letter from Edmond J. Forestall to Secretary of State Daniel Webster, referring to November 1839 transactions, stated that machinery of the Pensacola Railroad that had been hypothecated to the Florida Territory was shipped to New York and sold to the Montgomery Rail Road Company, but says nothing of the locomotives. It is unlikely the machinery included the engines. Taylor did not list the engines as among the assets to the Montgomery and West Point Rail Road Company. One engine was acquired by the Montgomery & West Point in each of 1839 and 1840, the former built by K. & G. Rogers and the latter by Jason Brooks.[12]

The message of Governor Reid on January 13, 1840 stated that "It is said" that the Pensacola Railroad locomotives had been removed from Florida by that date. Brown, citing the Pensacola Historical Society, observed that the two engines "were redeemed by northern bankers and returned to the builders". Taber asserted that the two engines were "Reclaimed by L.&C. in 1839. Unknown to whom resold to."[13]

No evidence has been located in L&C records, or elsewhere, that supports a return of the engines to L&C. To the contrary, reappearance of the Pensacola Railroad engine payment obligation on the L&C books in 1842 and 1843 supports the conclusion that the engines were not returned to L&C. That reappearance may have been in anticipation of L&C receiving some defaulted amounts. Possibly Jackson anticipated receiving funds from the BUS. Or William H. Chase may have rekindled a hope that the railroad would be revived or that the engines would be returned to L&C.

William H. Chase journeyed to Lowell in September 1840. He likely visited with L&C and Patrick Tracy Jackson. Which may have prompted Jackson to reinstate the Pensacola Railroad debt on the L&C books at year-end 1840, especially if the railroad still had possession of the engines, as indicated by Taylor in his response to the commissioner's interrogatories. It is possible this trip induced the decrease in the debt from $10,383 on July 31, 1839 to $9,783.23 in 1841 and 1842. The Pensacola Railroad was insolvent, and there is no indication that any asset liquidation proceeds made their way to L&C. Possibly, the decrease was forgiveness of accrued interest.

Taylor's responses to interrogatories regarding iron sales suggest another outcome. Proceeds from sales of Pensacola Railroad assets were probably credited against outstanding obligations to the Bank of Pensacola. If that were not the case, and the proceeds somehow made their way to the Bank of Pensacola (an unlikely scenario), it is likely that creditors of the bank, particularly the BUS or the Pensacola Association exercised a first preference against those proceeds (there being no indication that Florida exercised any such right).[14]

If the engines were shipped to New York but not to L&C, to whom were they shipped and to what end? The most likely recipient was Morris Robinson, Samuel Jaudon, or another BUS agent. Robinson was president of the BUS New York Branch in 1839 and 1840, when the engines were allegedly shipped to New York. Jaudon was officially residing in New York in this period, although he spent time in London as BUS agent, returning to the U.S. in 1841. Jaudon had responsibilities for liquidating BUS assets and may have received the engines as liquidator. In any case, it is likely the BUS would have applied the engine sale proceeds to either obligations due to it outside of the bonds or to the Bank of Pensacola's significant outstanding bond obligations. In any case, it is highly unlikely that L&C obtained any of the sale proceeds.[15]

Each of these scenarios leads to the same probable conclusion. That Locks & Canals eventually wrote of the Pensacola Railroad debt.[16]

---

It was during these tribulations with the Pensacola Railroad debt, amidst the 1839 depression, that Locks & Canals decided to sell locomotive engines to another struggling and financially stressed railroad: the Baltimore & Susquehanna. Taking lessons from the Pensacola Railroad debacle, Patrick Tracy Jackson devised a financing structure that, as further revised in the Rolling Stock Contracts with the Philadelphia & Reading, led to the development of the equipment financing structure that remains in use to the present day.

---

### Endnotes: Chapter Fifteen

[1] Pensacola RR AR (1836).

[2] *Extracts from Message of Governor Robert Raymond Reid – January 13, 1840*, in FL Executive Documents Volume IV, at 241. For authorization of the investigation of the Bank of Pensacola by the senate of the Territory of Florida, resolution set forth in FL Executive Documents IV at 254 *et seq.*

[3] Most biographical material on Walker Anderson is from Yonge (1933).

4   Walker (1848), at 66, and Whittier (1893), at 172-74 (the poem), Oickle (2011), Kittredge (1899), and Linton (1893).
5   Boyd & Reder (1981), at 1024-26.
6   FL Fed. Relations Comm. Report (1851), at 172.
7   Yonge (1933), at 181-82.
8   BoP Commissioner's Report, at 443 (custom-house inquiries) and 447. See *Bank of Pensacola*, 58 NILE'S NATIONAL REGISTER 310 (July 18, 1840), noting that issuance of the BoP Commissioner Report "had the effect of depreciating the value of its [Bank of Pensacola's] notes to such a degree as to render them almost unavailable to the holders."

   Brown (1959), at 11, citing the Pensacola Historical Society, references volume 86 of the RAILWAY AND LOCOMOTIVE HISTORICAL SOCIETY BULLETIN, which consists of a single article (Pettengill (1952), with the Pensacola Railroad prior to the Civil War discussed at 11 and 15-7) containing no information regarding the fate of the engines. Taber (2008), at 79, identifies two 2-2-0 engines built by L&C for the Pensacola Railroad in 1837 and made the quoted assertion. Clark (1924), at 47, Hay (1975), and Taber (2008), at 257, 269, and 540 cite two 2-2-0 engines built by L&C in 1837 were sold to the Marietta & Cincinnati: the *Rockingham* by the Boston & Maine and the *Meteor*, as the *Thomas James*, by the Boston & Worcester, each circa 1850. A remote possibility is that L&C reclaimed the engines and sold one to each of the Boston & Maine and the Boston & Worcester. That conclusion is contradicted by the sources cited in the text and is contrary to the L&C records regarding the Pensacola Railroad receivable in 1840 and 1842.

   For Walker Anderson, Yonge (1933), FL HJ (1850), at 172, Reese (1917), at 34, for Anderson's supreme court election, FL SJ (1850), at 311, for the prosecution of Jonathan Walker, Walker (1848), with the observations regarding Anderson and his wife at 66, and for the Oriental Brass Band, Clubbs (1959), at 391.
9   A note to the financial statements indicates $100,000 of iron rails and machinery were sold in the north to pay liabilities. It is unlikely that "machinery" included the engines given Taylor's response that "locomotives and other machinery" shipped in November of 1839. BoP Commissioner's Report, at 443. For the financial statements, BoP Commissioner's Report, at 442, including Taylor's transmittal letter.
10  Taylor also revealed that 1,000 tons of iron were shipped to New York, in November 1839, for sale. The sale proceeds (expected to approximate $95,000) were retained in New York as a reduction of Bank of Pensacola debt "contracted to enable the bank to resume specie payments in January, 1839". The Pensacola Railroad was credited with the amount of the sale proceeds against its debt to the Bank of Pensacola. It is unclear whether the valuation of iron in the financial statements provided by Taylor ($160,000) included $100,000 sold in the north or was determined after deduction for $100,000. What was reported, as derived from the commissioner's customs house inquiries, was that the Pensacola Railroad received 2,550 tons of iron in 1836 and 1837, that 2,200 tons were sold or shipped for sale (1,000 tons to the Montgomery & West Point, 100 tons to

the Tallahassee & St. Mark's, and 1,100 tons to New York in October and November), and that 350 tons remained in the Pensacola Railroad's possession as of April 1840. The $160,000 noted in the financial statement does not correlate with 350 tons of iron, based upon, among other things, Taylor's assertion that 1,000 tons would bring $95,000 in a New York sale. The $95 per ton pricing would yield an inventory of 1,684 tons, which may indicate that the financial statement figure was determined on the basis that the 1,100 tons shipped to New York were not yet sold (although that also does not correlate).

[11] BoP Commissioner's Report, at 468-70, for interrogatories regarding purchases and Pensacola Railroad possession of the engines and continuing possession. If the engines were not shipped to New York, they may have been retained in Pensacola and transferred to another railroad, such as the Pensacola & Perdido. No information supporting that conclusion has been discovered.

[12] For Forestall, Forestall Letter (1841). For Taylor's listing of assets conveyed to the Montgomery Rail Road, BoP Commissioner's Report, at 469. For the Montgomery &West Point locomotives, Brown (1959), at 43.

[13] For Reid's assertion, FL Gov. (1840), at 242. For the northern banks' redemption and return, Brown (1959), at 11. For Taber's assertion of engine return to L&C, Taber (2008), at 79. Brown Report (1840) was submitted to Governor Reid as a scathing indictment of the Bank of Pensacola, Pensacola Railroad, and New City developments.

[14] For Chase's trip to Lowell, Walby (2014), at 21. BoP Commissioner's Report, at 470: "materials on hand … Two locomotives and steam pile-driver…", as of April 27, 1840 (the date of Taylor's letter), contradicting his letter of April 2, 1840, at 443, that "[t]he locomotives and other machinery were shipped also to New York, in November, 1839."

[15] For Jaudon's return to the U.S., *Union Bank v. Call* (1854), at 413.

[16] The opinion of Gibb (1947), at 12, is that the Pensacola Railroad debt for the engines was likely written off.

# PART VI

## RESURRECTIONS

## Chapter Sixteen

### Envoi As Prelude

**Envoi**

Patrick Tracy Jackson arrived in Boston from Philadelphia on the night of December 12, 1845. A meeting of the Locks & Canals board of directors was held at 7½ Tremont Row at noon on Saturday, December 13. The agenda was Jackson's visit with Horace Binney. Jackson was present, as a director. In keeping with protocol, the results of the visit were presented by the new treasurer, John T. Morse.

The purpose of Jackson's consultation with Binney, as formulated by the L&C board of directors, pertained to the permissibility of disposing of the P&R debt under the Rolling Stock Contracts by assignment to a third party. Resolution of the disposition issue was anticlimactic. It went unmentioned in the minutes. The board meeting was devoted almost entirely to a plan developed by Jackson and Binney.

True to character, Jackson unilaterally expanded the scope and purpose of his consultation with Binney beyond the board mandate. Ridding L&C of the P&R debt was important. But only a threshold consideration.

The value of the debt was critical. Jackson needed to maximize the debt's value upon its disposition. Which entailed maximizing the probability of payment in full, and the timeliness of payment, even after L&C was relieved of its burden. Maximizing value was part of the plan.[1]

Resolving the disposition and valuation of the P&R debt did nothing to address infirmities in the P&R's financial structure and practices. Bostonians held equity and debt positions in the P&R that were jeopardized by the P&R's massive floating debt overhang. To Jackson's mind, the P&R's floating debt and financial practices were imprudent and unacceptable as a matter of business judgment and financial management. The Jackson-Binney plan directly targeted elimination of the floating debt.

Thus began the inexorable process of restructuring the P&R's finances and capital structure. The restructuring began modestly. The P&R Investigation Committee was formed in 1845 to report to P&R bondholders and stockholders. The committee was comprised of John Davis,[2] Robert Schuyler,[3] Amos Binney,[4] and W. Raymond Lee.[5] Each had close ties to Boston Associates and investors in L&C. The committee issued the P&R 1846 Report on March 30, 1846. The report addressed specific questions posed to it regarding the P&R's operations and financial condition, particularly its indebtedness. While the original purpose was broad (to motivate a reduction in floating debt), the methodological approach was narrow: to determine if the financial reports corresponded to the P&R's books and records. The investigation was limited to those books and records.[6]

London, Boston, and New York investors found inadequate the P&R's responses to their concerns, and those expressed in the P&R 1846 Report. Concurrently, public concern with excessive debt was mounting. By 1848, criticism of debt incurrence was widespread. Henry Varnum Poor, in an early writing as editor of the AMERICAN RAILROAD JOURNAL, addressed the P&R's debt profile expressly:[7]

> The experience of the Reading railroad, and some other similar enterprises, show that the safety of the capitalist is found in the fact, that the cost of the road is represented by share capital. Indebtedness of any sort is found to be a hindrance to the success of the enterprise, however well the interest is secured by a surplus of receipts over expenses. Every effort should therefore be made to secure the capital stock by the sale of shares, rather than resort to expedients by the hiring of money.

London, Boston, and New York investors eventually petitioned the P&R to appoint David A. Neal to investigate P&R finances. The Neal Report (1849) was commissioned on December 13, 1848 and issued on September 19, 1849. It supported comprehensive debt restructurings in 1848-1849 and thereafter. The P&R was remade commensurate with the vision of Patrick Tracy Jackson in 1845.[8]

**Prelude**

The structure used in the 1837 Pensacola Railroad engine sale transaction was a prelude to development of equipment finance structures. It contained no elements of equipment finance structures. It was a simple deferred payment sale. Title to the equipment was transferred at delivery. L&C took no collateral to secure repayment.

Failure of the Pensacola Railroad to make payment was not financially devastating for L&C. Despite the Panic of 1837 and the subsequent depression, L&C paid dividends every year from 1838 to 1844, other than 1842, when the Pensacola Railroad debt was likely written off. However, the transaction awakened Patrick Tracy Jackson to the necessity of robust structures to protect L&C's interests as a seller of rolling stock. Jackson was not one to sleep through a lesson. Nor was he oblivious to the roles of rolling stock builders as credit providers, financiers, and financial intermediaries.[9]

In 1839 L&C sold four locomotive engines to the Baltimore & Susquehanna. L&C adopted a conditional sale structure with deferred payment credit. Title was retained by an L&C agent: Charles Howard, the B&S president. Collateral included promissory notes and bonds, all saleable in secondary markets.[10]

The P&R Rolling Stock Contracts of 1842 and 1843 further improved the structure. Each was a conditional sale with deferred payment credit. Trusts were introduced as title holders. Novel collateral arrangements were introduced. Performance-based payments, calculated on tonnages of coal transported, were added. These were adapted from canal company arrangements developed by Lehigh Coal & Navigation during the cholera pandemic of 1832-1833 to induce boat captains to transport coal to Philadelphia despite cholera risks and to enable Lehigh C&N to control freight rates.[11]

Schuylkill Navigation adopted the L&C structure as the core of its 1845 boat loan and then improved the structure in boat loans of 1850, 1855, 1863, 1864, 1866, and 1868. In connection with a restructuring, SNC sought and obtained legislative protection for equipment financing arrangements. The SNC Creditors Act (1852) established a fundamental principle of equipment finance. It allowed railroads and canal companies to raise money for equipment acquisitions and secure its repayment by pledging the acquired equipment. The equipment was unavailable to other creditors. Up to 25% of the tolls and revenue from use of the equipment was dedicated exclusively to repayment of the money raised.[12]

SNC boat loan structures expanded to include acquisition of equipment and collateral beyond boats and railroad cars, including financial assets. Powers of boat loan trustees were enhanced. By 1863 boat loan trusts issued indebtedness and used issuance proceeds for purposes other than equipment acquisitions, such as payment of other SNC indebtedness and in mergers. Most boat loans introduced new structural elements. Nearly all remain in modern equipment finance structures.

The 1845 Schuylkill Navigation boat loan was cited by Francis Rawle in 1885 as an important development in equipment finance. More than Rawle knew. No single transaction or series of transactions contributed more to the development of equipment finance structures than the Schuylkill Navigation boat loans.[13]

The boat loan structure was taken up by Lehigh Coal & Navigation in 1868 for railroad equipment. It was styled as a "car trust" and then an "equipment trust". The documentary structure of 1868 is preserved in contemporary transactions, with additions for capital market issuances. The Central Railroad of New Jersey acquired the two Lehigh C&N trusts and replicated them in four car and equipment trusts. That legitimization ensured that the car and equipment trust structure would predominate continuously to the present.[14]

All this Patrick Tracy Jackson begat because of two locomotives lost in Florida.

## Endnotes: Chapter Sixteen

[1] P&R Corr. (January 16 and January 24, 1846). The P&R debt was $183,981.95 at the time of its disposition.

[2] Davis, a prominent lawyer, was a three-time Whig governor of Massachusetts and served in both houses of the U.S. Congress. He represented the defendants (the competing bridge) in the *Charles River Bridge* case. Gherardi Davis, a co-author of Davis & Browne (1894), was a descendant. For Davis, see Kinnicutt (1854), Roe (1901-1902), at 542, and Scheiber (1963). For Neal, Corning (1938), Kennedy (1957), at 100, 101 (including footnote 20), 102, 110-11, 117, and 121, Kennedy (1951-1), at 67 and 69. For his involvements for the Illinois Central and Michigan Central, Veenendaal (1996), at 58-61.

[3] Schuyler, a nephew of Alexander Hamilton from a wealthy family, was the first president of the New York and New Haven Railroad Company in 1846, a founder and president of the Illinois Central Railroad Company, an officer of the New Jersey Rail Road and Transportation Company (which named an 1847 Rogers-built 4-4-0 engine the *Robert Schuyler*), the Brooklyn and Jamaica Rail-road Company, the Saratoga and Washington Railroad Company, the Harlem Railroad Company, the Vermont Valley Railroad, and the Sangamon and Morgan Railroad Company, and a promoter of numerous other railroads. He was a lawyer, civil engineer, and New York broker and financier, with his brother George, in the firm of R. & G. L. Schuyler. He was a trustee of the Mutual Life Insurance Company of New York.

In the mid-1850s Robert Schuyler orchestrated one of the largest stock frauds in U.S. history.

For Schuyler, see Merchants' Magazine (1854, August), at 207-09, Withington (1958), Shaw (1979), Flesher, Previts & Samson (2006), Doggett's NYC Directory (1846), at 26, and, for the engine, Moshein & Rothfus (1992), at 31.

[4] Amos Binney was of a prominent Boston lineage, a medical doctor, a coal and iron merchant with his father's firm (C. J. F. Binney), a shareholder in the Amoskeag Manufacturing Company, an incorporator of the President, Directors and Company of the City Bank and the Boston Copper Mining Company, and a member of the boards of the Eastern Rail-road Company, the Norwich and Worcester Rail Road Company, the East Florida Railroad Company, the Manufacturer's Insurance Company, and the Tremont Insurance Company. Binney served on the Eastern Rail-road board with David A. Neal, who was intimately involved with the P&R and in the sale of railroad securities to Dutch interests on behalf of the Illinois Central Railroad Company and the Michigan Central Railroad Company. Among other relationships, John Elliott Thayer and John Bryant (the partner of and replacement director for William Sturgis, who also served on the L&C Board) each served as a director of the Eastern Rail-road between 1842 and 1848. Binney also served in the Massachusetts House of Representatives. Binney died in 1847. For Binney, see Kennedy (1957), at 101, Corning (1938), MA Law

(1822) Ch. C, MA Law (1833) Ch. LXXXVI, Browne (1915), at 227, Loring's Register (1840), at 33, 231, 244, and 246, Loring's Register (1847), at 125, 174, 182, and 183l, and East Florida Memorial (1835).

5  Lee was superintendent of the Boston & Providence and president of the Rutland and Burlington Railroad Company, and the Northern (Ogdensburgh) Railroad Company. Lee hired George Smith Griggs as head of locomotives for the Northern (Ogdensburgh). Griggs was trained by Paul Moody at Boston Manufacturing. Lee had a long and illustrious career in the U.S. railroad industry, including as a superintendent, commissioner, technical evaluator, director, investigator, and bond trustee. Lee was a founder of the New England Association of Railway Superintendents in 1848 and served as its president. He also served as a justice of the peace. Lee was active in the Episcopal Church in Boston. In 1861 Lee volunteered for military service and, as Colonel, led the Twentieth of the Massachusetts Volunteers. At the battle of Balls Bluff, Lee was taken prisoner and held at Richmond as a hostage confined to the county jail to stand for others. Lee was born in Salem, Massachusetts in 1807 and attended West Point Military Academy. He married the daughter of Thomas Amory, a prominent Boston merchant.

For Lee, see Railway Superintendents (1910), at 5-9, 16, 18, 20, 33, 57, 66, and 99, Railway Superintendents (1850), at iv, 17, 18, 20, 29, 34-43, Hancock (1836), at 65, NY RRC AR (1855), at 652-53, R&B AR (1854), at 3, A&K AR (1856), at 9-10, 12, 19, and 20-2 (report on settlement of the revenue sharing dispute involving the Androscoggin and Kennebec Railroad), NC Comm. Rep. (1849) (report to stockholders regarding expenditures, debts, claims, and construction), Northern AR (1855), Western RR Report (1843), at 88 (Lee was on the subcommittee that evaluated the Winans engines), R&B AR (1853), V&C Report (1877), at 149, Lanman (1862), at 199-200, 212-13, Jeffrey (1893), at 61-2, and 215-17, Forbes (1899), at 259, SB AR (1849), at 200, VC Deed (1854), Mason (1879), at 128, Axle Boxes (1849), at 478, MA DJ (1848), at 6 and 122, MA DJ (1849), at 43, 49, 130, and 131, MA DJ (1850), at 6, 37, 39, 44, 45, 46, 138, and 139, MA DJ (1851), at 6, 32-6, 127, 128, MA DJ (1852), at 6, 8, 12, 33, 34, 130, and 131, Adams (1846), at 107, Fisher (1938), Knight & Latrobe (1838), at 15-6 and 90-4, Monroe (1992), at 209, footnote 75, and *Vermont & Canada RR v. Vermont Central RR* (1855).

6  For the Committee of Investigations, P&R 1846 Report and Hare (1909-1914), at 23 and 33-4. For limiting consideration to the P&R books, see P&R 1846 Report at 3, 4, 7, 9, 10, 12, 15, 16, 18, 27 ("The Debt of the Company, *as exhibited by the books*, July 31, 1845…"; italics in original), 33 ("our services as substantially limited to an investigation of the books and papers"), 43, and 44. For public criticism of the P&R, Ellet (1845) and P&R Ellet Response (March 25, 1845). For public consideration of the Neal Report, ARJ (1849, October 13). For the internal investigation and first audits of managerial custodianship, Boockholdt (1983), at 71 and 79, observing that this occurred at the same time as the Companies Act in England required the formation of audit committees by certain companies. For the development of English company law, see Cottrell (1980), at 39-79.

7  The Poor quotation is from ARJ (1849, March 10).

8. Neal Report (1849). The request that Neal prepare the report was made by a group of ten investors who had large equity and debt holdings. The group included Thayer & Brother, McCalmont Brothers, Gihon & Company, George Peabody, John Murray Forbes, and William Dwight. Undated letter of 1848, HA 1572, Box 1182, Folder 919.

9. For the L&C dividends, Gibb (1950), at 98-102, with Table 4 on 101 listing the annual dividends.

10. The Locks & Canals transaction with the Baltimore & Susquehanna is discussed in McMillen (2022-3).

11. The Locks & Canals transactions under the Rolling Stock Contracts are discussed in detail in McMillen (2022-4). And see the LTCB Mortgage (1843).

12. The Schuylkill Navigation boat loans and their evolution are discussed in detail in McMillen (2022-5). For the SNC boat loan, SNC Boat Loan Proposal (1845), SNC Minutes (September 27 and 30, 1845), and SNC AR (1846), at 4-5. For the Lehigh Coal & Navigation scow boat transaction, *Lehigh C&N v. Field* (1844). For a subsequent Pennsylvania usage, *Farmers' Bank v. McKee* (1845). For use on the Erie Canal, *Strong v. Taylor* (1842), and on the Delaware and Hudson Canal, *Tuthill v. Wheeler* (1849).

13. Rawle (1885), footnote at 322, references the boat loans.

14. Discussed in McMillen (2022-5).

# Bibliography

## General Reference Information

### Principal Document Accessions and Collections

Baker Library, Harvard Graduate School of Business, Harvard University, Cambridge, Massachusetts
Berks History Center Museum and Henry Janssen Library, Reading, Pennsylvania
Boston Public Library, Boston, Massachusetts
British Library, London, England
British Library, Mechanical Curator Collection on Flickr
Christopher T. Baer, private collection
Digital Commonwealth, Worcester, Massachusetts
Florida Supreme Court, Tallahassee, Florida
The Frick Collections, New York, New York
Hagley Museum and Library, Archives and Manuscripts, Soda House at Eleutherian Mills, Wilmington, Delaware
Historical Society of Pennsylvania, Philadelphia, Pennsylvania
Historical Society of the Phoenixville Area, Phoenixville, Pennsylvania
Jenkins Law Library, Philadelphia, Pennsylvania
Lehigh County Historical Society, Allentown, Pennsylvania
The Library Company of Pennsylvania, Philadelphia, Pennsylvania
Library of Congress, Washington, D.C.
Lowell National Historical Park, Lowell, Massachusetts
Massachusetts Historical Society, Boston, Massachusetts
Michigan History Center, Archives of Michigan, Lansing, Michigan
The Metropolitan Museum of Art, New York, New York
National Canal Museum, Hugh Moore Park, Easton, Pennsylvania
National Gallery of Art, Washington, D.C.
National Library of Medicine, National Institutes of Health, Department of Health and Human Services of the United States of America, Bethesda, Maryland
National Museum of American History, Washington, D.C.
National Museum of Industrial History, Washington, D.C. and Bethlehem, Pennsylvania
National Portrait Gallery, London, England
National Portrait Gallery of the Smithsonian Institution, Washington, D.C.
New York Historical Society, New York, New York
New York Public Library, New York, New York

The Pennsylvania State Archives, Pennsylvania Historical and Museum Commission, Harrisburg, Pennsylvania

Railroad Museum of Pennsylvania, Strasburg, Pennsylvania

Reading Area Community College, Schuylkill Navigation Maps Project, Reading, Pennsylvania

Reading Railroad Heritage Museum, Hamburg, Pennsylvania

Rutgers, The State University of New Jersey, Mid-Atlantic Regional Center for the Humanities, THE ENCYCLOPEDIA OF GREATER PHILADELPHIA, Camden, New Jersey

State Library of Pennsylvania, Rare Collections, Harrisburg, Pennsylvania

University College London, Centre for the Study of the Legacies of British Slavery, Department of History, London, England, United Kingdom

University of Massachusetts Lowell Library, Lowell, Massachusetts

Worcester Art Museum, Worcester, Massachusetts

## Abbreviations

AL: State of Alabama

FL: Territory of Florida or State of Florida, as appropriate

HA 5012: Accession 5012, Reading Papers, Archives and Manuscripts, Soda House, Hagley Museum and Library, Wilmington, Delaware

Jackson Corr.: Patrick Tracy Jackson Correspondence, Locks & Canals files, Letter Book DA-2, Baker Library, Harvard Graduate School of Business, Harvard University, Cambridge, Massachusetts

L&C Machine Shop Ledgers (1838): machine shop ledger of Locks & Canals, FD-2, 1838-1839, Locks & Canals Records 1747-2008, Baker Library, Harvard Graduate School of Business, Harvard University, Cambridge Massachusetts

L&C Minutes ([date]): Minutes of the board of directors of The Proprietors of Locks and Canals on Merrimac River, available at (a) Directors' Records, 1792-1941, EA-1 Microfilm (DA-2), Baker Library, Harvard Graduate School of Business, Harvard University, Cambridge Massachusetts, and (b) Locks & Canals records, 1747-2008, Book DA-2, LOWE 5058, I Directors' Records, 1813-1955, Lowell National Historical Park, Lowell, Massachusetts

MA: Commonwealth of Massachusetts

MD: State of Maryland

ME: State of Maine

MI: State of Michigan

NH: State of New Hampshire

NY: State of New York

P&R Corr. ([date]): Correspondence Files of Executive Officers, Early (pre-1845) Company Correspondence, Reading Papers, Accession 1520, Box B-17, Archives and Manuscripts, Soda House, Hagley Museum and Library, Wilmington, Delaware

PA: Commonwealth of Pennsylvania

SNC Minutes ([date of meeting]): Minutes of the Board of Managers of Schuylkill Navigation Company, Pennsylvania State Historical and Museum Commission, Pennsylvania State Archives, Harrisburg, Pennsylvania, referenced by date of meeting; the minutes are stored on microfilm as follows: reel 2297, January 1, 1838 to January 5, 1846; reel 2298, January 6, 1846 to July 1, 1850; and reel 2300, 1850 to 1882

VA: Commonwealth of Virginia

## Credits for Figures

Figure 1: Patrick Tracy Jackson: in John Amory Lowell, *Memoir of the Late Patrick Tracy Jackson*, 18 THE MERCHANT'S MAGAZINE 355 (1848)

Figure 2: Stephenson *Planet* Class Engine, 1834: Nicolson Wood, TRAITÉ PRATIQUE DES CHEMINS DE FER DE NICOLSON WOOD, TRADUIT DE L'ANGLAIS (DEUXIÈME ÉDITION) PAR MM DE MONTRICHER ET DE FRANQUEVILLE, INGÉNIEURS DES PONTS ET CHAUSSÉES ET DE RUOLZ, PLANCHES, PARIS, CHEZ CARILLIAN-GOEURY ÉDITEUR-LIBRAIRE (1834)

Figure 3: *Bristol* Locomotive Engine: Charles H. Hildreth, *Railroads out of Pensacola*, 1833-1883, 37 THE FLORIDA HISTORICAL QUARTERLY 397 (1959), at 402; the picture is also at Edwin R. Clark, *Early Locomotive Building in Lowell, Mass.*, 7 THE RAILWAY AND LOCOMOTIVE HISTORICAL SOCIETY 25 (1924), with the picture at 46

Figure 4: Camden & Amboy, 1834: *This Planet. Camden & Amboy Railroad*, E. L. Henry, artist, photoengraving, Library of Congress of the United States of America, Prints and Photographs Division, digital id ppmsca 46196, https://hdl.loc.gov/loc.pnp/ppmsca.46196

Figure 5: Bank of Pensacola Bond, 1835: public domain

Figure 6: Nicholas Biddle, 1843: Auguste Edouart, National Portrait Gallery, gift of Robert L. McNeil, Jr., object NPG.91.126.104.A; cropped

Figure 7: Bank of the United States, 1838: built in 1821-1824, William Strickland, architectural designer, John Casper Wild, artist, lithography of Wild & Chevalier, 1838, originally published as plate 2 in J.C. Wild, VIEWS OF PHILADELPHIA, AND ITS VICINITY (1838), Library of Congress of the United States of America, Marian S. Carson Collection, Library of Congress Control Number 2021670221, Digital ID https://hdl.loc.gov/loc.wdl/wdl.9295

Figure 8: Thomas A. Biddle: George Peter Alexander Healy, painter, 1856, oil on canvas, Jay V. Hare, *History of the Reading*, 10 THE PILOT AND PHILADELPHIA & READING RAILWAY MEN 40 (October 1909); a copy is held by National Portrait Gallery, Smithsonian Institution, record number npg_1975-Q-8, listing Mutual Assurance Company as owner

Figure 9: Samuel Jaudon: *Samuel Jaudon*, by Thomas Sully, painter, New York Historical Society, 1921.2, oil on canvas, gift of Mrs. Augustus Cortlandt Van Rensselaer

Figure 10: William Bainbridge, circa 1814: *William Bainbridge*, Rembrandt Peale, artist, oil on canvas, National Portrait Gallery, Smithsonian Institution, object number NPG.79.172

Figure 11: James DePeyster Ogden and Charles Augustus Davis, 1839: *James DePeyster Ogden and Charles Augustus Davis, 1839*, Auguste Edouart, National Portrait Gallery, Smithsonian Institution, gift of Robert L. McNeil, Jr., object number NPG.91.126.81.A; cropped

Figure 12: *Cider Making*, by William Sidney Mount, 1840-1841: The Metropolitan Museum of Art, New York City, accession number 66126, Purchase, bequest of Charles Allen Munn, by exchange, 1966, public domain

Figure 13: Sampson Vryling Stoddard Wilder: *Sampson Vryling Stoddard Wilder*, John Vanderlyn, artist, 1808-1812, Worcester Art Museum, Object Number 1981.331, gift of Lawrence Alan Haines in memory of his father, Wilder Hayden Haines

Figure 14: Sampson Vryling Stoddard Wilder: from RECORDS FROM THE LIFE OF S. V. S. WILDER (1865), face plate; cropped

Figure 15: Morris Robinson: from J. Owen Stanton, MARKETING LIFE INSURANCE: ITS HISTORY IN AMERICA (1942), at page following 128; cropped

Figure 16: William Gibbs McNeill, from NATIONAL CYCLOPAEDIA OF AMERICAN BIOGRAPHY, VOLUME 9 (1899), at 48

Figure 17: Fort Pickens and Fort McRae: *Fort Pickens: Pensacola Harbor, Florida*, Currier & Ives, circa 1860, Library of Congress of the United States of America, Library of Congress Control Number 2001699182, Digital ID cph 3b50227 //hdl.loc.gov.loc.pnp/cph.3b50227

Figure 18: William H. Chase: by John Wesley Jarvis, public domain, Flickr, Attribution 2.0 Generic License; without modification

Figure 19: Egeria at the Fountain: *Cincinnati – Spring Grove Cemetery & Arboretum "Egeria – Roman Goddess of Childbirth and Water*, David Paul Ohmer, photographer, undated, Flickr, Attribution 2.0 Generic License; without modification

Figure 20: Dudley S. Gregory: from George H. Farrier, ed., MEMORIAL OF THE CENTENNIAL CELEBRATION OF THE BATTLE OF PAULUS HOOK, AUGUST 19TH, 1879; WITH A HISTORY OF THE EARLY SETTLEMENT AND PRESENT CONDITION OF JERSEY CITY, N. J. (1879), at 162; cropped

Figure 21: Walter Gregory Monument: Spring Grove Cemetery, THE CINCINNATI CEMETERY OF SPRING GROVE (1862), at 88; the monument is located in section 99, lot 6

Figure 22: Richard Keith Call: public domain, with a copy at the Florida Department of State

Figure 23: Endorsement of Bank of Pensacola Bond: text from BoP Commissioners Report, at 456

Figure 24: London Bond Agreement: public domain

Figure 25: Text of London Bond Agreement: public domain

Figure 26: Walker Anderson: public domain, with a copy at the Florida Supreme Court

Figure 27: *Still Engine #1*: *Still Engine #1*, Karin Laine McMillen, artist, a graphite on paper rendering of a wood-fired steam locomotive engine, the Baltimore, and its tender built by The Proprietors of Locks and Canals on Merrimac River for the Baltimore and Susquehanna Railroad Company in 1837; copyright 2018 and 2021 Karin Laine McMillen, used with permission

## Credits for Maps

Map 1: Pensacola, Territory of Florida: Crop of *Map of the Territory of Florida, From its Northern boundary to Lat: 27° 50' N., Connected with the Delta of the Mississippi, Annexed to the report of the Board of Internal Improvement dated Feby. 19th, 1829 relating to the Canal contemplated to connect the Atlantic with the Gulf of Mexico; and describing the Inland Navigation parallel to the Coast from the Mississippi to the Bay of Espiritu Santo; and from St. Mary's Harbour to St. Augustine*, drawn and compiled by W. H. Swift, Lt. Artillery (1829)

Map 2: Proposed Rail System: *Concentrated Rail Roads & Canals to Pensacola*, Lithograph of Graham & Price, 42 Nassau St. Cor Liberty New York, from William H. Chase, SALE OF TOWN LOTS OF PENSACOLA, WITH A DESCRIPTION OF THE PLACE, CLIMATE, &C. (1836)

Map 3: Graham Map of Proposed Railroad: *A map of part of Alabama & Florida, showing the route of the proposed Columbus & Pensacola Rail Road, accompanying the report of Major J. D. Graham, U.S. Topographical Engr. Feb. 6th, 1836, drawn chiefly from the original surveys in the Gen. Land Office at Washington by Wm. R. Palmer, U.S. Asst. Civil Engr.*, J. D. [James Duncan] Palmer, W. R. [William R.] Palmer, 1836, Library of Congress of the United States of America, Geography and Map Division, Library of Congress Control Number 98688639, Digital ID http://hdl.loc.gov/loc.gmd/g3971p.rr003880

# Citations to Laws

Citations to laws are to the session laws of the relevant state, territory, or other jurisdiction. Express reference is made in the bibliographical entry for territorial laws.

## SOURCES REFERENCED

### NUMERICAL

1835 Act: Florida Session Laws, Chap. 843, [No. xx], An Act to increase the capital of the Bank of Pensacola, and to amend the laws incorporating said Bank, and or [stet] other purposes, approved February 14, 1835

1837 Indenture: Indenture, dated January 30, 1837, among William H. Chase, Walker [stet] Gregory, John A. Cameron, Thomas M. Blount, Charles Augustus Davis, Morris Robinson, Sampson V. S. Wilder, Thomas Biddle, Elihu Chauncey, Samuel Jaudon, William L. Booth, The Pensacola Association, James H. Severich, Jackson Morton, James D. Graham, Henry Hyer, and Charles Le Baron, of the first part, William H. Chase, of the second part, Walker Gregory, of the third part, and William H. Chase, Morris Robinson, and Charles Augustus Davis, of the fourth part, Exhibit 31 of the *McGuire v. Blount* Certiorari (1903), at 319

### A

A&ER AR (1838): *The First Annual Report of the Directors of the Annapolis and Elk Ridge Railroad Company* (1838), in 9 (No. 340) AMERICAN RAILROAD JOURNAL 97 (August 15, 1839) (for the year ending October 8, 1838)

A&K AR (1856): *Report of the Directors to the Stockholders of the Androscoggin and Kennebec Railroad Company, Presented at the Annual Meeting in Waterville (June 25, 1856)*

Abbey (1937): Abbey, Kathryn T., *The Union Bank of Tallahassee: An Experiment in Territorial Finance*, 15 THE FLORIDA HISTORICAL QUARTERLY 207 (1937)

ACS (1849): *Receipts of the American Colonization Society*, 25 THE AFRICAN REPOSITORY 223 (December 1849)

ACS (1850): *Receipts of the American Colonization Society*, 26 THE AFRICAN REPOSITORY 382 (December 1850)

Adams (1846): Adams, George, ENVIRONS OF BOSTON: AN ALMANAC AND BUSINESS DIRECTORY OF THE CITIES OF CAMBRIDGE, CHARLESTOWN AND ROXBURY, AND THE TOWNS OF CHELSEA, DORCHESTER, BRIGHTON AND BROOKLINE, FOR THE YEAR 1846 (1846)

Adams (1848): \_\_\_\_\_, THE BOSTON DIRECTORY: CONTAINING THE CITY RECORD, GENERAL DIRECTORY OF CITIZENS, AND A SPECIAL DIRECTORY OF TRADES, PROFESSIONS, &C. 1848-9 (1848)

Adams (2011-1): Adams, Sean Patrick, *How Choice Fueled Panic: Philadelphians, Consumption, and the Panic of 1837*, 12 ENTERPRISE AND SOCIETY 761 (2011)

Adams (2011-2): \_\_\_\_\_, *Hard Times, Loco-Focos, and Buckshot Wars: The Panic of 1837 in Pennsylvania*, 11 PENNSYLVANIA LEGACIES 12 (2011)

AES AR (1828): American Education Society, *Twelfth Annual Report of the Directors of the American Education Society, Presented at the Annual Meeting in the City of New York, May 8, 1828* (1828)

African Repository (1875): *Death of Hon. Dudley S. Gregory*, 51 THE AFRICAN REPOSITORY 24 (January 1875)

Ahmat (1965): Ahmat, Sharom, *American Trade with Singapore, 1819-65*, 38 JOURNAL OF THE MALAYSIAN BRANCH OF THE ROYAL ASIATIC SOCIETY 241 (1965)

Aitkin (1953): Aitkin, Hugh G. J., *Yates and McIntyre: Lottery Managers*, 13 THE JOURNAL OF ECONOMIC HISTORY 36 (1953)

AL Law (1834) No. 11: No. 11, An Act To incorporate the subscribers to the Alabama, Florida, and Georgia Rail Road Company, approved December 12, 1834

AL Law (1837) No. 76: No. 76, An Act To amend an act, incorporating the Subscribers to the Alabama, Florida and Georgia Rail Road, approved December 23, 1837

American Slavery (1839): American Anti-Slavery Society, AMERICAN SLAVERY AS IT IS: TESTIMONY OF A THOUSAND WITNESSES (1839)

Ames (1970): Ames, Winslow, *The Transformation of Château-sur-Mer*, 92 JOURNAL OF THE SOCIETY OF ARCHITECTURAL HISTORIANS 291 (1970)

*Apalachicola Land & Development v. McRae* (1923): *The Apalachicola Land and Development Company, A Declaration of Trust, H. L. Flowers, H. D. Marks, S. E. Rice, Jr., R. R. Rice, C. E. Smith, Joseph Messina, J. J. Abbott, H. B. Robins and W. H. Collier, Trustees; and N. R. Hays, S. E. Teague, and H. L. Oliver v. W. A. McRae, Commissioner of Agriculture of the State of Florida, and T. R. Hodges, Shell Fish Commissioner of the State of Florida*, 86 Fla. 393, 98 So. 505, 1923 Fla. LEXIS 452 (1923)

Appleton (1858): Appleton, Nathan, INTRODUCTION OF THE POWER LOOM, AND ORIGIN OF LOWELL (1858)

Appleton's Biographies (1888): APPLETON'S CYCLOPAEDIA OF AMERICAN BIOGRAPHY, VOLUME II, James Grant Wilson and John Fiske, eds. (1888)

Archaeologia Americana (1836): Archaeologia Americana, TRANSACTIONS AND COLLECTIONS OF THE AMERICAN ANTIQUARIAN SOCIETY, VOLUME II (1836)

ARJ (1835, April 4): *The Alabama, Florida and Georgia Railroad*, 4 AMERICAN RAILROAD JOURNAL, AND ADVOCATE OF INTERNAL IMPROVEMENTS 196 (April 4, 1835)

ARJ (1849, March 10): *Railway Progress*, 22 AMERICAN RAILROAD JOURNAL 145 (March 10, 1849)

ARJ (1849, October 13): *Pennsylvania: Philadelphia and Reading Railroad*, 42 AMERICAN RAILROAD JOURNAL 645 (October 13, 1849)

ASCE (1892): American Society of Civil Engineers, eds., 18 PROCEEDINGS OF THE AMERICAN SOCIETY OF CIVIL ENGINEERS (1892)

*Associates of Jersey v. Davison* (1860): *The Associates of the Jersey Company v. Erastus Davison*, 5 Dutch. 415, 29 N.J.L 415, 1860 WL 5173, 1860 N.J. LEXIS 47 (1860)

ATS (1830): American Temperance Society, 1 THE TEMPERANCE SOCIETY RECORD (June 1830), at 10

ATS (1865): American Tract Society, RECORDS FROM THE LIFE OF S. V. S. WILDER (1865)

Axle Boxes (1849): letter of W. Raymond Lee to John Lightner, December 28, 1849, in *Lightner's Patent Axle Boxes*, 798 AMERICAN RAILROAD JOURNAL 494 (August 2, 1851) and in TESTIMONY RESPECTING THE PATEN AXLE BOXES INVENTED BY JOHN LIGHTNER (1850), at 3

## B

B&L AR (1834): *Third Annual Report of the Boston and Lowell Rail-Road Corporation*, Jan. 9th, 1834, in in REPORTS OF THE ANDOVER AND WILMINGTON, BOSTON AND LOWELL, BOSTON AND PROVIDENCE, AND BOSTON AND WORCHESTER RAIL ROAD CORPORATIONS, SENATE NO. 26, at 7 (1834)

B&L AR (1836): *Fifth Annual Report of the Boston and Lowell Rail-Road Corporation*, Jan. 1st, 1836, in REPORTS OF THE ANDOVER AND WILMINGTON, BOSTON AND LOWELL, BOSTON AND PROVIDENCE, BOSTON AND WORCHESTER, AND TAUNTON BRANCH RAIL-ROAD CORPORATIONS, SENATE NO. 49, at 16 (1836)

B&L AR (1837): *Sixth Annual Report of the Boston and Lowell Rail-Road Corporation*, in ANNUAL REPORTS OF THE RAIL-ROAD CORPORATIONS IN THE STATE OF MASSACHUSETTS FOR 1840, Senate No. 33, at 12 (1838)

B&L AR (1838): *Seventh Annual Report of the Boston and Lowell Rail-Road Corporation*, January 5, 1839, in ANNUAL REPORTS OF THE RAIL-ROAD CORPORATIONS IN THE STATE OF MASSACHUSETTS FOR 1838, at 13 (1838)

B&L AR (1839): *Eighth Annual Report of the Boston and Lowell Rail-Road Corporation*, January 1, 1840, in ANNUAL REPORTS OF THE RAIL-ROAD CORPORATIONS IN THE STATE OF MASSACHUSETTS FOR 1840, Senate No. 18, at 5 (1840)

B&L AR (1840): *Tenth Annual Report of the Boston and Lowell Rail-Road Corporation*, January 5, 1842, in ANNUAL REPORTS OF THE RAIL-ROAD CORPORATIONS IN THE STATE OF MASSACHUSETTS FOR 1840, Senate No. 17, at 5 (1841), which, at 6, corrects the numbering of annual reports from 1837 (printed as the Sixth, but should have been the Seventh onward)

B&L AR (1841): *Eleventh Annual Report of the Boston and Lowell Rail-Road Corporation*, in ANNUAL REPORTS OF THE RAIL-ROAD CORPORATIONS IN THE STATE OF MASSACHUSETTS FOR 1841, at 7 (1842)

B&L AR (1844): *Fourteenth Annual Report of the Boston and Lowell Rail-Road Corporation*, November 30, 1844, in ANNUAL REPORTS OF THE RAIL-ROAD CORPORATIONS IN THE STATE OF MASSACHUSETTS FOR 1844, SENATE NO. 46, at 7 (1845)

B&L Committee Report (1831): *Report of a Committee on the Boston and Lowell Rail Road* (1831)

B&R Cars Contract (1842): Agreement, dated March 30, 1842, between The Philadelphia and Reading Rail Road Company and Bradley & Rice, HA 1520, Box 1220, Folder 9025

Bagnall (1884): Bagnall, W. R., *Paul Moody*, 3 Contributions of The Old Residents Historical Association, Lowell, Mass 57 (1884)

Baker (2002): Baker, Pamela L., *The Washington National Road Bill and the Struggle to Adopt a Federal System of Internal Improvement*, 22 JOURNAL OF THE EARLY REPUBLIC 437 (2002)

Balch (1918): Balch, Edwin Swift, *The Art of George Catlin*, 57 PROCEEDINGS OF THE AMERICAN PHILOSOPHICAL SOCIETY 144 (1918)

Bald Eagle & Spring Creek Ann. Rep. (1836): *Report to the Stockholders of the Bald Eagle and Spring Creek Navigation Company* (June 18, 1836)

Baldwin Catalogue (1907): _____, ILLUSTRATED CATALOGUE OF LOCOMOTIVES AND DETAIL PARTS (Burnham, Williams & Company, undated, circa 1907)

Baldwin Works (1897): Baldwin Locomotive Works, HISTORY OF THE BALDWIN LOCOMOTIVE WORKS (1897)

Bank for Savings AR (1820): *First Report of the Bank for Savings in the City of New York* (1820)

Barkin (1981): Barkin, Solomon, *Management and Ownership in the New England Cotton Textile Industry*, 15 JOURNAL OF ECONOMIC ISSUES 463 (1981)

Barragy (1975): Barragy, Terrence J., *The Trading Age, 1792-1844*, 76 OREGON HISTORICAL QUARTERLY 197 (1975)

Barrett (1864): Barrett, Walter, THE OLD MERCHANTS OF NEW YORK CITY (1864)

Batson (1970): Batson, Trenton W., *The Troy Car Works: A History of Eaton and Gilbert*, 123 The RAILWAY AND LOCOMOTIVE HISTORICAL SOCIETY BULLETIN 5 (1970)

Bayou Sara (2019): Coastal Environments, Inc., THE LOST RIVER TOWN: HISTORY AND ARCHAEOLOGY OF BAYOU SARA (2019)

Becker, Fisher & Jackson (1930): Becker, Geo. P., Chas. E. Fisher and Francis Jackson, *Boston and Albany Locomotives 1932-1930*, 22 THE RAILWAY AND LOCOMOTIVE HISTORICAL SOCIETY BULLETIN 9 (1930)

Bell (1942): Bell, John F., *Frederick List, Champion of Industrial Capitalism*, 66 THE PENNSYLVANIA MAGAZINE OF HISTORY AND BIOGRAPHY 56 (1942)

Bell & Fisher (1929): Bell, J. Snowden, and Charles E. Fisher, *The New Castle Manufacturing Company*, 18 THE RAILWAY AND LOCOMOTIVE HISTORICAL SOCIETY BULLETIN 28 (1929)

Bennett (1994): Bennett, Swannee, *Rediscovering the Artists and Art of Early Arkansas 1820-1860*, 53 THE ARKANSAS HISTORICAL QUARTERLY 33 (1994)

Benton (1854): Benton, Thomas H., THIRTY YEAR'S VIEW, OR, A HISTORY OF THE WORKING OF THE AMERICAN GOVERNMENT FOR THIRTY YEARS, FROM 1820 TO 1850, VOLUME I (1854)

BH&H Tenders Contract (1843): Agreement, dated July 5, 1842, between Betts Harlan & Hollingsworth and the Philadelphia and Reading Rail Road Company, Hagley Archives, Reading Papers, Accession 1520, Box 1220, Folder 9018

BHS 1837 Panic (1933): *Reflections of the Panic of 1837*, 7 BULLETIN OF THE BUSINESS HISTORICAL SOCIETY 6 (1933)

BHS Whistler (1926): *Business History Sheds Light on the Origins of James A. McNeill Whistler*, 1 BULLETIN OF THE BUSINESS HISTORICAL SOCIETY 9 (1926)

*Biddle v. Morris* (1842): *Commonwealth of Pennsylvania, ex relatione N. Biddle v. Henry Morris, Esq. Sheriff of the City and County of Philadelphia, Commonwealth of Pennsylvania, ex rel. Joseph Cowperthwait, v. the same*, and *Commonwealth of Pennsylvania, ex rel. John Andrews v. the same*, JUDICIAL DECISIONS OF THE COURT OF GENERAL SESSIONS, IN THE CASE OF NICHOLAS BIDDLE AND OTHERS, VS. HENRY MORRIS *(Of March Term, 1842)*

Binney (1903): Binney, Charles Chauncey, THE LIFE OF HORACE BINNEY WITH SELECTIONS FROM HIS LETTERS (1903)

Bishop (1868): Bishop, J. Leander, A HISTORY OF AMERICAN MANUFACTURES FROM 1608 TO 1860 (1868)

Bittle (1966): Bittle, George C., *The Florida Militia's Role in the Battle of Withlacoochee*, 44 THE FLORIDA HISTORICAL QUARTERLY 303 (1966)

Boockholdt (1983): Boockholdt, James L., *A Historical Perspective on the Auditor's Role: The Early Experience of the American Railroads*, 10 THE ACCOUNTING HISTORIANS JOURNAL 69 (1983)

BoP Bond Sale Contract (1835): Contract and Agreement, dated December 2, 1835, between the Bank of Pensacola and William H. Chase, as agent for Thomas Biddle, Samuel Jaudon and Elihu

Chauncey as financial agents for the Pensacola Association, included in BoP Commissioner's Report, at 466-68

BoP Commissioner's Report: *Report of the Commissioner of the Bank of Pensacola, dated April 7, 1840, Document No. 111*, in CONDITION OF THE STATE BANKS, LETTER FROM THE SECRETARY OF THE TREASURY, HOUSE OF REPRESENTATIVES EXECUTIVE DOCUMENTS, TWENTY-SIXTH CONGRESS, SECOND SESSION, VOLUME 4, P 13, 438 ET SEQ. (1841)

BoP Financials (July 1837): *Semi-annual Statement No. 3, July 1, 1837*, in 4 (Issue 18) PENSACOLA GAZETTE 3 (July 8, 1837)

BoP Financials (December 1837): *Semi-annual statement of the Bank of Pensacola, December 30, 1837*, in BoP Commissioner's Report, at 451

BoP Financials (1838): *Semi-annual statement of the Bank of Pensacola, June 30, 1838*, in BoP Commissioner's Report, at 452

BoP Financials (1839): Semi-annual statement of the Bank of Pensacola, January 1, 1839, in BoP Commissioner's Report, at 453

BoP Indenture: Indenture, dated April 29, 1835, from the Bank of Pensacola to the Territory of Florida, in BoP Commissioner's Report, at 444-45

Boston Courier (1832, January 16): *Saturday, January 14, 1832: Legislature*, 7 (Issue 632) BOSTON COURIER 1 (January 16, 1832)

Boston Courier (1835, December 28): *Faneuil Hall Meeting*, 10 (Issue 781) BOSTON COURIER 1 (December 28, 1835)

Boston Courier (1838, November 5): *Amory Hall Nominations*, 12 (Issue 5115) BOSTON COURIER 3 (November 5, 1838)

Boston Courier (1838, November 8): *Amory Hall Nominations*, 12 (Issue 5116) BOSTON COURIER 2 (November 8, 1838)

Boyd & Reder (1981): Boyd, Joseph A., Jr., and Randall Reder, *A History of the Florida Supreme Court*, 35 UNIVERSITY OF MIAMI LAW REVIEW 1019 (1981)

Bradford (1880): Bradford, Samuel, Jr., THE AUTOBIOGRAPHY OR A BRIEF NARRATIVE OF THE LIFE OF SAMUEL BRADFORD, JUNIOR, CONTAINED IN SOME INCIDENTS IN THE LIFE OF SAMUEL BRADFORD, SENIOR, BY HIS SON (1880)

Bradlee (1918): Bradlee, Francis C., THE BOSTON AND LOWELL RAILROAD, THE NASHUA AND LOWELL RAILROAD, AND THE SALEM AND LOWELL RAILROAD (1918)

Breck (1843): Breck, Samuel, *A Historical Sketch of Continental Paper Money, Part II, Special Meeting, Second Session, 26th May, Half Past Seven O'Clock, P. M.*, 3 PROCEEDINGS OF THE AMERICAN PHILOSOPHICAL SOCIETY 57 (1843)

Breidenbach (2001): Breidenbach, Paul, *Art Patronage and Class Identity in a Border City: Cincinnati, 1828-1872*, unpublished Ph.D. dissertation, University of California, San Diego (2001)

Brevard (1908-1): Brevard, Caroline Mays, *Richard Keith Call*, 1, No. 3 PUBLICATIONS OF THE FLORIDA HISTORICAL SOCIETY 8 (1908)

Brevard (1908-2): Brevard, Richard Keith, *Richard Keith Call*, 1, No. 2 PUBLICATIONS OF THE FLORIDA HISTORICAL SOCIETY 2 (1908)

Brooks (1847): Brooks, Edward, A CORRESPONDENCE BETWEEN EDWARD BROOKS AND JOHN A. LOWELL, WITH REMARKS BY EDWARD BROOKS, REFERRING TO DOCUMENTS ANNEXED (1847)

Brown (1874): Brown, William H., THE HISTORY OF THE FIRST LOCOMOTIVES IN AMERICA (1874)

Brown (1959): Brown, Robert R., *Pioneer Locomotives of North America*, 101 THE RAILWAY AND LOCOMOTIVE HISTORICAL SOCIETY BULLETIN 7 (1959)

Brown (1993): Brown, John K., *The Baldwin Locomotive Works, the Capital Equipment Sector, and American Industrial Practice in the Nineteenth Century*, 22 BUSINESS AND ECONOMIC HISTORY 7 (1993)

Brown (1995-1): _____., THE BALDWIN LOCOMOTIVE WORKS, 1831-1915 (1995)

Brown (1995-2): Brown, Canter, Jr., *Race Relations in Territorial Florida*, 73 THE FLORIDA HISTORICAL QUARTERLY 287 (1995)

Brown Report (1840): Brown, T. S., *Private report of T. S. Brown to Governor Reid* (May 6, 1840), in Carter (1960), at 170

Browne (1915): Browne, George Waldo, THE AMOSKEAG MANUFACTURING CO. OF MANCHESTER, NEW HAMPSHIRE: A HISTORY (1915)

Bruce (1913): Bruce, H. Addington, ABOVE THE CLOUDS AND OLD NEW YORK: AN HISTORICAL SKETCH OF THE SITE AND A DESCRIPTION OF THE MANY WONDERS OF THE WOOLWORTH BUILDING (1913)

Buck (1925): Buck, Norman Sydney, THE DEVELOPMENT OF THE ORGANISATION OF ANGLO-AMERICAN TRADE 1800-1850 (1925)

Buckingham (1842): Buckingham, J. S., THE SLAVE STATES OF AMERICA, VOLUME 1 (1842)

Buley (1959): Buley, Carlyle, THE EQUITABLE LIFE ASSURANCE SOCIETY OF THE UNITED STATES (1959)

Burnett (1988): Burnett, Gene M., FLORIDA'S PAST: PEOPLE AND EVENTS THAT SHAPED THE STATE, VOLUME 2 (1988)

BUS Assignment (May 1841): Indenture, dated May 1, 1841, between the President, Directors and Company of the Bank of the United States, on the one hand, and James Dundas, Mordecai D. Lewis, Samuel W. Jones, Robert L. Pitfield, and Robert Howell, on the other hand

BUS Assignment (June 1841): Indenture, dated June 7, 1841, between the President, Directors and Company of the Bank of the United States, on the one hand, and John Bacon, Alexander Symington, and Thomas Robins, on the other hand

BUS Assignment (September 1841): Indenture, dated September 4, 1841, between the President, Directors and Company of the Bank of the United States, on the one hand, and James Robertson, Richard H. Bayard, James S. Newbold, Herman Cope, and Thomas S. Taylor, on the other hand, and supplemented and modified by the Indenture, dated September 7, 1841, among those same parties

BUS Auditors Report (October 28, 1853): REPORT (FILED, 28TH OCTOBER, 1853,) OF THE AUDITORS APPOINTED TO MAKE DISTRIBUTION OF THE BALANCE IN THE HANDS OF THE TRUSTEES OF THE BANK OF THE UNITED STATES, ACTING UNDER ASSIGNMENTS OF 4TH AND 6TH SEPTEMBER 1841, AS EXHIBITED BY THEIR 12TH ACCOUNT, FILED, 25TH JULY, 1853 (1853)

BUS Investigation (1841): *Report of the Committee of Investigations Appointed at the Meeting of the Stockholders of the Bank of the United States, Held January 4, 1841* (1841)

Busch & Gough (1996): Busch, Briton C., and Barry M. Gough, FUR TRADERS FROM NEW ENGLAND: THE BOSTON MEN IN THE NORTH PACIFIC, 1787-1800; THE NARRATIVES OF WILLIAM DANE PHELPS, WILLIAM STURGIS AND JAMES GILCHREST SWAN (1996)

Business Wire (2014): *175 Years Old and Still Buzzing: The Provident Bank Celebrates Milestone Anniversary in February*, BUSINESS WIRE (February 6, 2014), GALE|A357824414

## C

Calhoun Report (1827): REPORT OF THE COMMITTEE APPOINTED ON THE 29TH, DEC. 1825, ON A LETTER OF JOHN C. CALHOUN, VICE PRESIDENT OF THE UNITED STATES, ASKING AN INVESTIGATION OF HIS CONDUCT WHILE SECRETARY OF WAR, WITH ACCOMPANYING DOCUMENTS (February 13, 1827)

Calkins (1867): Calkins, Wolcott, *A Sketch of the Life, Mechanical Enterprise, and Christian Beneficence of Matthias W. Baldwin*, in MEMORIAL OF MATTHIAS W. BALDWIN (1867), 12 et seq.

Call (1837): Call, Richard Keith, *The Florida War: Governor Call to General Clinch*, 52 NILES' WEEKLY REGISTER 395-97 (August 19, 1837)

Campbell (1838): Campbell, William S., *Report on the Alabama, Florida and Georgia Rail-Road* (1838)

Campbell (1972): Campbell, Randolph, *Henry Clay and the Poinsett Pledge Controversy of 1826*, 28 THE AMERICAS 429 (1972)

Canada Law (1847) Ch. LXXII: Chapter LXXII, An Act to incorporate "The Lake Huron Silver and Copper Mining Company", July 28, 1847

Carlson (1964): Carlson, Robert E., *The Pennsylvania Improvement Society and its Promotion of Canals and Railroads, 1824-1826*, 31 PENNSYLVANIA HISTORY: A JOURNAL OF MID-ATLANTIC STUDIES 295 (1964)

Carter (1960): Carter, Clarence Edwin, THE TERRITORIAL PAPERS OF THE UNITED STATES, VOLUME XXVI, THE TERRITORY OF FLORIDA 1839-1845 (1960)

Chandler (1954): Chandler, Alfred D., Jr., *Patterns of Railroad Finance, 1830-50*, 28 THE BUSINESS HISTORY REVIEW 248 (1954)

Charvat (1937): Charvat, William, *American Romanticism and the Depression of 1837*, 2 SCIENCE AND SOCIETY 67 (1937)

*Chase v. New Orleans* (1836): *William H. Chase v. Mayor of the City of New Orleans et al.*, 9 La. 343, 1836 WL 827, 1836 La. LEXIS 78 (1836)

*Chase v. United States* (1856): *William H. Chase v. United States*, 1 U.S. Cong. Rep. C. C. 15, 1856 WL 4048, 1856 U.S. Ct. Cl. LEXIS 93 (1856)

*Chase v. United States* (1859): *William H. Chase v. United States*, 9 U.S. Cong. Rep. C. C. 221, 1860 WL 4878, 1859 U.S. Ct. Cl. LEXIS 82 (1859)

Chase (1849): Chase, William H., REPORT OF WILLIAM H. CHASE, CHAIRMAN OF THE COMMITTEE OF WAYS AND MEANS, MADE AT THE RAIL ROAD CONVENTION HELD IN THE CITY OF MONTGOMERY, DECEMBER 30, 1849, TO DEVISE WAYS AND MEANS FOR BUILDING A RAIL ROAD BETWEEN MONTGOMERY AND PENSACOLA (1849)

Chase (1860): \_\_\_\_\_, *The Secession of the Cotton States; Its Status; Its Advantages and Its Power* (1860), published in THE NEW YORK EXPRESS and THE OBSERVER in 1860, and collected in a volume entitled CIVIL WAR IN AMERICA 1860-64 (undated) and presented to senator Charles Sumner

Chase Brochure (1836): \_\_\_\_\_, William H., PENSACOLA: SALE OF TOWN LOTS AT PENSACOLA, WITH A DESCRIPTION OF THE PLACE, CLIMATE, &C. (1st October 1836)

Chase, Robinson & Davis Brochure (1837): \_\_\_\_\_, M. Robinson, and Charles Augustus Davis, PENSACOLA: SALE OF TOWN LOTS AT PENSACOLA (MARCH 1, 1837)

Cincinnati Astronomical Society (1844): *The Annual Address delivered before the Cincinnati Astronomical Society, June 3, 1844, by the Hon. Jacob Burnet, together with The Act of Incorporation, the Constitution of the Society, the Annual Reports, The Officers, and A Catalogue of the Stockholders* (1844)

Clark (1924): Clark, Edwin R., *Early Locomotive Building in Lowell, Mass.*, 7 THE RAILWAY AND LOCOMOTIVE HISTORICAL SOCIETY BULLETIN 25 (1924)

Clark (1942): Clark, Allen C., *Margaret Eaton (Peggy O'Neal)*, 44/45 RECORDS OF THE COLUMBIA HISTORICAL SOCIETY, WASHINGTON, D.C. (1942/1943)

Clark (1966): Clark, Malcolm C., *The Birth of an Enterprise: Baldwin Locomotive, 1831-1842*, 90 THE PENNSYLVANIA MAGAZINE OF HISTORY AND BIOGRAPHY 423 (1966)

Clark, Dodge (1945): Clark, Dodge & Co., CLARK, DODGE & CO., 1845-1945 (1945)

Clough (1946): Clough, Shepard B., A CENTURY OF AMERICAN LIFE INSURANCE: A HISTORY OF THE MUTUAL LIFE INSURANCE COMPANY OF NEW YORK, 1843-1945 (1946)

Clubbs (1959): Clubbs, Occie, *Pensacola in Retrospect*, 37 THE FLORIDA HISTORICAL QUARTERLY 377 (1959)

CNJ Annual Report (1860): *Thirteenth Annual Report of the Board of Directors to the Stockholders of the Central R. R. Co. of New Jersey, January 1, 1860*

CNJ Stock Offering (1853): *Central Railroad Co. of New Jersey $950,000 of Stock*, 9 AMERICAN RAILROAD JOURNAL 412 (June 25, 1853)

Coburn (1920): Coburn, Frederick W., HISTORY OF LOWELL AND ITS PEOPLE, VOLUME I (1920)

Cochran (1982): Cochran, Thomas C. *Philadelphia: The American Industrial Center, 1750-1850*, 106 THE PENNSYLVANIA MAGAZINE OF HISTORY AND BIOGRAPHY 323 (1982)

Cohen (1984): Cohen, Lucy M., CHINESE IN THE POST-CIVIL WAR SOUTH (1984)

*Cohens v. Virginia* (1821): *Cohens v. State of Virginia*, 19 U.S. 264, 6 Wheat. 264, 5 L.Ed. 257, 1821 LEXIS 362, 1821 WL 2186 (1821)

Cole (1928): Cole, Arthur H., *Statistical Background of the Crisis Period*, 10 THE REVIEW OF ECONOMICS AND STATISTICS 182 (1928)

Coleman (1988): Coleman, James C., FORT MCREE: "A CASTLE BUILT ON SAND" (1988)

Colvin (1902): Colvin, Fred H., *Locomotive Building in the United States*, 15 RAILWAY AND LOCOMOTIVE JOURNAL 60 (February 1902) and, as continued, 15 RAILWAY AND LOCOMOTIVE JOURNAL 144 (March 1902)

Connors (2014): Connors, Anthony J., INGENIOUS MACHINISTS: TWO INVENTIVE LIVES FROM THE AMERICAN INDUSTRIAL REVOLUTION (2014)

Cornell Law (1977): Cornell Law School, THE DEVELOPMENT OF THE LAW OF GAMBLING: 1776-1976 (1977)

Corning (1938): Corning, Howard, *The Autobiography of a Salem Merchant*, 12 BULLETIN OF THE BUSINESS HISTORICAL SOCIETY 33 (1938)

Cottrell (1980): Cottrell, P. L., INDUSTRIAL FINANCE 1830-1914: THE FINANCE AND ORGANIZATION OF ENGLISH MANUFACTURING INDUSTRY (1980)

Cowdrey & Williams (1944): Cowdrey, Bartlett, and Hermann Warner Williams, Jr., WILLIAM SIDNEY MOUNT, 1807-1868, AN AMERICAN PAINTER (1944)

Cowley (1868): Cowley, Charles, HISTORY OF LOWELL, SECOND EDITION (1868)

[Cox (2012): Cox, John Warren, *Benevolent Capitalists: Corporate Funding of Education in Waltham, Massachusetts 1814-1865*, unpublished Ph.D. dissertation, Boston College, Lynch School of Education (May 2012)

Crockett (1837): Crockett, David, THE LIFE OF MARTIN VAN BUREN, HEIR-APPARENT TO THE "GOVERNMENT," AND THE APPOINTED SUCCESSOR OF GENERAL ANDREW JACKSON, SIXTEENTH EDITION (1837)

Cupper (2007-1): Cupper, Dan, *Steam Locomotive Nomenclature*, 197 RAILROAD HISTORY 96 (2007).

Cupper (2007-2): \_\_\_\_\_, *American Locomotive Builders*, 197 RAILROAD HISTORY 99 (2007)

Curtis (1844): Curtis, Benjamin R., *Debts of the States*, 58 NORTH AMERICAN REVIEW 109 (1844)

Cutler (1972): Cutler, William W., III, *Status, Values and the Education of the Poor: The Trustees of the New York Public School Society, 1805-1853*, 24 AMERICAN QUARTERLY 69 (1972)

## D

D&B Cars Contract (1842): Agreement, dated March 30, 1842, between the Philadelphia and Reading Rail Road Company and Davenport & Bridges, HA 1520, Box 1220, Folder 9016

D&B Iron Car Contract (1844): Articles of Agreement, dated January 14, 1844, between the President and Managers of the Philadelphia & Reading Rl. Rd. Co. and Davenport and Bridges, Hagley Archives, Reading Papers, Accession 1520, Box 1220, Folder 9016

D&B-F Cars Contract (1842): Agreement, dated March 30, 1842, between The Philadelphia and Reading Rail Road Company and Davenport & Bridges, HA 1520, Box 1220, Folder 9016

D&H (1925): THE DELAWARE AND HUDSON COMPANY, A CENTURY OF PROGRESS: HISTORY OF THE DELAWARE AND HUDSON COMPANY 1823 – 1923 (1925)

D&H History (1906): THE DELAWARE AND HUDSON COMPANY, CORPORATE HISTORY OF THE DELAWARE AND HUDSON COMPANY AND SUBSIDIARY COMPANIES, VOLUME I (1906)

D&S Coal AR (1852): *Report of the President and Directors of the Dauphin & Susquehanna Coal Co. to the Stockholders, December 1852* (1852)

Dahl (1974): Dahl, Curtis, *The Clergyman, the Hussy, and Old Hickory: Ezra Stiles Ely and the Peggy Eaton Affair*, 52 JOURNAL OF PRESBYTERIAN HISTORY 137 (1974)

Dalzell (1987): Dalzell, Robert F., Jr., ENTERPRISING ELITE: THE BOSTON ASSOCIATES AND THE WORLD THEY MADE (1987)

*Davis v. Garr* (1851): *Davis and others v. Garr, administrator, &c.*, 6 N.Y. 124, 2 Seld. 124, 55 AmDec. 387, 1851 WL 5536, 1851 N.Y. LEXIS 111 (1851)

Davis (1834): Davis, Charles A., LETTERS OF J. DOWNING (1834)

Davis (1835): \_\_\_\_\_, LETTERS OF MAJOR DOWNING (1835)

Davis (1978): Davis, Harold Eugene, *One Hundred and Fifty Years of the American Peace Society*, 2 WORLD AFFAIRS 92 (1978)

Davis & Browne (1849): Davis, Gherardi, and G. Morgan Browne, Jr., CAR TRUSTS IN THE UNITED STATES (1894)

De Bow (1854): De Bow, J. D. B., ENCYCLOPAEDIA OF THE TRADE AND COMMERCE OF THE UNITED STATES, MORE PARTICULARLY OF THE SOUTHERN AND WESTERN STATES (1854)

Dean (1998): Dean, Love, LIGHTHOUSES OF THE FLORIDA KEYS (1998)

Delaware Coal Corporate Documents (1834): CHARTER AND BY-LAWS OF THE DELAWARE COAL COMPANY, INCORPORATED, APRIL 8, 1833, John C. Clark, printer (1834)

Democratic Review (1843): *Biographical Memoir of Albert Gallatin*, THE DEMOCRATIC REVIEW (June 1843)

Democratic Whig Convention (1839): *Proceedings of the Democratic Whig National Convention, which assembled at Harrisburg, Pennsylvania, on the Fourth of December, 1839, for the purpose of Nominating Candidates for President and Vice President of the United States* (1839)

Dengler v. Kiehner (1850): *Dengler v. Kiehner*, 13 Pa. 38, 53 Am. Dec. 441, 1 Harris, 37, 1850 Pa. LEXIS 6, 1849 WL 5817 (1850)

Denham (1995): Denham, James M., *From a Territorial to a State Judiciary: Florida's Antebellum Courts and Judges*, 73 THE FLORIDA HISTORICAL QUARTERLY 443 (1995)

Denham (2011): \_\_\_\_\_, *Crime and Punishment in Antebellum Pensacola*, 90 THE FLORIDA HISTORICAL QUARTERLY 13 (2011)

Depew (1895): Depew, Chauncy M., ed., ONE HUNDRED YEARS OF AMERICAN COMMERCE, 1795-1895 (1895)

Devine (1983): Devine, Warren D., Jr., *From Shafts to Wires: Historical Perspective on Electrification*, 43 THE JOURNAL OF ECONOMIC HISTORY 347 (1983)

Dewey (1910): Dewey, Davis R., STATE BANKING BEFORE THE CIVIL WAR, at 32, included as National Monetary Commission, Document No. 841, SENATE RECORDS, 61$^{ST}$ CONGRESS, 2D SESSION, UNITED STATES OF AMERICA (1910)

Dewhurst (1950), P. C., *The "Norris" Locomotive—Its Origins and Vogue in America*, 79 THE RAILWAY AND LOCOMOTIVE HISTORICAL SOCIETY BULLETIN 6 (1950)

Dexter (1911-IV): Dexter, Franklin Bowditch, BIOGRAPHICAL SKETCHES OF THE GRADUATES OF YALE COLLEGE, WITH ANNALS OF THE COLLEGE HISTORY, VOLUME IV, JUNE, 1778-SEPTEMBER, 1792 (1911)

Dexter (1911-V): \_\_\_\_\_, BIOGRAPHICAL SKETCHES OF THE GRADUATES OF YALE COLLEGE, WITH ANNALS OF THE COLLEGE HISTORY, VOLUME V, JUNE, 1792-SEPTEMBER, 1805 (1911)

Dibble (1971): Dibble, Ernest F., *War Averters: Seward, Mallory, and Fort Pickens*, 49 THE FLORIDA HISTORICAL QUARTERLY 232 (1971)

Dibble (1974): \_\_\_\_\_, ANTE-BELLUM PENSACOLA AND THE MILITARY PRESENCE (1974)

Dippie (1990): Dippie, Brian W., CATLIN AND HIS CONTEMPORARIES: THE POLITICS OF PATRONAGE (1990)

Dippie (1994): \_\_\_\_\_, *Government Patronage: Catlin, Stanley, and Eastman*, 44 MONTANA: THE MAGAZINE OF WESTERN HISTORY 40 (1994)

DIP (1831): JOURNAL OF THE PROCEEDINGS OF THE FRIENDS OF DOMESTIC INDUSTRY, IN GENERAL CONVENTION MET AT THE CITY OF NEW YORK, OCTOBER 26, 1831

Disturnell (1846): Disturnell, John, A GUIDE BETWEEN WASHINGTON, BALTIMORE, PHILADELPHIA, NEW YORK AND BOSTON; CONTAINING A DESCRIPTION OF THE PRINCIPAL PLACES; RAILROAD AND STEAMBOAT ROUTES; TABLES OF DISTANCES, ETC. ALSO, ROUTES OF TRAVEL FROM BOSTON TO BUFFALO, AND FROM NEW YORK TO MONTREAL (June 1846)

DL&W AR (1857): *Fourth Annual Report of the Board of Managers of the Delaware, Lackawanna & Western Rail-Road Co. to the Stockholders, January 1857* (1857)+

Dodd (1954): Dodd, Edwin Merrick, AMERICAN BUSINESS CORPORATIONS UNTIL 1860 (1954)

Dodd (1945): Dodd, Dorothy, *Florida in 1845 Statistics – Economic Life – Social Life*, 24 THE FLORIDA HISTORICAL QUARTERLY 3 (1945)

Dodd (1931): \_\_\_\_\_, *The New City of Pensacola: A Real Estate Development of 1835-1837*, 9 THE FLORIDA HISTORICAL QUARTERLY 224 (1931)

Dodd (1929): \_\_\_\_\_, *Railroad Projects in Territorial Florida*, unpublished M.A. thesis, Florida State College for Women (1929)

Doggett's NYC Directory (1846): DOGGETT'S NEW-YORK CITY DIRECTORY, FOR 1846 AND 1847, FIFTH PUBLICATION (1846)

Doherty (1950), Doherty, Herbert J., Jr., *Union Nationalism in Florida*, 29 THE FLORIDA HISTORICAL QUARTERLY 83 (1950)

Doherty (1953), \_\_\_\_\_, *Richard K. Call vs. the Federal Government on the Seminole War*, 31 THE FLORIDA HISTORICAL QUARTERLY 163 (1953)

Doherty (1961): \_\_\_\_\_, RICHARD KEITH CALL: SOUTHERN UNIONIST (1961)

Doherty (1959): Doherty, Herbert J., Jr., *Ante-Bellum Pensacola: 1821-1860*, 37 THE FLORIDA HISTORICAL QUARTERLY 337 (1959)

Dougherty (1915): Dougherty, J. Hampden, CONSTITUTIONAL HISTORY OF THE STATE OF NEW YORK, SECOND EDITION (1915)

Dome (1970): Dome, Steam, *Locomotives Built at Auburn Additional Information*, 123 THE RAILWAY AND LOCOMOTIVE HISTORICAL SOCIETY BULLETIN 78 (1970)

Dorfman (1951): Dorfman, Joseph, *A Note on the Interpenetration of Anglo-American Finance, 1837-1841*, 11 THE JOURNAL OF ECONOMIC HISTORY 140 (1951)

Dorfman (1961): \_\_\_\_\_, *Chancellor Kent and the Developing American Economy*, 61 COLUMBIA LAW REVIEW 1290 (1961)

Dovell & Richardson (1955), Dovell, J. E., and J. G. Richardson, HISTORY OF BANKING IN FLORIDA, 1828-1954 (1955)

Dover Gazette (1835, June 2): *Lowell Rail Road*, 10 (Issue 27) DOVER GAZETTE & STRAFFORD ADVERTISER 3 (1835, June 2)

Doyle (1841): Doyle, Thomas, FIVE YEARS IN A LOTTERY OFFICE; OR AN EXPOSITION ON THE LOTTERY SYSTEM IN THE UNITED STATES (1841)

Drake (1879): Drake, Francis S., DICTIONARY OF AMERICAN BIOGRAPHY, INCLUDING MEN OF THE TIME (1879)

Dunbar (1915-II): Dunbar, Seymour, A HISTORY OF TRAVEL IN AMERICA, VOLUME II (1915)

Dunbar (1915-III): \_\_\_\_\_, A HISTORY OF TRAVEL IN AMERICA, VOLUME III (1915)

*Duncan v. Jaudon* (1873): *Duncan v. Jaudon*, 82 U.S. 165, 21 L. Ed. 142, 15 Wall. 165, 1872 WL 142, 1872 U.S. LEXIS 1244 (1873)

Dysart (1982): Dysart, Jane E., *Another Road to Disappearance: Assimilation of Creek Indians in Pensacola, Florida, during the Nineteenth Century*, 61 THE FLORIDA HISTORICAL QUARTERLY 37 (1982)

## E

East Florida Memorial (1835): *Memorial to Congress by the President and Directors of the East Florida Railroad Company, December 14, 1835*, in Clarence Edwin Carter, ed., THE TERRITORIAL PAPERS OF THE UNITED STATES, VOLUME XXV, THE TERRITORY OF FLORIDA 1834-1839 (1960), at 212-13

Eaton (1824): Eaton, John Henry, THE LIFE OF ANDREW JACKSON, MAJOR-GENERAL IN THE SERVICE OF THE UNITED STATES: COMPRISING A HISTORY OF THE WAR IN THE SOUTH FROM THE

Commencement of the Creek Campaign, to the Termination of Hostilities Before New Orleans (1824)

Eaton (1932): Eaton, Margaret L., The Autobiography of Peggy Eaton (1932)

Eisler (2013): Eisler, Benita, The Red Man's Bones: George Catlin, Artist and Showman (2013)

Eisterhold (1973): Eisterhold, John A., *Lumber and Trade in Pensacola and West Florida: 1800-1860*, 51 The Florida Historical Quarterly 267 (1973)

Ellet (1845): Ellet, Charles, Jr., The Reading Railroad Company (1845)

Ellsworth (1974): Ellsworth, Lucius F., *Raiford and Abercrombie: Pensacola's Premier Antebellum Manufacturer*, 52 The Florida Historical Quarterly 247 (1974)

Ellsworth (1976): Ellsworth, Linda, *The History of a House*, 31 History News 169 (1976)

Emancipator (1842, July 28): *The Florida Banking System*, 7 Emancipator and Free American 1 (July 28, 1842)

Engines Contract: Agreement, dated March 9, 1843, between the Philadelphia and Reading Rail Road Company and The Proprietors of Locks and Canals on Merrimack River, HA 1520 Box 1220, Folder 9022

English (1996): English, William B., *Understanding the Costs of Sovereign Default: American State Debts in the 1840s*, 86 The American Economic Review 259 (1996)

Evans (1795): Evans, Oliver, The Young Mill-Wright and Miller's Guide (1795)

*Evans v. Eaton* (1818): *Evans v. Eaton*, 16 U.S. 454, 3 Wheat. 454, 4 L. Ed. 433, 1818 WL 2427, 1818 U.S. LEXIS 370 (1822)

*Evans v. Eaton* (1822): *Evans v. Eaton*, 20 U.S. 356, 7 Wheat. 356, 5 L. Ed. 472, 1822 WL 2199, 1822 U.S. LEXIS 266 (1822)

*Evans v. Hettich* (1822): *Evans v. Hettich*, 20 U.S. 453, 7 Wheat. 453, 5 L. Ed. 496, 1822 WL 2195, 1822 U.S. LEXIS 267 (1822)

*Evans v. Jordan & Morehead* (1815): *Evans v. Jordan and Morehead*, 13 U.S. 199, 9 Cranch. 199, 3 L. Ed. 704, 1815 WL 1462, 1815 U.S. LEXIS (1815)

Ezell (1960): Ezell, John Samuel, Fortune's Merry Wheel: The Lottery in America (1960)

# F

F&L Insurance (1854): *Fire and Life Insurance! Liverpool and London Company*, advertisement, Charles Cobb, American Railway Guide, and Pocket Companion, For the United States (July 1854), at 4

*Farmers' Bank v. McKee* (1845): *Farmers' Bank of Bucks County v. McKee*, 2 Pa. 318, 1845 WL 5247, 1845 Pa. LEXIS 343 (1845)

Farrier (1879): Farrier, George H., Memorial of the Centennial Celebration of the Battle of Paulus Hook, August 19th, 1879; With a History of the Early Settlement and Present Condition of Jersey City, N. J. (1879)

FCC Stockholders (1837): *List of Stockholders in Franklin Coal Company, Read in Senate, March 22, 1837*, Journal of The Senate of Pennsylvania, Session 1836-37, Volume II 461 (1836-37),

Feld (1967): Feld, Stuart P., *"In the Midst of 'High Vintage'"*, 25 The Metropolitan Museum of Art Bulletin 292 (1967)

Financial Register (1838, June 6): *Resumption of Specie Payments in Philadelphia*, 1 The Financial Register of the United States 398 (June 6, 1838)

Financial Register (1838, October 17): *Domestic Intelligence*, 2 THE FINANCIAL REGISTER OF THE UNITED STATES 253 (October 17, 1838)

Firm Histories (2007): *Histories of Individual Firms*, 197 RAILROAD HISTORY 24 (2007)

Fisher (1929): Fisher, Chas. E., *The Michigan Central R. R.*, 19 THE RAILWAY AND LOCOMOTIVE HISTORICAL SOCIETY BULLETIN 4 (1929)

Fisher (1938), _____, *Locomotives of the New Haven R. R.*, 47 THE RAILWAY AND HISTORICAL SOCIETY BULLETIN 79 (1938)

Fisher (1940): _____, *Moncure Robinson*, 53 THE RAILWAY AND LOCOMOTIVE HISTORICAL SOCIETY 19 (1940)

Fisher (1942): _____, *Locomotive Builders of the United States*, 58 THE RAILWAY AND LOCOMOTIVE HISTORICAL SOCIETY BULLETIN 55 (1942)

Fisher (1947): _____, *Whistler's Railroad: The Western Railroad of Massachusetts*, 69 THE RAILWAY AND LOCOMOTIVE HISTORICAL SOCIETY BULLETIN 8 (1947)

Fisher (1962): Fisher, Barbara, *Maritime History of the Reading, 1833-1905*, 86 THE PENNSYLVANIA MAGAZINE OF HISTORY AND BIOGRAPHY 160 (1962)

Fishlow (1965): Fishlow, Albert, AMERICAN RAILROADS AND THE TRANSFORMATION OF THE ANTE-BELLUM ECONOMY (1965)

FL AG (1845, November 18): Letter of Joseph Branch, Office of the Attorney General of the State of Florida, dated November 18, 1845, to the General Assembly of Florida, in FL SJ (1845), at 23 *et seq.*

FL AG (1845, December 16): Letter of Joseph Branch, Office of the Attorney General of the State of Florida, dated December 16, 1845, to the House of Representatives of Florida, in FL SJ (1845), at 163

FL Bank Comm. Rep. (1840): *Report of the Committee on Banks, February 25, 1840*, in US House Executive Documents (1841), at 278-92

FL Department of State: Department of State of the State of Florida, at https://dos.myflorida.com/florida-facts/florida-history/florida-governors/richard-keith-call/

FL Executive Documents IV: INDEX TO THE EXECUTIVE DOCUMENTS, TWENTY-SIXTH CONGRESS, SECOND SESSION (1841)

FL Fed. Relations Comm. Report (1851): Walker Anderson, Chairman of the Committee on Federal Relations, *Report*, JOURNAL OF THE PROCEEDINGS OF THE HOUSE OF REPRESENTATIVES OF THE GENERAL ASSEMBLY OF THE STATE OF FLORIDA AT ITS FIFTH SESSION, BEGUN AND HELD AT THE CAPITOL IN THE CITY OF TALLAHASSEE, ON MONDAY, TWENTY-FIFTH NOVEMBER, 1850 (1851), at 166-73 (1850)

FL Gov. (1840): *Extracts from the message of Governor Reid—January 13, 1840*, in US House Executive Documents (1840), at 241 et seq.

FL Gov. (1842): *Governor's Message*, Journal of the Senate of the Territory of Florida, at its Fourth Session, Begun and Held in the City of Tallahassee, on Monday, January 3, 1842, at 6 *et seq.*

FL Gov. (1843): *Governor's Message of January 5, 1843*, JOURNAL OF THE PROCEEDINGS OF THE LEGISLATIVE COUNCIL OF THE TERRITORY OF FLORIDA AT ITS FOURTH SESSION, BEGUN AND HELD IN THE CITY OF TALLAHASSEE ON MONDAY, JANUARY 2ND, 1843, at 10 *et seq.*

FL HJ (1842): A JOURNAL OF THE PROCEEDINGS OF THE LEGISLATIVE COUNCIL, OF THE TERRITORY OF FLORIDA, AT ITS TWENTIETH SESSION, BEGUN AND HELD IN THE CITY OF TALLAHASSEE, ON MONDAY THE THIRD DAY OF JANUARY EIGHTEEN HUNDRED AND FORTY-TWO (1842)

FL HJ (1850): *Report of the Committee on Foreign Relations, read December 30, 1850,* HOUSE JOURNAL: A JOURNAL OF THE PROCEEDINGS OF THE HOUSE OF REPRESENTATIVES OF THE GENERAL ASSEMBLY OF THE STATE OF FLORIDA AT ITS FIFTH SESSION, BEGUN AND HELD AT THE CAPITAL, IN THE CITY OF TALLAHASSEE ON MONDAY, TWENTY-FIFTH NOVEMBER 1850 (1851), at 166

FL Judiciary Committee Report (1840): *Report of the Committee on the Judiciary to the Legislative Council of the Territory of Florida*, in US House Executive Documents (1841), at 257

FL Law (1831): Florida Territory Legislative Council Laws, An Act to incorporate a bank by the name and style of the Bank of Pensacola, passed January 19, 1831, rejected by the governor on January 31, 1831, and reconsidered and passed by the Council on February 31, 1831

FL Law (1833) Ch. 697: Florida Territory Legislative Council Laws, Chapter 697, No. 40, An Act to Incorporate the subscribers to the Union Bank of Florida, passed and approved, February 13, 1833

FL Law (1833) 699: Florida Territory Legislative Council Laws, Chapter 699, An Act to extend the time limited by law for the subscribing for the stock of the Bank of Pensacola, passed January 16, 1833, which was vetoed on January 23, and passed over the veto on January 29, 1833

FL Law (1833) Veto Message: Veto Message: Florida Territory Legislative Council Laws, veto message of January 24, 1833, at 22

FL Law (1834) No. 11: Florida Territory Legislative Council Laws, No. 11, An Act To incorporate the subscribers to the Alabama, Florida and Georgia Rail Road Company, approved, December 12, 1834

FL Law (1834) Ch. 774: Florida Territory Legislative Council Laws, Chapter 774-No. 35, An act to incorporate the College of Pensacola, Passed, February 8th, 1834, approved, February 14th, 1834.

FL Law (1834) Ch. 792: Florida Territory Legislative Council Laws, Chapter 792, Number 53, An act to incorporate the Florida, Alabama, and Georgia Rail Road Company, Passed February 14, 1834, Approved February 15, 1834

FL Law (1834) Ch. 820: Florida Territorial Legislative Council Laws, Chapter 820, No. 81, An act supplemental to the several acts incorporating the Bank of Pensacola, approved February 11, 1834

FL Law (1835) Ch. 825: Florida Territory Legislative Council Laws, Chapter 825, [Number ii], An Act to incorporate the Pensacola and Perdido Rail Road and Canal Company, passed February 10, 1835 and approved February 14, 1835

FL Law (1835) Ch. 826: Florida Territory Legislative Council Laws, Chapter 826, [No. iii], An Act to Incorporate the Southern Life Insurance and Trust Company, passed February 12, 1835, approved February 14, 1835

FL Law (1835) Ch. 843: Chap. 843, [No. xx], An Act to increase the capital of the Bank of Pensacola, and to amend the laws incorporating said Bank, and or [stet] other purposes, approved February 14, 1835

FL Law (1835) Ch. 848: Florida Territory Legislative Council Laws Chapter 848 [No. xx], An Act to increase the capital of the Bank of Pensacola, and to amend the laws incorporating said Bank, and for other purposes, Passed February 13th, 1835, approved February 14th, 1835

FL Law (1835) Ch. 870: Florida Territory Legislative Council Laws, Chapter 870, An Act to authorize the Alabama, Florida, and Georgia Rail Road Company to continue their Road from the line between the State of Alabama and Territory of Florida, to the waters of Pensacola Bay, Passed February 5th, 1835, approved February 9th, 1835

FL Law (1836) Ch. 973: Florida Territory Legislative Council Laws, Chapter 973 [No. LXII], An Act to Incorporate the Florida Insurance and Banking Company, passed February 14, 1836, rejected February 15, 1836, reconsidered and passed by the requisite majority

FL Law (1838) No. 38: Florida Territory Legislative Council Laws, No. 38, An Act supplemental to the several Acts incorporating the Bank of Pensacola, passed February 9, 1838 and approved February 10, 1838,

FL Law (1838) No. 60: Florida Territory Legislative Council Laws, Act No. 60, An Act to incorporate the Pensacola City Company, February 11, 1838

FL Law (1840) No. 40: Florida Territory Legislative Council Laws, No. 40, An Act to repeal the second section of the act approved 10th February, 1838, supplemental to several acts incorporating the Bank of Pensacola, and to revive the 8th section of an act to increase the capital of the Bank of Pensacola, and to amend the laws incorporating said bank, and for other purposes, approved 14th February, 1835, approved March 2, 1840

FL Law (1842) Res. 9: Florida Territory Legislative Council Laws, Joint Legislative Resolution No. 9, A Resolution respecting the Faith Bonds and Guarantees, adopted by the Senate on February 3, 1842 and the House of Representatives on February 23, 1842

FL Law (1853) Ch. 504, No. 25: Florida Territory Legislative Council Laws, Chapter 504, No25, An Act to authorize William H. Chase and Jasper Strong to cut a Canal connecting the Waters of the Perdido River and the Grand Lagoon, approved January 8, 1853

FL LCJ (1843): JOURNAL OF THE LEGISLATIVE COUNCIL OF THE TERRITORY OF FLORIDA, BEGUN AND HELD IN THE CITY OF TALLAHASSEE, ON MONDAY THE SECOND DAY OF JANUARY, EIGHTEEN HUNDRED AND FORTY-THREE (1843)

FL SJ (1840): A JOURNAL OF THE PROCEEDINGS OF THE SENATE OF THE TERRITORY OF FLORIDA AT ITS SECOND SESSION BEGUN AND HELD AT THE CITY OF TALLAHASSEE, ON MONDAY THE SIXTH DAY OF JAN., EIGHTEEN HUNDRED AND FORTY (1840)

FL SJ (1842): DOCUMENTS ACCOMPANYING THE MESSAGE OF THE GOVERNOR, JOURNAL OF THE PROCEEDINGS OF THE SENATE OF THE LEGISLATIVE TERRITORY OF FLORIDA AT ITS FOURTH SESSION BEGUN AND HELD AT THE CITY OF TALLAHASSEE, ON MONDAY THE THIRD DAY OF JANUARY, 1842 (1842)

FL SJ (1845): A JOURNAL OF THE PROCEEDINGS OF THE SENATE OF THE FIRST GENERAL ASSEMBLY OF THE STATE OF FLORIDA AT ITS FIRST SESSION, BEGUN AND HELD IN THE CITY OF TALLAHASSEE, ON MONDAY, JUNE 23, 1845 AT THE CAPITOL (1845)

FL SJ (1850): Letter from Neill McPherson, Secretary of the Senate, dated January 14, 1851, to Thomas Brown, Governor of Florida, in SENATE JOURNAL: A JOURNAL OF THE PROCEEDINGS OF THE SENATE OF THE GENERAL ASSEMBLY OF THE STATE OF FLORIDA, AT ITS FIFTH SESSION, BEGUN AND HELD AT THE CAPITOL, IN THE CITY OF TALLAHASSEE, ON MONDAY, NOVEMBER 25, A. D. 1850 (1850)

Flesher, Previts & Samson (2006): Flesher, Dale L., Gary J. Previts, and William D. Samson, *Early American Corporate Reporting and European Capital Markets: The Case of the Illinois Central Railroad, 1851-1861*, 33 THE ACCOUNTING HISTORIAN'S JOURNAL 3 (2006)

Floridian (1840, August 1): *Editorial*, 12 THE FLORIDIAN & JOURNAL 3 (August 1, 1840)

Forbes (1899): Forbes, John Murray, LETTERS AND RECOLLECTIONS OF JOHN MURRAY FORBES, VOLUME I, Sarah Forbes Hughes, ed. (1899)

Ford & Ford (1881): Ford, Henry A., and Kate B. Ford, HISTORY OF CINCINNATI, OHIO, WITH ILLUSTRATIONS AND BIOGRAPHICAL SKETCHES (1881)

Forestall Letter (1841): Letter, dated November 8, 1841, from Edmund J. Forestall to Daniel Webster, in THE TERRITORIAL PAPERS OF THE UNITED STATES, VOLUME XXVI, THE TERRITORY OF FLORIDA 1839-1845 (2006), Edwin Carter, ed.

Frederico (1945-I): Frederico, P. J., *The Patent Trials of Oliver Evans, Part I*, 27 JOURNAL OF THE PATENT LAW SOCIETY 586 (1945)

Frederico (1945-II): \_\_\_\_\_, *The Patent Trials of Oliver Evans, Part II*, 27 JOURNAL OF THE PATENT LAW SOCIETY 657 (1945)

## G

Gaskell (1952): Gaskell, G. H., *The Origin of Locomotive Class Names*, 87 THE RAILWAY AND LOCOMOTIVE HISTORICAL SOCIETY BULLETIN 83 (1952)

Gatell (1964): Gatell, Frank Otto, *Spoils of the Bank War: Political Bias in the Selection of Pet Banks*, 70 THE AMERICAN HISTORICAL REVIEW 35 (1964)

Gatell (1966): \_\_\_\_\_, *Sober Second Thoughts on Van Buren, the Albany Regency, and the Wall Street Conspiracy*, 53 THE JOURNAL OF AMERICAN HISTORY 19 (1966)

Gates (1969): Gates, Paul W., *Frontier Land Business in Wisconsin*, 52 THE WISCONSIN MAGAZINE OF HISTORY 306 (1969)

Geller (1916): Geller, Carl, *Cotton Speculation in America*, in LAMB'S TEXTILE INDUSTRIES OF THE UNITED STATES, VOLUME I, E. Everton Foster, ed. (1916)

Gephart (1909): Gephart, William F., *Transportation and Industrial Development in the Middle West*, 34 COLUMBIA UNIVERSITY STUDIES IN HISTORY, ECONOMICS AND PUBLIC LAW (1909)

Gibb (1947): Gibb, George Sweet, *Three Early Railroad Contracts*, 21 BULLETIN OF THE BUSINESS HISTORICAL SOCIETY 10 (1947)

Gibb (1950): \_\_\_\_\_, THE SACO-LOWELL SHOPS: TEXTILE MACHINERY BUILDING IN NEW ENGLAND 1813-1949 (1950)

Gilbart (1840): Gilbart, James William, AN INQUIRY INTO THE CAUSES OF THE PRESSURE ON THE MONEY MARKET DURING THE YEAR 1839 (1840)

Goodman (1966): Goodman, Paul, *Ethics and Enterprise: The Values of the Boston Elite, 1800-1860*, 18 AMERICAN QUARTERLY 437 (1966)

Goodrich (1950): Goodrich, Carter, *The Revulsion Against Internal Improvements*, 2 THE JOURNAL OF ECONOMIC HISTORY 15 (1950)

Goodrich (1960): \_\_\_\_\_, GOVERNMENT PROMOTION OF AMERICAN CANALS AND RAILROADS, 1800-1890 (1960)

Goodrich (1961): \_\_\_\_\_, ed., CANALS AND AMERICAN ECONOMIC DEVELOPMENT (1961)

Govan (1940): Govan, Thomas Payne, *An Ante-Bellum Attempt to Regulate the Price and Supply of Cotton*, 17 THE NORTH CAROLINA HISTORICAL REVIEW 302 (1940)

Govan (1959): \_\_\_\_\_, NICHOLAS BIDDLE: NATIONALIST AND PUBLIC BANKER, 1786-1844 (1959)

Gray (1933): Gray, Lewis Cecil, HISTORY OF AGRICULTURE IN THE SOUTHERN UNITED STATES TO 1860, VOLUME II (1933)

Green-Wood Cemetery (1844): GREEN-WOOD CEMETERY: ITS RULES, REGULATIONS, ETC. (1844)

*Gregory v. NYLE&W* (1888): *Gregory v. The New York, Lake Erie and Western Railroad Company*, 40 N.J. Eq. 38, 13 Stewart 38, 1888 N.J. Ch. LEXIS 51, 1885 WL 605 (1885), also available in John H. Stewart, *Equity Jurisdiction in Case of Foreign Corporations: Gregory v. New York Etc. R. Co.*, 22 THE CENTRAL LAW JOURNAL (1874-1927) 110 (1886)

Gregory (1938): Gregory, Grant, ANCESTORS AND DESCENDANTS OF HENRY GREGORY (1938)

Gregory (1975): Gregory, Frances W., NATHAN APPLETON: MERCHANT AND ENTREPRENEUR, 1779-1861 (1975)

Gregory (1983): Gregory, _____, *A Tale of Three Cities: The Struggle for Banking Stability in Boston, New York, and Philadelphia*, 56 NEW ENGLAND QUARTERLY 3 (1983)

*Gregory's Executrix v. Shelby College* (1859): *Gregory's Executrix v. Trustees of Shelby College, &c.*, 59 Ky. 589, 2 Met. 589, 1859 Ky. LEXIS 173, 1860 WL 7967 (1859)

Gregory & Catlin Bond Letter (March 12, 1836): *To His Excellency, John H. Eaton, Gov. of Florida*, 7 FLORIDIAN & JOURNAL 2 (March 12, 1836), a letter of Walter Gregory and James Catlin announcing sale of the bonds by the Bank of Pensacola.

Griffin (1957): Griffin, Clifford S., *Religious Benevolence as Social Control*, 1815-1860, 44 THE MISSISSIPPI VALLEY HISTORICAL REVIEW 423 (1957)

Grinath, Wallis & Sylla (1997): Grinath, Arthur, III, John Joseph Wallis, and Richard Sylla, *Debt, Default and Revenue Structure: The Early American State Debt Crisis in the Early 1840s*, NATIONAL BUREAU OF ECONOMIC RESEARCH Historical Paper 97 (March 1997), available at https://papers.ssrn.com/sol3/papers.cfm?abstract_id=225060

Gunderson (1957-I): Gunderson, Robert Gray, THE LOG-CABIN CAMPAIGN (1957)

Gunderson (1957-II): _____, *Log-Cabin Canvass, Hoosier Style*, 53 INDIANA MAGAZINE OF HISTORY 245 (1957)

## H

Haberly (1948): Haberly, Lloyd, PURSUIT OF THE HORIZON: A LIFE OF GEORGE CATLIN, PAINTER & RECORDER OF THE AMERICAN INDIAN (1948)

Hamilton (1957): Hamilton, Holman, *Texas Bonds and Northern Profits: A Study in Compromise, Investment, and Lobby Influence*, 43 THE MISSISSIPPI VALLEY HISTORICAL REVIEW 579 (1957)

Hammond (1947): Hammond, Bray, *The Chestnut Street Raid on Wall Street*, 1839, 61 THE QUARTERLY JOURNAL OF ECONOMICS 605 (1947)

Hancock (1836): Hancock, J., THE MERCHANT AND TRADER'S GUIDE, AND STRANGER'S MEMORANDUM BOOK, FOR THE YEAR OF OUR LORD 1836, CALCULATED FOR BOSTON AND ITS VICINITY (1836)

Hansen (1915): Hansen, Alvin H., *Wholesale Prices for the United States, 1801-1840*, 14 PUBLICATIONS OF THE AMERICAN STATISTICAL ASSOCIATION 112 (1915)

Hare (1909): Hare, Jay V., *History of the Reading*, 10 THE PILOT AND PHILADELPHIA & READING RAILWAY MEN 40 (October 1909)

Hare (1909-1914): _____, HISTORY OF THE READING: THE COLLECTED ARTICLES OF MR. JAY V. HARE (ONE TIME SECRETARY OF THE READING COMPANY) WHICH APPEARED AS A SERIAL IN THE PILOT and Philadelphia & Reading Railway Men Beginning in May 1909 – Ending February 1914 (1966)

Harford (1879): Harford, W. M., A Short Sketch of the Life and Services of Jonathan Walker, the Man with a Branded Hand, with a Poem by John G. Whittier and an Address by Hon. Parker Pillsbury, on of Walker's anti-slavery friends, and a funeral oration by Rev. F. E. Kittredge (1879)

Harris (1837): Harris, Thomas, The Life and Services of Commodore William Bainbridge, United States Navy (1837)

Harris (2000): Harris, Ron, Industrializing English Law: Entrepreneurship and Business Organization 1720-1844 (2000)

Harrison (1872): Harrison, Joseph, Jr., The Locomotive Engine, and Philadelphia's Share in its Early Development (1872)

Hart (1946): Hart, George M., *History of the Locomotives of the Reading Company*, 67 The Railway and Historical Society Bulletin 9 (1946)

Hartford (2001): Hartford, William F., Money, Morals, and Politics: Massachusetts in the Age of The Boston Associates (2001)

Hartman (1940): Hartman, E. J., *Josiah White and the Lehigh Canal*, 7 Pennsylvania History: A Journal of Mid-Atlantic Studies 225 (1940)

Harvey (1977): Harvey, Katherine A., ed., The *Lonaconing Journals: The Founding of a Coal and Iron Community, 1837-1840*, 67 Transactions of the American Philosophical Society 1 (1977)

Hauptman & Hamell (2003): Hauptman, Laurence M., and George Hamell, *George Catlin: The Iroquois Origins of His Indian Art*, 84 New York History 125 (2003)

Hay (1975): Hay, Warren, History of Locomotive Building in Lowell, Mass. (1975)

Hazard's Register (1832, January 27): *Delaware and Raritan Canal Company, and Camden and Amboy Rail-Road and Transportation Company*, 9 Hazard's Register of Pennsylvania 49 (January 27, 1832)

Hazard's Register (1835, December 26): *New York Sufferers* and *Meeting of Citizens With Reference to the New York Sufferers*, each 16 Hazard's Register of Pennsylvania 411 (December 26, 1835)

Heale (1976): Heale, M. J., *From City Fathers to Social Critics: Humanitarianism and Government in New York, 1790-1860*, 63 The Journal of American History 21 (1976)

Heeney (1910): Heeney, Georgette, *Colonial Lotteries in America*, unpublished M.L. dissertation, University of California (1910)

Hemstreet (1900): Hemstreet, Charles, *Philip Hone and the Union Club*, 55 The Home Journal 5 (July 19, 1900)

Heydinger (1954): Heydinger, Earl J., *The English Influence on American Railroads*, 91 Bulletin of the Railway and Locomotive Historical Society 41 (1954)

*Hereford v. Chase* (1841): *John B. Hereford v. William H. Chase*, 40 Va. 196, 1 Rob. 212, 1841 La. LEXIS 94, 1842 WL 2664 (1841)

Hidy (1939): Hidy, Muriel E., *George Peabody, Merchant and Financier, 1829-1854*, unpublished Ph.D. dissertation, Radcliffe College (1939)

Hidy (1941): Hidy, R. W., *The Organization and Functions of Anglo-American Merchant Bankers, 1815-1860*, 1 The Journal of Economic History, Supplement: The Tasks of Economic History 53 (1941)

Hidy (1946): _____, *Cushioning a Crisis in the London Money Market*, 20 BULLETIN OF THE BUSINESS HISTORICAL SOCIETY 131 (1946)

Hight (1990): Hight, Kathryn S., *"Doomed to Perish": George Catlin's Depictions of Mandan*, 49 ART JOURNAL 119 (1990)

Hildreth (1840): Hildreth, Richard, THE PEOPLE'S PRESIDENTIAL CANDIDATE; OR THE LIFE OF WILLIAM HENRY HARRISON OF OHIO (1840)

Hildreth (1959): Hildreth, Charles H., *Railroads out of Pensacola, 1833-1883*, 37 THE FLORIDA HISTORICAL QUARTERLY 397 (1959)

Holloway (1889): Holloway, Laura C., FAMOUS AMERICAN FORTUNES AND THE MEN WHO MADE THEM (1889)

Holton (1989): Holton, James L., THE READING RAILROAD: HISTORY OF A COAL AGE EMPIRE: VOLUME 1: THE NINETEENTH CENTURY (1989)

Hone (1828): Hone, Philip, *Delaware and Hudson Canal*, 7 SATURDAY EVENING POST 2 (October 25, 1828)

Hone (1841): _____, *Art. II—Commerce and Commercial Character*, 20 HUNT'S MERCHANTS' MAGAZINE AND COMMERCIAL REVIEW 129 (February 1841)

Hone (1889): _____, THE DIARY OF PHILIP HONE 1828-1851, VOLUME I, Bayard Tuckerman, ed. (1889)

Hone (1927): _____, THE DIARY OF PHILIP HONE 1828-1851, VOLUME I, Allan Nevins, ed. (1927)

Hoskins (1937): Hoskins, F. W., *The St. Joseph Convention: The Making of Florida's First Constitution*, 16 THE FLORIDA HISTORICAL QUARTERLY 33 (1937)

Hoskins (1938-1): _____, *The St. Joseph Convention: The Making of Florida's First Constitution (Continued)*, 16 THE FLORIDA HISTORICAL QUARTERLY 242 (1938)

Hoskins (1938-2): _____, *The St. Joseph Convention: The Making of Florida's First Constitution (The Fourth and Last Installment)*, 17 THE FLORIDA HISTORICAL QUARTERLY 125 (1938)

House of Commons Return (1840): *Return to an Order of the Honourable The House of Commons, dated 12 March 1840;—for, Copies of all Communications between the Board of Treasury, or the India Board, or any other Public Department, and the Parties or their Agents who are Holders of Certificates or Bills granted by the Chief Superintendent at Canton for Opium surrendered to the Chinese Authorities; together with an Account of the Number of such Bills or Certificates, and of the Amount in Sterling Value which they represent* (1840)

Howard (1863): Howard, Frank Key, FOURTEEN MONTHS IN AMERICAN BASTILES (1863)

Howard (1873): Howard, George W., THE MONUMENTAL CITY, ITS PAST HISTORY AND PRESENT RESOURCES (1873)

Howe (2007): Howe, Daniel Walker, WHAT HATH GOD WROUGHT: THE TRANSFORMATION OF AMERICA, 1815-1848 (2007)

Hudson (1975): Hudson, Joseph B., Jr., *The Political Origins of William Sidney Mount's Cider Making*, 10 METROPOLITAN MUSEUM JOURNAL 107 (1975)

Hulbert (1901): Hulbert, Archer Butler, THE OLD NATIONAL ROAD: A CHAPTER OF AMERICAN EXPANSION (1901)

Hulbert (1903): _____, HISTORIC HIGHWAYS OF AMERICA, VOLUME 4: BRADDOCK'S ROAD AND THREE RELATIVE PAPERS (1903)

Hulbert (1904): _____, HISTORIC HIGHWAYS OF AMERICA, VOLUME 10: THE CUMBERLAND ROAD (1904)

Hulse (2010): Hulse, Thomas, *Military Slave Rentals, the Construction of Army Fortifications, and the Navy Yard in Pensacola, Florida, 1824-1863*, 88 THE FLORIDA HISTORICAL QUARTERLY 497 (2010)

## J

Jack Downing Letter (1836, May 30): letter, dated May 30, 1836, from a New York investor in the Bank of Pensacola and Pensacola Railroad, likely Charles Augustus Davis, to a member of the U.S. Congress and reprinted in 24 DAILY NATIONAL INTELLIGENCER 3 (June 9, 1836), the letter being characterized by the publisher as being "in a sort of Jack Downing style"

Jackson (1966): Jackson, Carlton, *The Internal Improvement Vetoes of Andrew Jackson*, 25 TENNESSEE HISTORICAL QUARTERLY 261 (1966)

Jackson-Stevenson Letter (1839): Letter, dated February 9, 1939, addressed to Robert Stevenson, copy printed in 4 THE RAILWAY AND LOCOMOTIVE HISTORICAL SOCIETY BULLETIN 45 (1923)

Jarvis (1994): Jarvis, Robert M., *The History of Florida's State Flag*, 18 NOVA LAW REVIEW 1036 (1994)

Jaher (1972): Jaher, Frederic Cople, *Nineteenth-Century Elites in Boston and New York*, 6 JOURNAL OF SOCIAL HISTORY 32 (1972)

*Jameson v. Gregory's Executor* (1863): *Jameson v. Gregory's Executor*, 61 Ky. 363, 4 Met. 363, 1863 Ky. LEXIS 78, 1863 WL 2578 (1863)

Jaudon Family (1890): AN ACCOUNT OF THE JAUDON FAMILY (1890)

*Jaudon v. National City Bank* (1871): *Jaudon v. National City Bank*, 13 F. Cas. 376, 8 Blatchf. 430, 1871 U.S. App. LEXIS 1701 (1871)

*Jaudon v. Wertheym* (1842): *Commonwealth of Pennsylvania ex re. Samuel Jaudon v. Joseph H. Wertheym*, OPINION OF THE HON. ARCHIBALD RANDALL, JUDGE OF THE COURT OF COMMON PLEAS, IN THE CASE OF SAMUEL JAUDON (1842)

Jay (1905): Jay, John, MEMORIALS OF PETER A. JAY, COMPILED FOR HIS DESCENDANTS (1905)

JCCB (1896): Journal of Commerce and Credit Bulletin, Editor, A HISTORY OF BANKING IN ALL THE LEADING NATIONS, VOLUME I (1896)

Jeffrey (1893): Jeffrey, William H., RICHMOND PRISONS 1861-1862 (1893)

Jenkins (1846): Jenkins, John S., HISTORY OF POLITICAL PARTIES OF THE STATE OF NEW YORK, FROM THE ACKNOWLEDGMENT OF THE INDEPENDENCE OF THE UNITED STATES TO THE CLOSE OF THE PRESIDENTIAL ELECTION IN EIGHTEEN HUNDRED FORTY-FOUR (1846)

Jenkins (1852): _____, LIVES OF THE GOVERNORS OF THE STATE OF NEW YORK (1852)

Jeremy (1973): Jeremy, David J., *Innovation in American Textile Technology during the Early 19th Century*, 14 TECHNOLOGY AND CULTURE 40 (1973)

Johnson (1965): Johnson, Dudley Sady, *The Railroads of Florida, 1865-1900*, unpublished Ph.D. dissertation, The Florida State University (1965)

Jonathan Jackson Will (1806): *The Will of Jonathan Jackson, Boston, Apr. 22, 1806, and Related Documents: "Memorandum of the Disposition of Certain Personal Estate," Nov. 30, 1807, and "Inventory and Appraisement of the Estate of Jonathan Jackson," Mar. 16, 1810*, in Porter (1937), at 380-90

Jordan (1948): Jordan, Philip, THE NATIONAL ROAD (1948)

Joy (1878): Joy, Charles A., *The History of the Locomotive and of the Railway System of Modern Times*, 6 FRANK LESLIE'S POPULAR MAGAZINE 626 (November 878)

## K

Karp (2011): Karp, Matthew J. Karp, *Slavery and American Sea Power: The Navalist Impulse in the Antebellum South*, 77 THE JOURNAL OF SOUTHERN HISTORY 283 (2011)

Keller (1985): Keller, Morton, *The Personality of Cities: Boston, New York, Philadelphia*, 97 PROCEEDINGS OF THE MASSACHUSETTS HISTORICAL SOCIETY 1 (1985)

Kelly (1946): Kelly, Ralph, *Matthias W. Baldwin (1795-1866) Locomotive Pioneer!*, Issue 472 NEWCOMEN SOCIETY OF NORTH AMERICA (1946)

Kennedy (1951-1): Kennedy, Charles J., *The Early Business History of Four Massachusetts Railroads*, 25 BULLETIN OF THE BUSINESS HISTORICAL SOCIETY 52 (1951)

Kennedy (1951-2): _____, *The Early Business History of Four Massachusetts Railroads – II*, 25 BULLETIN OF THE BUSINESS HISTORICAL SOCIETY 84 (1951)

Kennedy (1951-3): _____, *The Early Business History of Four Massachusetts Railroads – III*, 25 BULLETIN OF THE BUSINESS HISTORICAL SOCIETY 188 (1951)

Kennedy (1951-4): _____, *The Early Business History of Four Massachusetts Railroads – IV*, 25 BULLETIN OF THE BUSINESS HISTORICAL SOCIETY 207 (1951)

Kennedy (1957): Kennedy, Charles J., *The Eastern Rail-road Company to 1855*, 31 THE BUSINESS HISTORY REVIEW 92 (1957)

Keuchel (1970): Keuchel, Edward F., *Coal-Burning Locomotives: A Technological Development of the 1850's*, 94 THE PENNSYLVANIA MAGAZINE OF HISTORY AND BIOGRAPHY 484 (1970)

Kim & Wallis (2005): Kim, Namsuck, and John Joseph Wallis, *The Market for American State Government Bonds in Britain and the United States, 1830-43*, 58 THE ECONOMIC HISTORY REVIEW 736 (2005)

Kinnicutt (1854): Kinnicutt, Thomas, NOTICE OF THE LIFE AND CHARACTER OF HON. JOHN DAVIS (1854)

Kirkland (1945): Kirkland, Edward C., *The "Railroad Scheme" of Massachusetts*, 5 THE JOURNAL OF ECONOMIC HISTORY 145 (1945)

Kittredge (1899): Kittredge, Frank Edward, THE MAN WITH THE BRANDED HAND, AN AUTHENTIC SKETCH OF THE LIFE AND SERVICES OF CAPT. JONATHAN WALKER (1899)

Knight & Latrobe (1838): Knight, J., and Benj. H. Latrobe, REPORT UPON THE LOCOMOTIVE ENGINES, AND THE POLICE AND MANAGEMENT OF SEVERAL OF THE PRINCIPAL RAIL ROADS IN THE NORTHERN AND MIDDLE STATES, BEING A SEQUEL TO THE REPORT OF THE 8TH OF JANUARY, 1838, UPON RAILWAY STRUCTURES (1838)

Konkle (1933): Burton Alva, *Enos Bronson, 1774-1823*, 57 THE PENNSYLVANIA MAGAZINE OF HISTORY AND BIOGRAPHY 355 (1933)

Kriedman (1965): Kriedman, Herbert, *New York's Philip Hone: Businessman-Politician-Patron of Arts and Letters*, unpublished Ph.D. dissertation, New York University (1965)

## L

L&C Minutes ([date]): Minutes of the board of directors of The Proprietors of Locks and Canals on Merrimac River, available at (a) Directors' Records, 1792-1941, EA-1 Microfilm (DA-2), Baker Library, Harvard Graduate School of Business, Harvard University, Cambridge Massachusetts, and (b) Locks & Canals records, 1747-2008, Book DA-2, LOWE 5058, I Directors' Records, 1813-1955, Lowell National Historical Park, Lowell, Massachusetts

Lamoreaux (1996): Lamoreaux, Naomi R., Insider Lending: Banks, Personal Connections, and Economic Development in New England (1996)

Lamoreaux, Raff & Temin (2003): _____, Daniel M. G. Raff, and Peter Temin, *Beyond Markets and Hierarchies: Toward a New Synthesis of American Business History*, 108 The American Historical Review 404 (2003)

Landon (1956): Landon, George Cooke, *Philip Hone and His New York, 1828-1851*, unpublished M.A. dissertation, University of Wyoming (1956)

Langbein (1993): Langbein, John H., *Chancellor Kent and the History of Legal Literature*, 93 Columbia Law Review 547 (1993)

Lanman (1862): Lanman, Charles, Journal of Alfred Ely, A Prisoner of War in Richmond (1862)

Larson (1935): Larson, Henrietta M., *William Sturgis, Merchant and Investor*, 9 Bulletin of the Historical Society 76 (1935)

Larson (1936): _____, Jay Cooke, Private Banker (1936)

Larson (2001): Larson, John Lauritz, Internal Improvement: National Public Works and the Promise of Popular Government in the Early United States (2001)

Latner (1977): Latner, Richard, *The Eaton Affair Reconsidered*, 36 Tennessee Historical Quarterly 332 (1977)

Latrobe Letter (1840): Letter of Jno. H. B. Latrobe, President of the Maryland State Colonization Society, February 17, 1840, to Charles Howard, William R. Stuart, and Franklin Anderson, regarding interrogatories from the Committee on Colored Population of the House of Delegates of the State of Maryland, in *Report of the Committee on Colored Population, February 25, 1840*, in Documents of the House of Delegates, Legislature of Maryland, December Session Eighteen Hundred and Thirty-Nine, February 26, 1840, Document Z (1840)

Lathrop (1937): Lathrop, Elise, Early American Inns and Taverns, New Edition (1937)

Lauer (2008): Lauer, Josh, *From Rumor to Record: Credit Reporting and the Invention of Financial Identity in Nineteenth-Century America*, 49 Technology and Culture 301(2008)

Law Reporter (1843): *Obituary Notices*, 5 Law Reporter (May 1842 – April 1843, inclusive)

LC (1916): *Celebration of Christ Church, Pensacola, Fla.*, The Living Church 468 (February 3, 1917)

Legal Opinion (1871): *Fraudulent Negotiation: The Daughter of Commodore Bainbridge in Court*, 1 Legal Opinion, Real Estate and Insurance Bulletin 95 (April 15, 1871)

*Lehigh C&N v. Field* (1844): *Lehigh Coal and Navigation Company v. Field*, 8 Watts & Serg. 232, 1844 WL 5107, 1844 Pa. LEXIS 181 (1844)

Linton (1893): Linton, W. J., Life of John Greenleaf Whittier (1893)

Lepler (2013): Lepler, Jessica M., The Many Panics of 1837: People, Politics, and the Creation of a Transatlantic Financial Crisis (2013)

Lepore (2018): Lepore, Jill, These Truths: A History of the United States (2018)

Lindsey (1996): Lindsey, Jack L. *The Cadwalader Family during the Early Nineteenth Century*, 91 Philadelphia Museum of Art Bulletin 384 (1996)

Lippincott (1914): Lippincott, Isaac, *A History of River Improvement*, 22 The Journal of Political Economy 630 (1914)

London Bond Agreement: Bank of Pensacola, Florida, Six Percent. Stock, a copy of which is set forth in Figure 24, with the text set forth in Figure 25

Long (1883): Long, Ellen Call, FLORIDA BREEZES; OR, FLORIDA, OLD AND NEW (1883; facsimile reproduction of 1962)

Longworth's Almanac (1834): LONGWORTH'S AMERICAN ALMANAC, NEW-YORK REGISTER, AND CITY DIRECTORY FOR THE FIFTY-NINTH YEAR OF AMERICAN INDEPENDENCE (1834)

Loring (1864): Loring, Charles G., *Memoir of the Hon. William Sturgis*, 7 PROCEEDINGS OF THE MASSACHUSETTS HISTORICAL SOCIETY 420 (1864)

Loring's Register (1840): THE MASSACHUSETTS REGISTER, AND UNITED STATES CALENDAR, FOR 1840 (1840)

Loring's Register (1847): LORING'S MASSACHUSETTS REGISTER OR RECORD BOOK OF VALUABLE INFORMATION FOR THE YEAR 1847 (1847)

Louisiana Landholders (1988): *Large Landholders of Rapides Parish, 1850*, 29 LOUISIANA HISTORY: THE JOURNAL OF THE LOUISIANA HISTORICAL ASSOCIATION 388 (1988)

*Lowell v. L&C* (1843): *Lowell v. Proprietors of Locks & Canals*, 48 Mass. 1, 7 Met. 1, 1843 Mass. LEXIS 103 (1843)

Lowell (1848): Lowell, John Amory, *The Late Patrick Tracy Jackson*, 18 THE MERCHANT'S MAGAZINE 355 (1848)

Lowell City Documents (1846): THE CHARTER WITH ITS AMENDMENTS, AND THE REVISED ORDINANCES OF THE CITY OF LOWELL, TOGETHER WITH SUNDRY LAWS OF THE COMMONWEALTH (1846)

Lowenthal (1997): Lowenthal, Larry, FROM THE COALFIELDS TO THE HUDSON: A HISTORY OF THE DELAWARE & HUDSON CANAL (1997)

LTCB Mortgage (1843): Indenture, dated March 9, 1843, between The Philadelphia and Reading Rail Road Company and Nathan Appleton, William Sturgis, and William McKee, as trustees, HA 1520, Box 1220, Folder 9022

## M

*M'Intyre v. Parks* (1841): *Archibald M'Intyre v. Samuel Parks and another*, 44 Mass. 207, 3 Met. 207, 1841 Mass. LEXIS 111 (1841)

MA DJ (1848): JOURNAL OF THE PROCEEDINGS OF THE FIFTY-EIGHTH ANNUAL CONVENTION OF THE DIOCESE OF MASSACHUSETTS: HOLDEN IN TRINITY CHURCH, BOSTON, WEDNESDAY AND THURSDAY, JUNE 14, 16, 1848 (1848)

MA DJ (1849): JOURNAL OF THE PROCEEDINGS OF THE FIFTY-NINTH ANNUAL CONVENTION OF THE DIOCESE OF MASSACHUSETTS: HOLDEN IN TRINITY CHURCH, BOSTON, WEDNESDAY AND THURSDAY, MAY 16, 17, 1849 (1849)

MA DJ (1850): JOURNAL OF THE PROCEEDINGS OF THE SIXTIETH ANNUAL CONVENTION OF THE DIOCESE OF MASSACHUSETTS: HOLDEN IN TRINITY CHURCH, BOSTON, WEDNESDAY AND THURSDAY, MAY 15, 16, 1850 (1850)

MA DJ (1851): JOURNAL OF THE PROCEEDINGS OF THE SIXTY-FIRST ANNUAL CONVENTION OF THE DIOCESE OF MASSACHUSETTS: HOLDEN IN TRINITY CHURCH, BOSTON, WEDNESDAY AND THURSDAY, MAY 20, 21, 1851 (1851)

MA DJ (1852): JOURNAL OF THE PROCEEDINGS OF THE SIXTY-SECOND ANNUAL CONVENTION OF THE DIOCESE OF MASSACHUSETTS: HOLDEN IN TRINITY CHURCH, BOSTON, WEDNESDAY AND THURSDAY, MAY 19, 20, 1852 (1852)

MA Law (1792) Ch. XVI: Chapter XVI, An Act Incorporating Dudley Atkins Tyng, Esq. and Others, for the Purpose of Rendering Merrimack-River Passable with Boats, Rafts and Masts, from the Divisional Line of New-Hampshire and Massachusetts, to the Tide Waters of said River, by the Name of the Proprietors of the Locks and Canals on Merrimack-River, dated May 30, 1792

MA Law (1813) Ch. XCII: Chapter XCII, An Act to incorporate The Boston Manufacturing Company, approved February 23, 1813

MA Law (1820) Ch. XCIX: Chapter XCIX, Resolve on the petition of Benjamin R. Nichols, approved February 9th, 1820

MA Law (1822) Ch. C: Chapter C, An Act to incorporate the President, Directors and Company of the City Bank, approved February 23, 1822

MA Law (1822) Ch. XLVI: Chapter XLVI, An Act to incorporate Merrimack Manufacturing Company, approved February 6, 1822

MA Law (1825) Ch. XLVII: Chapter XLVII, An Act Relating to the Locks and Canals on Merrimack River, approved January 27, 1825

MA Law (1830) Ch. IV: Chapter IV, An Act to establish the Boston and Lowell Rail Road Corporation, approved June 5, 1830

MA Law (1831) Ch. LVI: Chapter LVI, An Act to incorporate the Boston and Providence Rail-Road Corporation, adopted June 21, 1831 and approved June 22, 1831

MA Law (1833) Ch. XXV: Chapter XXV, An Act to incorporate the Lycoming Coal Company, approved February 11, 1833

MA Law (1833) Ch. CXVI: Chapter CXVI, An Act to establish the Western Rail Road Corporation, passed March 8 and approved by the governor on March 15, 1833

MA Law (1833) Ch. LXXXVI: Chapter LXXXVI, An Act to incorporate the Boston Copper Mining Company, approved March 9, 1833

MA Law (1836) Ch. CXXVIII: Chapter CXXVIII, An Act to establish the City of Lowell

MA R&C Report (1838): *Massachusetts Report of the Committee on Railways and Canals, On An Order Relative to the Public Use of Railroads, Accepted by the Senate, April 15, 1837* (1838)

Macesich (1960): Macesich, George, *Sources of Monetary Disturbances in the United States, 1834-1845*, 20 THE JOURNAL OF ECONOMIC HISTORY 407 (1960)

Madison (1974): Madison, James H., *The Evolution of Commercial Credit Reporting Agencies in Nineteenth-Century America*, 48 THE BUSINESS HISTORY REVIEW 164 (1974)

Maggor (2017): Maggor (2017): Maggor, Noam, BRAHMIN CAPITALISM: FRONTIERS OF WEALTH AND POPULISM IN AMERICA'S FIRST GILDED AGE (2017)

Mahoney (2000): Mahoney, Paul G., *Contract or Concession? An Essay on the History of Corporate Law*, 34 GEORGIA LAW REVIEW 873 (2000)

Mail Indenture (1849): Indenture, dated February 6, 1849, between Edward K. Collins, James Brown, Elisha Riggs, Williams S. Wetmore, and Stewart Brown, of the first part, Prosper M. Wetmore, of the second part, and the United States of America, by John Y. Mason, Secretary of the Navy, of the third part, in EXECUTIVE DOCUMENTS PRINTED BY ORDER OF THE SENATE OF THE UNITED STATES DURING THE FIRST SESSION OF THE THIRTY-SECOND CONGRESS, 1851-52, VOLUME III, at 50 (there are numerous other similar indentures involving Wetmore in this volume)

Mail Route Petition (1837): *Petition to Congress by Citizens of Pensacola*, NA:HF, 24 Cong. 2 sess: DS, THE TERRITORIAL PAPERS OF THE UNITED STATES, VOLUME XXV, THE TERRITORY OF FLORIDA 1834-1839 (1960), at 364

Malone (2009): Malone, Patrick M., WATERPOWER IN LOWELL: ENGINEERING AND INDUSTRY IN NINETEENTH CENTURY AMERICA (2009)

Malone & Parrott (1998): \_\_\_\_\_, and Charles A. Parrott, *Greenways in the Industrial City: Parks and Promenades along the Lowell Canals*, 24 IA. THE JOURNAL OF THE SOCIETY FOR INDUSTRIAL ARCHEOLOGY 19 (1998)

Manders & Rentfro (2011): Manders, Damon, and Brian Rentfro, ENGINEERS FAR FROM ORDINARY: THE U.S. ARMY CORPS OF ENGINEERS IN ST. LOUIS (September 1, 2011)

Marszalek (1996): Marszalek, John F., *The Eaton Affair: Society and Politics*, 55 TENNESSEE HISTORICAL QUARTERLY 6 (1996)

Martin (1943): Martin, Sidney Walter, *Richard Keith Call, Florida Territorial Leader*, 21 THE FLORIDA HISTORICAL QUARTERLY 332 (1943)

Martin & Sinclair (1974): Martin, Kenneth R., and Bruce Sinclair, *A Pennsylvanian in the Wilmington Whaling Trade, 1841-1844*, 41 PENNSYLVANIA HISTORY: A JOURNAL OF MID-ATLANTIC STUDIES 27 (1974)

Mason (1879): Mason, George C., THE LIFE AND WORKS OF GILBERT STUART (1879)

Maxwell (1870): Maxwell, Sidney D., THE SUBURBS OF CINCINNATI: SKETCHES HISTORICAL AND DESCRIPTIVE (1870; reprinted in 1974)

McCracken (1959): McCracken, Harold, GEORGE CATLIN AND THE OLD FRONTIER (1959)

McFaul (1972): McFaul, John M., THE POLITICS OF JACKSONIAN FINANCE (1972)

McFarland (1953): McFarland, Daniel Miles, *North Carolina Newspapers, Editors and Journalistic Politics, 1815-1835*, 30 THE NORTH CAROLINA HISTORICAL REVIEW 376 (1953)

McGrane (1933): McGrane, Reginald C., *Some Aspects of American State Debts in the Forties*, 38 THE AMERICAN HISTORICAL REVIEW 673 (1933)

McGrane (1935): \_\_\_\_\_, FOREIGN BONDHOLDERS AND AMERICAN STATE DEBTS (1935)

McGrane (1965): \_\_\_\_\_, THE PANIC OF 1837: SOME FINANCIAL PROBLEMS OF THE JACKSONIAN ERA (1965)

*McGuire v. Blount* (1905): *McGuire v. Blount*, 199 U.S. 142, 26 S. Ct. 1, 50 L. Ed. 125, 1905 U.S. LEXIS 1040 (1905)

*McGuire v. Blount* (1903): *McGuire et al. v. Blount et al.*, 121 F. 1020, 56 C.C.A. 682, 1903 U.S. App. LEXIS 4723 (5th Cir. 1903)

*McGuire v. Blount* Certiorari (1903): Petition For a Writ of Certiorari, filed with the U.S. Supreme Court on October 28, 1903 in McGuire v. Blount (1903)

*McGuire v. Blount* Plaintiff Brief (1903): Brief for Plaintiffs in Error, to the U.S. Supreme Court, in McGuire v. Blount (1903)

McHenry (1863): McHenry, George, COTTON TRADE: ITS BEARING UPON THE PROSPERITY OF GREAT BRITAIN AND COMMERCE OF THE AMERICAN REPUBLICS: CONSIDERED IN CONNECTION WITH THE SYSTEM OF NEGRO SLAVERY IN THE CONFEDERATE STATES (1863)

McMillen (2022-1): McMillen, Michael J.T., TRACKS OF THE MOHEGAN: A SECOND ENGINE MYSTERY (2021)

McMillen (2022-2): \_\_\_\_\_, The History of Equipment Finance, Volume 1, 1832-1833: Literature, Law, Coal in the Time of Cholera (2022)

McMillen (2022-3): \_\_\_\_\_, The History of Equipment Finance, Volume 2, 1839-1840: Locks & Canals and Baltimore & Susquehanna (2022)

McMillen (2022-4): \_\_\_\_\_, The History of Equipment Finance, Volume 3, 1841-1849: Locks & Canals and Philadelphia & Reading (2022)

McMillen (2022-5): \_\_\_\_\_, The History of Equipment Finance, Volume 4, 1845-1897: Boat Loans, Philadelphia Car & Equipment Trusts, Central of New Jersey (2022)

MD Archives (JIC): *Jacob I. Cohen, Jr. (1789-1869),* Archives of Maryland (Biographical Series), available at

https://msa.maryland.gov/megafile/msa/speccol/sc3520/013400/013489/html/13489bio.html

MD Law (1835) Ch. 328: Chapter 328, An act to Incorporate the George's Creek Mining Company

MD Law (1836) Ch. 382: Chapter 382, A supplement to an act to Incorporate the George's Creek Mining Company, passed June 1, 1836

Merchants' Magazine (1844, May): *The Commerce of Boston,* 10 The Merchants' Magazine, and Commercial Review 421 (May 1844)

Merchants' Magazine (1849, June): *Life Saving Benevolent Association,* 20 The Merchants' Magazine and Commercial Review 674 (June 1849)

Merchants' Magazine (1854, August): 31 Hunt's Merchants' Magazine 145 (August 1854)

Merchants' Magazine (1865, March): *Hon. William Sturgis, of Boston,* 52 The Merchants' Magazine and Commercial Review 169 (March 1865)

Meredith (1934): Meredith, L. Douglas, *The Early Development of Financial Merchandising,* 3 American Marketing Journal 155 (1934)

Merrill (1946): Merrill, Louis Taylor, *Mill Town on the Merrimack,* 19 The New England Quarterly 19 (1946)

MES AR (1837): *First Annual Report of the Morrison Education Society, Read 27th September, 1837* (1837)

MES AR (1842): *Fourth Annual Report of the Morrison Education Society, Read September 28th, 1842* (1842)

MHS (1880): *Notice of Benjamin R. Nichols,* 2 Proceedings of the Massachusetts Historical Society, 1835-1855 427 (1880)

Miles (1845): Miles, Henry A., Lowell, As It Was, And As It Is (1845)

Minnigerode (1927): Minnigerode, Meade, Certain Rich Men: Stephen Girard—John Jacob Astor—Jay Cooke—Daniel Drew—Cornelius Vanderbilt—Jay Gould—Jim Fisk (1927)

Minority Report (1832): *Reports of The Minority of the Committee, and of Mr. Adams, (One of the Members of the Committee,) Appointed to Examine the Books and Proceedings of the Bank of the United States* (1832)

Monroe (1992): Monroe, Elizabeth Brand, The Wheeling Bridge Case: Its Significance in American Law and Technology (1992)

MONY (2021): *The Mutual Life Insurance Company Of New York,* Encyclopedia.com, https://www.encyclopedia.com/books/politics-and-business-magazines/mutual-life-insurance-company-new-york (last visited January 13, 2022)

*Moody v. Fiske* (1820): *Moody v. Fiske*, 17 F. Cas. 655, 2 Mason 112, 1 Robb. Pat. Cas. 312, 1820 U.S. App. LEXIS 241 (1820)

Morison (1920): Morison, Samuel Eliot, *Boston Traders in the Hawaiian Islands, 1789-1823*, 54 PROCEEDINGS OF THE MASSACHUSETTS HISTORICAL SOCIETY 9 (October 1920)

Morley (2016): Morley, John, *The Common Law Corporation: The Power of the Trust in Anglo-American Business History*, 116 COLUMBIA LAW REVIEW 2145 (2016)

Morris (2012): Morris, Charles A., THE DAWN OF INNOVATION: THE FIRST AMERICAN INDUSTRIAL REVOLUTION (2012)

Morris & Maguire (1980): Morris, Allen, and Amelia Rea Maguire, *The Unicameral Legislature in Florida*, 58 THE FLORIDA HISTORICAL QUARTERLY 303 (1980)

Moshein & Rothfus (1992): Moshein, Peter, and Robert R. Rothfus, *Rogers Locomotives: A Brief History and Construction List*, 167 RAILROAD HISTORY 12 (1992)

Mott (1900): Mott, Edward Harold, BETWEEN THE OCEAN AND THE LAKES: THE STORY OF ERIE (1900)

Moulton (1914): Moulton, Harold G., WATERWAYS VERSUS RAILWAYS (1914; publication of a 1912 Ph.D. dissertation)

Mount – Suffolk Museum (1968): The Suffolk Museum at Stony Brook, Long Island, WILLIAM SIDNEY MOUNT, 1807-1868 (1968)

Muirheid (1909): Muirheid, Walter G., ed., JERSEY CITY OF TODAY: ITS HISTORY, PEOPLE, TRADES, COMMERCE, INSTITUTIONS & INDUSTRIES (1909)

## N

NC Comm. Rep. (1849): *Report of a Committee to the Norfolk County Railroad Company, June 25, 1849*

Neal Report (1849): Neal, David A., *Report to the Managers of the Philadelphia and Reading Rail Road Company* (September 19, 1849), included as an appendix to the P&R AR (1849)

New Orleans Ship Register (1942): *The Survey of Federal Archives in Louisiana, Division of Community Service Programs, Work Projects Administration*, SHIP REGISTERS AND ENROLLMENTS OF NEW ORLEANS, LOUISIANA, VOLUME II, 1821-1830 (1942)

New Yorker (1838): *New Banks*, 5 THE NEW YORKER 298 (July 28, 1838)

Niles' Register (1832, September 15): *Bank of the U. S.*, 43 NILE'S NATIONAL REGISTER 40 (September 15, 1832)

Niles' Register (1836, June 11): 50 NILES' WEEKLY REGISTER 251 (June 11, 1836)

Niles' Register (1838, July 14): 54 NILES' NATIONAL REGISTER 205 (July 14, 1838)

Niles' Register (1841, January 16): *Bank of the United States*, 59 NILE'S NATIONAL REGISTER 308 (January 16, 1841), at 310

NJ AG Report (1845): *Attorney General's Report, January 1, 1845*, Document No. 1, Documents Accompanying The Governor's Message, Submitted January 15th, 1845, in JOURNAL OF THE PROCEEDINGS OF THE FIRST SENATE OF THE STATE OF NEW JERSEY, CONVENED AT TRENTON ON THE FOURTEENTH DAY OF JANUARY, A. D. ONE THOUSAND EIGHT HUNDRED AND FORTY-FIVE, BEING THE SIXTY-NINTH SESSION (1845)

NJCU (undated): New Jersey City University, *Dudley S. Gregory*, NJCU JERSEY CITY PAST AND PRESENT, available athttps://njcu.libguides.com/gregory

Nolte (1854): Nolte, Vincent, Fifty Years in Both Hemispheres or, Reminiscences of the Life of a Former Merchant (1854)

North (1961): North, Douglas C., The Economic Growth of the United States, 1790-1860 (1961)

Northern AR (1855): *Report of the Directors of the Northern Rail Road Company from Ogdensburgh to Rouse's Point, New York, Submitted to the Stockholders July 25, 1855* (1855)

Northern Central AR (1857): *Second Annual Report of the President and Directors to the Stockholders of the Northern Central Railway Company* (1857)

NY Herald (1857, September 22): *Died - Gregory*, 22 (Issue 263) The New York Herald 5 (September 22, 1857)

NY Commercial Information (1823): Commercial Information Relative to the State of New York (1823)

NY Law (1842) Ch. 217: Chapter 217, An Act to incorporate Atlantic Mutual Insurance Company in the city of New-York, passed April 11, 1842

NY Law (1846) Ch. 145: Chapter 145, An Act to incorporate the Ocean Steam Navigation Company, May 8, 1846

NY Observer (1865, March 9): *S. V. S. Wilder, Esq.*, 43 New York Observer and Chronicle 2 (March 9, 1865)

NY RRC AR (1855): Annual Report of the Railroad Commissioners of the State of New York and of the Reports of the Railroad Corporations, Made to the Board, for the Year Ending September 30, 1855 (1856)

NY Spectator (1835, June 4): *Lowell Rail Road*, 38 New York Spectator 3 (1835, June 4), reprinting a report of June 2 of the Lowell Courier

NY Times (1874, December 9): *Obituary, Dudley S. Gregory*, 24 (No. 7248) The New York Times 4 (December 9, 1874)

NY Times (1874, December 12): *Funeral of the Late Dudley S. Gregory*, 24 (No. 7251) The New York Times 3 (December 12, 1874)

NY Times (1875, January 22): *The Will of Dudley S. Gregory*, 24 (No. 7286) The New York Times 12 (January 22, 1875)

## O

Oberg (1985): Oberg, Barbara, *New York State and the "Specie Crisis" of 1837*, 14 Business and Economic History 37 (1985)

Ohio Statesman (1842, November 23): *Bank of Pensacola*, 6 (Issue 21) The Ohio Statesman 4 (November 23, 1842)

Oickle (2011): Oickle, Alvin F., The Man with the Branded Hand: The Life of Jonathan Walker, Abolitionist (2011)

Osborne (1921): Osborne, Richard B., *Professional Biography of Moncure Robinson*, reprinted in 1 The William and Mary Quarterly 237 (1921)

## P

P&R 1846 Report: *Report of a Committee of Investigation into the Affairs of the Philadelphia and Reading Rail Road Company (March 30, 1846)* (1846)

P&R AR (1849): *Report of the President and Managers of the Philadelphia and Reading Rail Road Company to the Stockholders (January 8, 1849)* (1849)

P&R Ellet Response (March 25, 1845): Norris, Samuel, and Lewis R. Ashurst, *To the Stock and Bond-Holders of The Philadelphia and Reading Railroad Company*, 74 (Issue 1864) THE NORTH AMERICAN AND DAILY ADVERTISER 2 (March 25, 1845)

PA HJ (1851): *Document No. 13, Statement, Showing the several Banks of this Commonwealth, chartered or rechartered since the 1st of January, 1830, that have paid bonuses for their charters; the years when chartered, the authorized capital of each, and the amount of bonuses paid: together with the several permanent loans of the Commonwealth; by whom the same were taken; the rate per cent. Premium of each; and the amount of the several premiums received at the State Treasury since the same time*, JOURNAL OF THE SIXTY FIRST HOUSE OF REPRESENTATIVES OF THE COMMONWEALTH OF PENNSYLVANIA: COMMENCED AT HARRISBURG, TUESDAY THE SEVENTH DAY OF JANUARY, IN THE YEAR OF OUR LORD ONE THOUSAND EIGHT HUNDRED AND FIFTY-ONE, AND OF THE COMMONWEALTH OF THE SEVENTY-FIFTH, VOLUME II 157 (1851)

PA Law (1819) Chap. CLX: Chapter CLX, An Act Supplementary to an act, entitled "An act to incorporate the Union Canal Company of Pennsylvania", approved March 29, 1819

PA Law (1826) Ch. XI: Chapter XI, An Act To authorize the Governor to incorporate a company to make a lock navigation on the East branch of the river Schuylkill, called Little Schuylkill, approved February 20, 1826

PA Law (1826) Ch. CIX: Chapter CIX, A Supplement To the act, entitled "An act to authorize the Governor to incorporate a company to make a lock navigation on the East branch of the river Schuylkill, called Little Schuylkill", approved April 10, 1826

PA Law (1828) No. 47: No. 47, A Supplement To an act, entitled "An act to incorporate the Pennsylvania and Ohio Canal Company", approved February 7, 1828

PA Law (1829) No. 76: No. 76 An Act To authorize the Governor to incorporate the Philadelphia and Reading rail road company

PA Law (1832) No. 229: No. 229, Authorizing the Governor to incorporate the Strasburg rail-road, the Williamsport and Elmira rail-road, the Marietta and Columbia rail-road, the Portsmouth and Lancaster rail-road, and incorporating a company to make the Oxford rail-road, approved June 9, 1832

PA Law (1833) No. 132: No. 132, An Act To incorporate the Lycoming Coal Company, approved April 8, 1833

PA Law (1836) No. 22: No. 22, An Act To repeal the state tax on real and personal property, and to continue and extend the involvements of the state by railroads and canals, and to charter a state bank, to be called the United States Bank, approved February 18, 1836

PA Law (1836) No. 123: No. 123, An Act To incorporate the Lebanon Valley railroad company, approved April 1, 1836

PA Law (1836) No. 198: No. 198, An Act To incorporate the Preston Retreat, and relative to the sale of lands of St. John's church, in Norristown, Montgomery county, and for other purposes, approved June 16, 1836

PA Law (1836) Pamphlet: Act of 18th February, 1836, Pamph. p. 36, An Act to repeal the state tax on real and personal property, and to continue and extend the improvements of the state by rail roads and canals, and to charter a state bank, to be called the United States Bank, Passed February 18, 1836, and Approved February 18, 1836

PA Law (1837) No. 69: No. 69, An Act Supplementary to the act entitle "An act authorizing the Governor to incorporate the Wallenpaupack Improvement company," and for other purposes, approved April 1, 1837

PA Law (1839) No. 159: No. 159, To incorporate the "West Branch" Franklin Rail-Road Company, approved June 24, 1839

PA SJ (1836-1837): *List of Stockholders in the Bald Eagle and Spring Creek Navigation Company, as returned on oath, to the Auditor General, by the President and Treasurer of the Company, the first week of January last, viz:*, and *List of Stockholders in the Union Canal Company of Pennsylvania, the amount of stock held by each and their places of residence, as far as is known, on the twenty-first day of March, 1837*, and *List of Names and Residence of the Stockholders in the Danville and Pottsville Rail-road Company, and the number of Shares held by each, on the 25th day of March, 1837* each in JOURNAL OF THE SENATE OF PENNSYLVANIA, SESSION 1836-37, VOLUME II (1836-37), at 459-61, 465-70, and 475-80, respectively

Palmer (1837): Palmer, J. Horsley, THE CAUSES AND CONSEQUENCES OF THE PRESSURE UPON THE MONEY MARKET; WITH A STATEMENT OF THE ACTION OF THE BANK OF ENGLAND FROM 1$^{ST}$ OCTOBER, 1833, TO THE 27$^{TH}$ DECEMBER, 1836 (1837)

Patent List (1874): LIST OF PATENTS FOR INVENTIONS AND DESIGNS, ISSUED BY THE UNITED STATES, FROM 1790 TO 1847, WITH THE PATENT LAWS AND NOTES OF DECISIONS OF THE COURTS OF THE UNITED STATES FOR THE SAME PERIOD (1847)

Patrick (1979): Patrick, James, *The Architecture of Adolphus Heiman: Part I: Castellated and Grecian, 1837-1853*, 38 TENNESSEE HISTORICAL QUARTERLY 167 (1979)

PDR (1842): *Nicholas Biddle, the late president of the United States Bank of Pennsylvania, and other distinguished actors lately attached to that institution, have been presented by the Grand Jury of the count of Philadelphia "for entering into a conspiracy to defraud," etc, as will be seen by the following presentment of the Grand Jury, to which are added a few remarks touching the concern*, 1 THE PEOPLE'S DEMOCRATIC RECORD 86 (1842)

PDS (1836): *Eleventh Annual Report of the Board of Managers of the Prison Discipline Society, Boston, May 1836*, Prison Discipline Society (1836)

*Peabody v. George's Creek C&I* (1913): *Peabody v. George's Creek Coal & Iron Co.*, 120 Md. 659, 87 A. 1097, 1913 Md. LEXIS 156 (1913)

Pearce (1980): Pearce, George F., THE U.S. NAVY IN PENSACOLA: FROM SAILING SHIPS TO NAVAL AVIATION, 1825-1930 (1980)

Pearce (2000): \_\_\_\_\_, PENSACOLA DURING THE CIVIL WAR: A THORN IN THE SIDE OF THE CONFEDERACY (2000)

Penitentiary System Report (1822): *Report on the Penitentiary System in the United States prepared under a resolution of the Society for the Prevention of Pauperism in the City of New York* (1822)

Pennington (1938): Pennington, Edgar Legare, *The Episcopal Church in Florida, 1763-1892*, 7 HISTORICAL MAGAZINE OF THE PROTESTANT EPISCOPAL CHURCH 3 (1938)

Pensacola City Company Indenture (May 13, 1870): Indenture, May 13, 1870, between Samuel Jaudon and Nathaniel Thurston, trustees for the Pensacola City Company (unincorporated joint stock association) and Samuel Jaudon and Nathaniel Thurston, trustees for the Pensacola City Company, Exhibit 32, *McGuire v. Blount* Certiorari (1903)

Pensacola Gazette (1826, April 8): *Laws of Florida*, 3 (Issue 6) PENSACOLA GAZETTE 1 (April 8, 1826)

Pensacola Gazette (1833, July 5): *Bank of Pensacola*, 9 (Issue 50) PENSACOLA GAZETTE 2 (July 5, 1833)

Pensacola Gazette (1836, January 9): A*t an Election held on the 4th inst. For Directors of the Alabama, Florida, and Georgia Rail Road Company*, 2 (Issue 44) PENSACOLA GAZETTE 2 (January 9, 1836)

Pensacola Gazette (1836, April 9-1): *Married*, 3 (Issue 5) PENSACOLA GAZETTE 2 (April 9, 1836)

Pensacola Gazette (1836, April 9-2): *Notice to Rail Road Contractors*, 3 (Issue 5) PENSACOLA GAZETTE 2 (April 9, 1836)

Pensacola Gazette (1836, May 7): 3 (Issue 9) PENSACOLA GAZETTE 1 (1836, May 7); first column

Pensacola Gazette (1837, April 15): *Notice to Labourers & Slave Holders*, 4 (Issue 6) PENSACOLA GAZETTE 4 (April 15, 1837)

Pensacola Gazette (1837, April 22): *Notice to Labourers & Slave Holders*, 4 (Issue 7) PENSACOLA GAZETTE 4 (April 22, 1837)

Pensacola Gazette (1837, May 6): *Notice to Labourers & Slave Holders*, 4 (Issue 9) PENSACOLA GAZETTE 4 (May 6, 1837)

Pensacola Gazette (1837, May 13): *Notice to Labourers & Slave Holders*, 4 (Issue 10) PENSACOLA GAZETTE 4 (May 13, 1837)

Pensacola Gazette (1837, May 20): *Notice to Labourers & Slave Holders*, 4 (Issue 11) PENSACOLA GAZETTE 4 (May 20, 1837)

Pensacola Gazette (1837, May 27): *Notice to Labourers & Slave Holders*, 4 (Issue 12) PENSACOLA GAZETTE 4 (May 27, 1837)

Pensacola Gazette (1837, July 8): *Semi-Annual Statement No. 3, July 1, 1837, Bank of Pensacola in Acct with Sundries*, 4 (Issue 18) PENSACOLA GAZETTE 3 (July 8, 1837)

Pensacola Gazette (1838, February 17): *Notice*, 4, (Issue 56) PENSACOLA GAZETTE 1 (February 17, 1838)

Pensacola Gazette (1839, November 23): *Married*, 6 (Issue 34) PENSACOLA GAZETTE 3 (November 23, 1839)

Pensacola Gazette (1842, March 5): *District of West Florida*, 8 (Issue 49) PENSACOLA GAZETTE 3 (March 5, 1842)

Pensacola Gazette (1844, December 7): *At a meeting of the citizens of Pensacola, called for the purpose of reviving the project of the Alabama, Georgia and Florida Rail Road*, 11 (Issue 36) PENSACOLA GAZETTE 2 (December 7, 1844)

Pensacola Gazette (1849, October 20): *Rail-Road Meeting*, 16 (Issue 30) PENSACOLA GAZETTE 2 (October 20, 1849)

Pensacola RR AR (1836): *Semi-Annual Report of the Directors of the Alabama, Florida & Georgia Rail Company* (July 1, 1836)

Perkins (1931): Perkins, D. W., *Chapter VI—Panic of 1837-39* and *Chapter VII—Panic of 1841*, WALL STREET PANICS 1813-1930 (1931), at 33-40 and 41-6, respectively

Persey (1990): Persey, Edward Jay, *Lowell and the Industrial City in Nineteenth-Century America*, 5 OAH MAGAZINE OF HISTORY 5 (1990)

Pettengill & Simmons (1952): Pettengill, George W., Jr. and B. F. Simmons, *The Story of the Florida Railroads 1834-1903*, 86 THE RAILWAY AND LOCOMOTIVE HISTORICAL SOCIETY BULLETIN 1 (1952)

Philadelphia (1824): PHILADELPHIA IN 1824; OR, A BRIEF ACCOUNT OF THE INSTITUTIONS AND PUBLIC OBJECTS IN THIS METROPOLIS: BEING A COMPLETE GUIDE FOR STRANGERS, AND AN USEFUL COMPENDIUM FOR THE INHABITANTS (1824)

Pine (1921): John B., THE STORY OF GRAMERCY PARK 1831-1921 (1921)

Pollack (1931): Pollack, Queena, PEGGY EATON, DEMOCRACY'S MISTRESS (1931)

Poor (1860): Poor, Henry V., HISTORY OF THE RAILROADS AND CANALS OF THE UNITED STATES OF AMERICA (1860), three volumes

Porter (1937): Porter, Kenneth Wiggins, THE JACKSONS AND THE LEES: TWO GENERATIONS OF MASSACHUSETTS MERCHANTS 1765-1844 (1937)

PR-BW Engines Contract (1844): Articles of Agreement, dated February 21, 1844, between The Philadelphia and Reading Rail Road Company and Baldwin and Whitney, in Hagley Archives, Accession 1520, Box 1220, Folder 9028

PR-BW Engines Contract (1845): Articles of Agreement, dated January 3, 1845, between The Philadelphia and Reading Rail Road Company and Baldwin and Whitney, in Hagley Archives, Accession 1520, Box 1220, Folder 9028

PR-BW Engines Contract (1846): Articles of Agreement, dated March 21, 1846, The Philadelphia and Reading Rail Road Company and Matthias W. Baldwin, in Hagley Archives, Accession 1520, Box 1220, Folder 9028

Priest (1973): Priest, George L., *Law and Economic Distress: Sangamon County, Illinois, 1837-1844*, 2 THE JOURNAL OF LEGAL STUDIES 469 (1973)

Prince & Taylor (1982): Prince, Carl E., and Seth Taylor, *Daniel Webster, the Boston Associates, and the U. S. Government's Role in the Industrializing Process, 1815-1830*, 2 JOURNAL OF THE EARLY REPUBLIC 283 (1982)

PRR Petition (1835): *Petition to Congress by the Alabama, Georgia, and Florida Railroad Company*, NA:HF, 23 Cong., 2 sess.: DS, January 5, 1835

PSA (1844): *Sixteenth Anniversary of the American Peace Society*, 5 THE ADVOCATE OF PEACE 210 (1844)

PSA (1871): *How a Single Person, Perhaps, Prevented War Between Two Great Nations*, 3 ADVOCATE OF PEACE (1847-1884) 91 (1871)

PSAH (1907): *History of the American Peace Society and Its Work*, 69 THE ADVOCATE OF PEACE 15 (1907)

PSAM (1837): *Annual Meeting of the American Peace Society*, 1 THE ADVOCATE OF PEACE 17 (1837)

PSS AR (1830): *Twenty-fifth Annual Report of the Trustees of the Public School Society of New-York* (1830)

# R

R&B AR (1853): *Annual Report of the Rutland and Burlington Railroad [stet] Corporation for the fiscal Year Ending May 31, 1853* (1853)

R&B AR (1854): *Seventh Annual Report of the Directors of the Rutland and Burlington Railroad Company, Submitted to the Stockholders, Sept. 20, 1854*

Railway Superintendents (1850): REPORTS AND OTHER PAPERS OF THE NEW ENGLAND ASSOCIATION OF RAILROAD SUPERINTENDENTS, FROM THE COMMENCEMENT OF THE SOCIETY TO JANUARY 1ST, 1850 (1850)

Railway Superintendents (1910): RECORDS OF THE NEW ENGLAND ASSOCIATION OF RAILWAY SUPERINTENDENTS: ORGANIZED IN BOSTON, MASSACHUSETTS APRIL 5, 1848, DISSOLVED, OCTOBER 1, 1857 (1910)

Railway Times (1861, February 23): *The Erie Railway Company*, 13 RAILWAY TIMES 72 (February 23, 1861)

Raitz (1996): Raitz, Karl, ed., THE NATIONAL ROAD (1996)

Randolph (1931): Randolph, Bessie C., *Foreign Bondholders and the Repudiated Debts of the Southern States*, 25 THE AMERICAN JOURNAL OF INTERNATIONAL LAW 63 (1931)

Ratchford (1941): Ratchford, B. U., AMERICAN STATE DEBTS (1941)

Rawle (1885): Rawle, Francis, *Car Trust Securities*, REPORT OF THE EIGHTH ANNUAL MEETING OF THE AMERICAN BAR ASSOCIATION (1885)

Redlich (1968): Redlich, Fritz, THE MOLDING OF AMERICAN BANKING: MEN AND IDEAS (1968 reprint of 1947 publication as revised in 1951)

Reese (1917): Reese, J. H., FLORIDA FLASHLIGHTS: A THOUSAND AND ONE FACTS CONCERNING THE HISTORY, DEVELOPMENT, RESOURCES AND POSSIBILITIES OF THE GREAT PENINSULA STATE (1917)

Register of Officers (1833): REGISTER OF ALL OFFICERS AND AGENTS, CIVIL, MILITARY, AND NAVAL IN THE SERVICE OF THE UNITED STATES (1833)

Reiger (1968): Reiger, John F., *Secession of Florida from the Union: A Minority Decision?*, 46 THE FLORIDA HISTORICAL QUARTERLY 358 (1968)

Remini (1981): Remini, Robert, ANDREW JACKSON AND THE COURSE OF AMERICAN FREEDOM, 1822-1832, VOLUME II (1981)

Repudiation (1842, April 9): *Repudiation*, 1 WEEKLY GLOBE 288 (April 9, 1842), quoting the NEW YORK AMERICAN.

Rezneck (1935): Rezneck, Samuel, *The Social History of an American Depression*, 40 THE AMERICAN HISTORICAL REVIEW 662 (1935)

RF&P AR (1865): *Richmond, Fredericksburg and Potomac Railroad*, 38 AMERICAN RAILROAD JOURNAL 1143 (December 2, 1865)

RF&P AR (1872): *Richmond, Fredericksburg and Potomac Railroad*, 44 AMERICAN RAILROAD JOURNAL 990 (1872)

Rich (1975): Rich, Robert Stanley, *Politics and Pedigrees: The Wealthy Men of Boston, 1798-1852*, unpublished Ph.D. dissertation, University of California, Los Angeles (1975)

Richardson (1900): Richardson, James D., ed., A COMPILATION OF THE MESSAGES AND PAPERS OF THE PRESIDENTS 1789-1897 (1900)

Riley-Taylor (2013): Riley-Taylor, Zena S., *Losing Home: Why Rural Northwest Florida Needs to Be Saved*, unpublished M.A. thesis at Florida State University (2013)

Rippy (1935): Rippy, J. Fred, JOEL R. POINSETT: VERSATILE AMERICAN (1935)

Roberts (1897): Roberts, James A., A CENTURY IN THE COMPTROLLER'S OFFICE, STATE OF NEW YORK (1897)

Roberts (2013): Roberts, Alasdair, AMERICA'S FIRST GREAT DEPRESSION: ECONOMIC CRISIS AND POLITICAL DISORDER AFTER THE PANIC OF 1837 (2013)

*Rockwell v. Wilder* (1842): *Rockwell v. Wilder*, 45 Mass. 556, 4 Met. 556, 1842 Mass. LEXIS 182 (1842), 1843 WL 4088

Roe (1901-1902): Roe, Alfred S., *The Governors of Massachusetts*, 25 THE NEW ENGLAND MAGAZINE 523 (1901-1902)

Roe & Lytle (1941): Roe, Joseph W., and Charles W. Lytle, FACTORY EQUIPMENT (second edition, 1941)

Roehm (1966): Roehm, Marjorie Catlin, THE LETTERS OF GEORGE CATLIN AND HIS FAMILY: A CHRONICLE OF THE AMERICAN WEST (1966)

Rolling Stock Contracts: the Running Gear Contract and the Engines Contract

Ross (1906): Ross, A. Franklin, THE HISTORY OF LOTTERIES IN NEW YORK (1906?)

Rousseau (2002): Rousseau, Peter L., *Jacksonian Monetary Policy, Specie Flows, and the Panic of 1837*, 62 THE JOURNAL OF ECONOMIC HISTORY 457 (2002)

Rubin (1961): Rubin, *Julius, Canal or Railroad? Imitation and Innovation in Response to the Erie Canal in Philadelphia, Baltimore, and Boston*, 51 TRANSACTIONS OF THE AMERICAN PHILOSOPHICAL SOCIETY 1 (1961)

Rucker (1991): Rucker, Brian R., *West Florida's Creek Indian Crisis of 1837*, 69 THE FLORIDA HISTORICAL QUARTERLY 315 (1991)

Running Gear Contract: Agreement, dated March 3, 1842, between the Philadelphia and Reading Rail Road Company and The Proprietors of Locks and Canals on Merrimack River, HA 1520, Box 1220, Folder 9022

*Russell v. Wetmore* (1845): *Charles H. Russell et al. v. William S. Wetmore*, Superior Court, in Samuel Owen, ed., THE NEW YORK LEGAL OBSERVER, CONTAINING REPORTS OF CASES DECIDED IN THE COURTS OF EQUITY AND COMMON LAW, AND IMPORTANT DECISIONS IN THE ENGLISH COURTS VOLUME III (1845), at 318-26

## S

SA (1888): *Our First Imported Locomotive*, 59 SCIENTIFIC AMERICAN 153 (September 8, 1888)

Sackett (1895): Sackett, William Edgar, MODERN BATTLES OF TRENTON, BEING A HISTORY OF NEW JERSEY'S POLITICS AND LEGISLATION FROM THE YEAR 1868 TO THE YEAR 1894 (1895)

Sagle (1947): Sagle, Lawrence W., *Ross Winans*, 70 THE RAILWAY AND LOCOMOTIVE HISTORICAL SOCIETY BULLETIN 7 (1947)

Sagle (1972): _____, *America's Oldest Railroad Shops – Mt. Clare*, 127 RAILROAD HISTORY 22 (1972)

Sanford (1911): Sanford, Carlton E., THOMAS SANFORD, EMIGRANT TO NEW ENGLAND: ANCESTRY, LIFE AND DESCENDANTS 1632-4 (1911)

Sanford (1924): Sanford, R. H., *A Pioneer Locomotive Builder*, 8 RAILWAY AND LOCOMOTIVE HISTORICAL SOCIETY BULLETIN 7 (1924)

SB AR (1849): *Sixth Annual Report of the Stoughton Branch Railroad Corporation*, in Senate of the Commonwealth of Massachusetts, ANNUAL REPORTS OF THE RAILROAD CORPORATIONS IN THE STATE OF MASSACHUSETTS (1849), at 200

Schakenbach (2011): Schakenbach, Lindsay, *From Discontented Bostonians to Patriotic Industrialists: The Boston Associates and the Transcontinental Treaty, 1790-1825*, 84 THE NEW ENGLAND QUARTERLY 377 (2011)

Scharf & Westcott II (1884): Scharf, J. Thomas, and Thompson Westcott, HISTORY OF PHILADELPHIA: 1609-1884, VOLUME II (1884)

Scharf & Westcott III (1884): _____ and _____, HISTORY OF PHILADELPHIA: 1609-1884, VOLUME III (1884)

Scheiber (1963): Scheiber, Harry N., *Some Documents on Jackson's Bank War*, 30 PENNSYLVANIA HISTORY: A JOURNAL OF MID-ATLANTIC STUDIES 46 (1963)

Schene (1975): Schene, Michael G., *Robert and John Grattan Gamble: Middle Florida Entrepreneurs*, 54 THE FLORIDA HISTORICAL QUARTERLY 61 (1975)

Scott (1893): Scott, William A., THE REPUDIATION OF STATE DEBTS (1893)

Searight (1894): Searight, Thomas B., THE OLD PIKE: A HISTORY OF THE NATIONAL ROAD WITH INCIDENTS, ACCIDENTS, AND ANECDOTES THEREON (1894)

Select Committee Report (1837): *Report No. 303, Military Academy—West Point, March 1, 1837*, UNITED STATES HOUSE OF REPRESENTATIVES, 24TH CONGRESS, 2D SESSION (1837)

Shallat (2008): Shallat, Todd A., *American Gibraltar: Army Engineers and the Quest for a Scientific Defense of the Nation, 1815-1860*, 66 ARMY HISTORY 4 (2008)

Shaw (1979): Shaw, Robert B., *The Great Schuyler Stock Fraud*, 141 RAILROAD HISTORY 5 (1979)

Shelling (1938): Shelling, Richard I., *Philadelphia and the Agitation in 1825 for the Pennsylvania Canal*, 62 THE PENNSYLVANIA MAGAZINE OF HISTORY AND BIOGRAPHY 175 (1938)

Shlakman (1935): Shlakman, Vera, ECONOMIC HISTORY OF A FACTORY TOWN: A STUDY OF CHICOPEE, MASSACHUSETTS (1935)

Schlesinger (1945): Schlesinger, Arthur M. Jr., THE AGE OF JACKSON (1945)

Silberstein-Loeb (2015): Silberstein-Loeb, Jonathan, *The Transatlantic Origins of the Business Trust*, 36 THE JOURNAL OF LEGAL HISTORY 192 (2000)

Sinclair (1907): Sinclair, Angus, DEVELOPMENT OF THE LOCOMOTIVE ENGINE (1907)

Smiles (1868): Smiles, Samuel, THE LIFE OF GEORGE STEPHENSON AND OF HIS SON ROBERT STEPHENSON; COMPRISING ALSO A HISTORY OF THE INVENTION AND INTRODUCTION OF THE RAILWAY LOCOMOTIVE (1868)

Smith (1899): Smith, John F., ed., OUR COUNTRY AND ITS PEOPLE: DESCRIPTIVE AND BIOGRAPHICAL RECORD OF MADISON COUNTRY, NEW YORK (1899)

Smith (1953): Smith, Walter Buckingham, ECONOMIC ASPECTS OF THE SECOND BANK OF THE UNITED STATES (1953)

Smith (2009): Smith, Mark A., ENGINEERING SECURITY: THE CORPS OF ENGINEERS AND THIRD SYSTEM DEFENSE POLICY, 1815-1861 (2009)

SNC AR (1846): *Report of the President and Managers of the Schuylkill Navigation Company, to the Stockholders. January 5th, 1846* (1846); a selectively redacted copy is available at 11 JOURNAL OF THE FRANKLIN INSTITUTE 157 (1846)

SNC Boat Loan Proposal (1845): Proposal for a loan set forth in SNC Minutes (1845, September 30), at 533-34

SNC Creditors Act (1852): Pennsylvania Session Laws, No. 178, For the protection of the creditors of the Schuylkill Navigation Company (April 7, 1852) (1852)

SNC Minutes ([date of meeting]): Minutes of the Board of Managers of Schuylkill Navigation Company, Pennsylvania State Historical and Museum Commission, Pennsylvania State Archives, Harrisburg, Pennsylvania, referenced by date of meeting; the minutes are stored on microfilm as follows: reel 2297, January 1, 1838 to January 5, 1846; reel 2298, January 6, 1846 to July 1, 1850; and reel 2300, 1850 to 1882

Sodhy (1965): Sodhy, Pamela, *United States Consuls in Singapore 1859-1880*, 56 JOURNAL OF THE MALAYSIAN BRANCH OF THE ROYAL ASIATIC SOCIETY 241 (1965)

*Sortwell v. Hughes* (1852): *Sortwell et al. v. Hughes*, 22 F. Cas. 801, 1 Curt. 244, 1852 U.S. App. LEXIS 353 (1852)

*Southmayd v. McLaughlin* (1873): *Southmayd v. McLaughlin*, 24 N.J. Eq. 181, 9 C. E. Green 181, 1873 N.J. Ch. LEXIS 4, 1873 WL 6843 (1873)

Spencer (1973): Lilly Spencer Martin, 1822-1902: The Joys of Sentiment, Exhibition Catalogue, National Collection of Fine Arts, Smithsonian Institution, June 15-September 3, 1973 (1973)

Sprague (1858): Sprague, William B., A Sermon Addressed to the Second Presbyterian Congregation, Albany, Sunday Afternoon, May 9, 1856, on the Occasion of the Death of the Hon. Archibald McIntyre (1858)

Spring Grove Cemetery (1862): The Cincinnati Cemetery of Spring Grove: Reports, Forms, Etc., Enlarged Edition (1862)

Stalson (1842): Stalson, J. Owen, The Marketing of Life Insurance: Its History in America (1942)

Stanton ((1942): Stanton, J. Owen, Marketing Life Insurance: Its History in America (1942)

Stapleton (1991): Stapleton, Darwin H., *The Transfer of Early Industrial Technologies to America with Especial Reference to the Role of the American Philosophical Society*, 135 Proceedings of the American Philosophical Society 286 (1991)

*State v. Hawthorn* (1835): *State of Missouri v. Jacob Hawthorn*, 9 Mo. 389, 1845 WL 3785, 1845 Mo. LEXIS 104 (S. Ct. Mo. 1845)

*State v. Jersey City* (1871): *The State of New Jersey, Dudley S. Gregory et al. v. Mayor and Alderman of Jersey City*, 34 N.J.L. 429, 5 Vroom 429, 1871 WL 6745, 1871 N.J. Sup. Ct. LEXIS 51 (1871)

*State v. Jersey City* (1873): *The State of New Jersey, Dudley S. Gregory and others v. The Mayor and Alderman of Jersey City*, 36 N.J.L. 166, 7 Vroom 166, 1873 WL 6874, 1873 N.J. Sup. Ct. LEXIS 52 (1873)

*State v. Jersey City* (1880): *The State of New Jersey, Garret E. Winants et al. v. Jersey City and Henry A. Booraem*, 42 N.J.L. 349, 1880 N.J. Sup. Ct. LEXIS 61, 1880 WL 7746 (1880)

*State v. Maury* (1851): *State of Delaware v. John W. Maury, Kendal M. Lewis, Stephen Green, and William Tunnell*, 2 Del. Ch. 141, 1851 WL 1089, 1851 Del. Ch. LEXIS 1 (1851)

*State v. McWilliams* (1879): *State of Missouri v. John McWilliams*, 7 Mo. App. 99, 1879 WL 8064, 1879 Mo. App. LEXIS 54 (1879)

*State v. Miller* (1872): *The State of Missouri v. George Miller*, 50 Mo. 129, 1872 WL 7697, 1872 Mo. LEXIS 237 (S. Ct. Mo. 1872)

*State v. Morrow* (1857): *The State of Missouri v. David I. Morrow*, 26 Mo. 131, 1857 WL 5365, 1857 Mo. LEXIS 26 (S. Ct. Mo. 1857)

*State v. Platt* (1844): *The State of Delaware v. George Platt and The State of Delaware v. James Rogers*, 4 Del. 154, 4 Harr. 154, 1844 WL 541, 1844 Del. LEXIS 16 (1844)

*State ex rel. AG v. Miller* (1876): *The State of Missouri, ex rel. The Attorney General v. George C. Miller*, 1 Mo. App. 48, 1876 WL 9550, 1876 Mo. LEXIS 14 (1876)

*State ex rel. AG v. Miller* (1877): *The State of Missouri, ex rel. The Attorney General v. Miller et al.*, 66 Mo. 328, 1877 WL 8766, 1877 Mo. LEXIS 44 (S. Ct. Mo. 1877)

Sterling (1998): Sterling, Eric, *George Catlin*, in American Travel Writers, 1850-1915, Donald Ross and James Schramer, eds., Dictionary of American Biography 189 (1998), GALE|H1200007776

*Strong v. Taylor* (1842): *Strong v. Taylor*, 2 Hill 326, 1842 N.Y. LEXIS 38 (1842)

*Strong v. Willis* (1850): *Jasper Strong v. George Willis et al.*, 3 Fla. 124, 52 Am. Dec. 364, 1850 WL 1217, 1850 Fla. LEXIS 9 (1850)

Sturgis (1822): Sturgis, William, *Examination of the Russian Claims to the Northwest Coast of America*, 15 NORTH AMERICAN REVIEW 370 (1822)

Sturgis (1845): \_\_\_\_\_, THE OREGON QUESTION: SUBSTANCE OF A LECTURE BEFORE THE MERCANTILE LIBRARY ASSOCIATION, DELIVERED JANUARY 22, 1845 (1845)

Sturgis (1978): \_\_\_\_\_, THE JOURNAL OF WILLIAM STURGIS, S. W. Jackman, ed. (1978)

Sumner (1896): Sumner, William Graham, A HISTORY OF BANKING IN THE UNITED STATES (1896)

Sylla (1976): Sylla, Richard, *Forgotten Men of Money: Private Bankers in Early U.S. History*, 36 THE JOURNAL OF ECONOMIC HISTORY 173 (1976)

# T

Taber (2008): Taber, Thomas T., III, ANTEBELLUM AMERICAN RAILROAD COMPENDIUM 1830-1860 (2008)

Taylor (1951): Taylor, George Rogers, THE TRANSPORTATION REVOLUTION, 1815-1860 (1951)

Taylor Letter (June 8, 1841): Letter of William B. Taylor, cashier of the Bank of Pensacola, to Walker Anderson, June 8, 1841, responding to inquiries of the investigative committee for the Bank of Pensacola, in JOURNAL OF THE PROCEEDINGS OF THE SENATE OF THE TERRITORY OF FLORIDA, AT ITS FOURTH SESSION, BEGUN AND HELD IN THE CITY OF TALLAHASSEE, ON MONDAY, JANUARY 3, 1842, DOCUMENTS ACCOMPANYING THE MESSAGE OF THE GOVERNOR 52 (1842)

Temin (1969): Temin, Peter, THE JACKSONIAN ECONOMY (1969)

Territorial Papers (1842): TERRITORIAL PAPERS OF THE UNITED STATES, FLORIDA TERRITORY, PART ELEVEN, PAPERS RELATING TO THE ADMINISTRATION OF GOVERNOR REID, 1839-1841 (1842)

*The Armitrage Brearly* (1877): *The Armitrage Brearly* and *The Dudley S. Gregory*, 1 F. Cas. 1130, 9 Ben. 108, 1877 U.S. Dist. LEXIS 85 (1877)

Thompson (1941): Thompson, Lawrence, *The Printing and Publishing Activities of the American Tract Society from 1825 to 1840*, 35 THE PAPERS OF THE BIBLIOGRAPHICAL SOCIETY OF AMERICA 81 (1941)

Totten Letter (1842): Totten, Joseph G., Letter from Joseph G. Totten, Chief Engineer, U.S. Army Corps of Engineers, to William H. Chase, March 7, 1840, in TERRITORIAL PAPERS OF THE UNITED STATES, FLORIDA TERRITORY, PART ELEVEN, PAPERS RELATING TO THE ADMINISTRATION OF GOVERNOR REID, 1839-1841 (1842), at 121

Treasury Building (1960): United States of America Department of the Treasury, HISTORICAL HIGHLIGHTS: U.S. TREASURY BUILDING (1960)

Treasury Steam-Engines Letter (1838): *Steam-Engines*, Letter from The Secretary of the Treasury, H. Doc. No. 21, 25th Cong., 3d sess., December 13, 1838

Tucker (1889): Tucker, William Howard, HISTORY OF HARTFORD, VERMONT, JULY 4, 1761-APRIL 4, 1889 (1889)

Turner (2003): Turner, Gregg M., A SHORT HISTORY OF FLORIDA RAILROADS (2003)

*Tuthill v. Wheeler* (1849): *Tuthill v. Wheeler*, 6 Barb. 362, 1849 N.Y. App. Div. LEXIS 191 (1849)

Twaddell (1946): Twaddell, Elizabeth, *The American Tract Society, 1814-1860*, 15 CHURCH HISTORY 116 (1946)

*Tyler v. Tuel* (1810): *Tyler and Others v. Tuel*, 10 U.S. 324, 6 Cranch. 324, 3 L. Ed. 237, 1810 WL 1609, 1810 U.S. LEXIS 346 (1810)

Tyson (1833): Tyson, Job R., A Brief Survey of the Great Extent and Evil Tendencies of the Lottery System, as Existing in the United States (1833)

Tyson v. George's Creek C&I (1911): *Tyson v. George's Creek Coal & Iron Co.*, 115 Md. 564, 81 A. 41. 1911 Md. LEXIS 174 (1911)

Tyson (1834): Tyson, J. R., A Discourse before the Young Men's Colonization Society of Pennsylvania (1834)

## U

UCNY Catalogue (1844): Catalogue of the Officers and Students of the University of the City of New York, 1843-'44 (1844)

UCNY Faculty Circular (1851): *Circular of the Faculty of Science and Letters of the University of the City of New York* (June 1851)

Unger (2013): Unger, David Stephen, *A Place of Work: The Geography of an Early Nineteenth Century Machine Shop*, unpublished Ph.D. dissertation, Harvard University (2013)

Union Bank v. Call (1854): *Union Bank of Florida v. Call*, 5 Fla. 409, 1854 WL 1272, 1854 Fla. LEXIS 3 (1854)

UNJRR&C AR (1869): *Report of the United Delaware and Raritan Canal Company, Camden and Amboy Railroad and Transportation Company, and New Jersey Railroad and Transportation Company, to the Stockholders, and the Proceedings at the Annual Meeting of the Stockholders of the Camden and Amboy R. R. and Trans. Co., Held at Camden, Wednesday, April 28th, 1869* (1869)

U.S HJ (1842): Journal of the House of Representatives of The United States at the Third Session of the Twenty-Seventh Congress begun and held at the City of Washington in The Territory of Columbia, December 5, 1842, and in the Sixty-Seventh Year of the Independence of the United States (1843)

US House BUS Report (1832): Bank of the United States, Report No. 460, United States House of Representatives, 22d Congress, 1st Session, April 30, 1832 (1832)

U.S. House Bank Report (1838): *Reports on the Bank Question, Twenty-Second Congress, First Session, House of Representatives of the United States of America, March 14, 1838* (1838), included as an Appendix to The Bank Question, 11 The Quarterly Review 245 (1838), at xv et seq. (the Appendix follows page 512 of the volume)

US House Executive Documents (1841): *Condition of the State Banks*, United States House of Representatives, Treasury Department, The Executive Documents, Twenty-Sixth Congress, Second Session, Volume 4, Doc. No. 111 (1841)

US Law (1865) Ch. XCII: U.S. Statutes at Large, 13 Stat. 510, Chapter XCII, An Act to Incorporate the Freedman's Savings and Trust Company, approved March 3, 1865

## V

V&C Report (1877): *Report of Special Masters in the case of Vermont and Canada R. R. Co. vs. Vermont Central R. R. Co. and Others, Filed April 24, 1877*

VA Law (1846) Ch. 113: Chapter 113, An Act to incorporate the Richmond and Ohio railroad company, passed February 2, 1846

VA Public Works Report (1839): *Twenty-Fourth Annual Report of the Board of Public Works, to the General Assembly of Virginia, with the Accompanying Documents, November 1, 1839* (1839)

*Van Keuren v. McLaughlin* (1868): *Van Keuren and others v. McLaughlin and others*, 19 N.J. Eq. 187, 4 C.E. Green 187, 1868 WL 94, 1868 N.J. Ch. LEXIS 29, 1868 WL 94 (1868)

Van Oss (1893): Van Oss, S. F., AMERICAN RAILROADS AS INVESTMENTS (1893)

VC Deed (1854): Deed of Surrender to Trustees of the First Mortgage, dated May 12, 1854, from the Vermont Central Railroad Company to John Smith, William Raymond Lee, and John S. Eldridge, in CHARTERS OF THE VERMONT CENTRAL, VERMONT AND CANADA, AND CENTRAL VERMONT RAILROADS: THE VERMONT AND CANADA LEASE, THE FIRST AND SECOND MORTGAGES AND DEEDS OF SURRENDER OF THE VERMONT CENTRAL RAILROAD COMPANY, ORDERS AND DECREES IN THE CAUSE VERMONT AND CANADA R. R. CO. VS. VERMONT CENTRAL R. R. CO. ET AL, at 45-8

Veeder (1970): Veeder, Paul L., III, *The Outbuildings and Grounds of Château-sur-Mer*, 29 JOURNAL OF THE SOCIETY OF ARCHITECTURAL HISTORIANS 307 (1970)

Veenendaal (1996): Veenendaal, Augustus J., Jr., SLOW TRAIN TO PARADISE: HOW DUTCH INVESTMENT HELPED BUILD AMERICAN RAILROADS (1996)

*Vermont & Canada RR v. Vermont Central RR* (1855), in CHARTERS OF THE VERMONT CENTRAL, VERMONT AND CANADA, AND CENTRAL VERMONT RAILROADS: THE VERMONT AND CANADA LEASE, THE FIRST AND SECOND MORTGAGES AND DEEDS OF SURRENDER OF THE VERMONT CENTRAL RAILROAD COMPANY, ORDERS AND DECREES IN THE CAUSE VERMONT AND CANADA R. R. CO. VS. VERMONT CENTRAL R. R. CO. ET AL (1855), at 61 *et seq.*

von Gerstner (1842-1843): von Gerstner, Franz Anton Ritter, FRANZ ANTON VON GERSTNER'S DIE INNERN COMMUNICATIONEN (1842-1843), Frederick C. Gamst, ed., David J. Diephouse and John C. Decker, trans. (1997)

Van Oss, S. F., AMERICAN RAILROADS AS INVESTMENTS (1893)

Vose (1887): Vose, George L., A SKETCH OF THE LIFE OF GEORGE W. WHISTLER, CIVIL ENGINEER (1887)

## W

Walby (2014): Walby, David L., WILLIAM HENRY CHASE: UNIQUELY AMERICAN (2014)

Walker (1848): Walker, Jonathan, THE TRIAL AND IMPRISONMENT, AT PENSACOLA, FLORIDA, FOR AIDING SLAVES TO ESCAPE FROM BONDAGE, WITH AN APPENDIX CONTAINING A SKETCH OF HIS LIFE (1848)

Wallis (2001): Wallis, John Joseph, *What Caused the Crisis of 1839?*, Historical Paper 133, NATIONAL BUREAU OF ECONOMIC RESEARCH (April 2001)

Wallis, Sylla & Grinath (2004): \_\_\_\_\_, Richard E. Sylla, and Arthur Grinath III, *Sovereign Debt and Repudiation: The Emerging-Market Debt Crisis in the U.S. States, 1839-1843*, NATIONAL BUREAU OF ECONOMIC RESEARCH, Working Paper 10753 (September 2004)

Warner (1940): Warner, Paul T., *The Development of the Anthracite-Burning Locomotive*, 52 THE RAILWAY AND LOCOMOTIVE SOCIETY BULLETIN 11 (1940)

Waters (1917): Waters, Wilson, HISTORY OF CHELMSFORD MASSACHUSETTS (1917)

Watkins (1908): Watkins, James L., KING COTTON: A HISTORICAL AND STATISTICAL REVIEW 1790 TO 1908 (1908)

Wealthy Philadelphians (1846): A MERCHANT OF PHILADELPHIA, MEMOIRS AND AUTO-BIOGRAPHY OF SOME OF THE WEALTHY CITIZENS OF PHILADELPHIA, WITH A FAIR ESTIMATE OF THEIR ESTATES – FOUNDED UPON A KNOWLEDGE OF FACTS (1846)

Weaver (1833): *Bank of the United States, List of Presidents, Cashiers, and Directors of the Bank of the United States, and its Branches, in the Office on the 30th of September, 1833,* in REGISTER OF ALL OFFICERS AND AGENTS, CIVIL, MILITARY, AND NAVAL, IN THE SERVICE OF THE UNITED STATES, ON THE THIRTIETH OF SEPTEMBER, 1823 165 (1833) [stet as to "1823" in the title]

Weaver (2018): Weaver, John, A LEGACY IN BRICK AND STONE: AMERICAN COASTAL DEFENSE FORTS OF THE THIRD SYSTEM, 1816-1867 (2018)

Weekly Globe (1842, August 27): *We Recommend a Change of State Policy*, 1 WEEKLY GLOBE 608 (August 27, 1842)

*Wendover v. Lexington* (1854): *Wendover v. The City of Lexington*, 54 Ky. 258, 15 B. Mon. 258, 1854 LEXIS 71, 1854 WL 3835 (1854)

West Point Reminiscences (1886): REMINISCENCES OF WEST POINT IN THE OLDEN TIME AND REGISTER OF GRADUATES OF THE UNITED STATES MILITARY ACADEMY, CORRECTED TO SEPTEMBER 1ST, 1886, WITH AN INDEX, [section entitled "Register of Graduates" following page 40 (1886)

Western RR Report (1843): *Proceedings of the Western Railroad Corporation, with a Report of the Committee of Investigation* (1843)

Wetmore (1841): Wetmore, William S., *A Plan of a National Bank*, 4 HUNT'S MERCHANT'S MAGAZINE AND COMMERCIAL REVIEW 528 (June, 1841)

Wetmore (1861): Wetmore, James Carnahan, THE WETMORE FAMILY OF AMERICA, AND ITS COLLATERAL BRANCHES: WITH HISTORICAL, BIOGRAPHICAL & GENEALOGICAL NOTICES (1861)

White (1907): James T. White & Company, publisher, THE NATIONAL CYCLOPAEDIA OF AMERICAN BIOGRAPHY, VOLUME IX (1907)

White (1963): White, John H., Jr., *The Centipede*, 109 THE RAILWAY AND LOCOMOTIVE HISTORICAL SOCIETY BULLETIN 11 (1963)

White (1968-1): _____, A HISTORY OF THE AMERICAN LOCOMOTIVE: ITS DEVELOPMENT: 1830-1880 (1968)

White (1968-2): _____, *Old Ironsides, Baldwin's First Engine*, 118 THE RAILWAY AND LOCOMOTIVE HISTORICAL SOCIETY BULLETIN 85 (1968)

White (1972): _____, EARLY AMERICAN LOCOMOTIVES (1972)

White (1980-1): _____, *Who Was Ezra Miller?*, 150 RAILROAD HISTORY 115 (1980)

White (1980-2): _____, *Railroad Car Builders of the United States*, 138 RAILROAD HISTORY 5 (1980)

White (1980-3): _____, *Holmes Hinkley and the Boston Locomotive Works*, 142 RAILROAD HISTORY 27 (1984)

White (1984): _____, *Once the Greatest of Builders: The Norris Locomotive Works*, 150 RAILROAD HISTORY 17 (1984)

White & Edson (1974): _____, and W. D. Edson, *Richmond Locomotive Builders*, 130 RAILROAD HISTORY 68 (1974)

Whittier (1893): Whittier, John Greenleaf, THE EARLY POEMS OF JOHN GREENLEAF WHITTIER (1893)

Wiernik (1912): Wiernik, Peter, HISTORY OF JEWS IN AMERICA FROM THE PERIOD OF DISCOVERY OF THE NEW WORLD TO THE PRESENT TIME (1912)

Wilder (1865): Wilder, Sampson Vryling Stoddard, RECORDS FROM THE LIFE OF S. V. S. WILDER (1865)

Wilkins (1989): Wilkins, Mira, THE HISTORY OF FOREIGN INVESTMENT IN THE UNITED STATES TO 1914 (1989)

Wilson (1852): Wilson, Henry, THE DIRECTORY OF THE CITY OF NEW-YORK, FOR 1852-1853 (1852)

Wilson (1879): Wilson, W. Hasell, NOTES ON INTERNAL IMPROVEMENTS OF PENNSYLVANIA (1879)

Wilson & Fiske (1889): Wilson, James Grant, and John Fiske, eds., APPLETON'S CYCLOPAEDIA OF AMERICAN BIOGRAPHY, VOLUME II (1889)

Wilson's NYC Directory (1864): WILSON'S NEW YORK CITY COPARTNERSHIP DIRECTOR, FOR 1864-'65 (1864)

Wiltse (1973): Wiltse, Charles M., *Daniel Webster and the British Experience*, 85 PROCEEDINGS OF THE MASSACHUSETTS HISTORICAL SOCIETY 58 (1973)

Withington (1958): Withington, Sidney, *The Strange Case of Robert Schuyler*, 98 THE RAILWAY AND LOCOMOTIVE HISTORICAL SOCIETY BULLETIN 32 (1958)

Wong (1996): Wong, Vivian Wu, *Somewhere between White and Black: The Chinese in Mississippi*, 10 OAH MAGAZINE OF HISTORY 33 (1996)

Wood (1834): Wood, Nicolson, TRAITÉ PRATIQUE DES CHEMINS DE FER DE NICOLSON WOOD, TRADUIT DE L'ANGLAIS (DEUXIÈME ÉDITION) PAR MM DE MONTRICHER ET DE FRANQUEVILLE, INGÉNIEURS DES PONTS ET CHAUSSÉES ET DE RUOLZ, PLANCHES, PARIS, CHEZ CARILLIAN-GOEURY ÉDITEUR-LIBRAIRE (1834)

Wood (1997): Wood, Kirsten E., *"One Woman So Dangerous to Public Morals": Gender and Power in the Eaton Affair*, 17 JOURNAL OF THE EARLY REPUBLIC 237 (1997)

Worth (1866): Worth, Gorham A., RANDOM RECOLLECTIONS OF ALBANY, FROM 1800 TO 1808, THIRD EDITION (1866)

*Wright v. Delafield & Curtis* (1857): *Wright v. Delafield and Curtis, trustees, &c., Berrien and others*, 23 Barb. 498, 1857 N.Y. App. Div. LEXIS 13 (1857)

Wyatt-Brown (1966): Wyatt-Brown, Bertram, *God and Dun & Bradstreet, 1841-1851*, 40 THE BUSINESS HISTORY REVIEW 432 (1966)

## Y

YMCSP (1836): Young Men's Colonization Society of Pennsylvania, 12 AFRICAN REPOSITORY AND COLONIAL JOURNAL 125 (April 1836)

Yonge (1933): Yonge, Julia J., *Walker Anderson, 1801-1857*, 11 THE FLORIDA HISTORICAL QUARTERLY 173 (1933)

Yonge (1959): Yonge, Julien C., *Pensacola in the War for Southern Independence*, 37 THE FLORIDA HISTORICAL QUARTERLY 357 (1959)

Young (1904): Young, Jeremiah Simeon, A POLITICAL AND CONSTITUTIONAL STUDY OF THE CUMBERLAND ROAD (1904)

# Index

## A

agency structure, 5, 40, 65, 73, 88, 115
Allen, Solomon, 114, 115
American Life and Trust Company, 87
Anderson, Walker, 47, 49, 60, 103, 131, 133, 137, 138, 139, 140, 141, 143, 144, 158, 171, 180, 195, 199
   secession, 140
Andrews, Henry, 25
Appleton Manufacturing Company, 4
Appleton, Nathan, 12, 17, 24, 25, 31, 33, 34, 38, 175, 181
Appleton, William, 3, 31, 76, 85, 86

## B

B&R Cars Contract Contract (1842), 41, 161
Bainbridge, William, 74, 75, 157, 176, 180
Baker, Nathaniel F., 104
Baldwin Locomotive Works, 7, 21, 23, 28, 32, 161, 164, 165, 179, 190
Baltimore & Susquehanna railroad, xi, 12, 13, 21, 23, 24, 36, 63, 115, 143, 150, 154, 184
Bank of Pensacola, 36, 37, 45, 46, 47, 48, 49, 50, 53, 54, 55, 56, 57, 58, 59, 60, 63, 64, 65, 85, 97, 99, 103, 105, 106, 109, 111, 117, 121, 122, 123, 124, 127, 128, 129, 130, 131, 133, 134, 135, 137, 139, 140, 141, 143, 144, 145, 157, 158, 159, 162, 163, 172, 173, 175, 178, 181, 186, 188, 189, 195
   bonds, 45, 49, 53, 55, 59, 121, 123, 124, 127, 128, 131, 134, 159
   bonds and Florida Committee on Banks, 135
   bonds payment location, 55, 124, 127
   legal opinions on bonds and guarantee, 133
   share sales and ownership, 45, 47, 55, 63, 64, 65
   share voting, 65, 67, 68
   Territorial guarantee, 130
   Territorial guarantee of bonds, 53, 54, 55, 59, 123, 124
Bank of Pensacola bonds, 45, 55, 121, 123, 128, 134, 137
   endorsement, 123, 124
   original bond sales, 59, 123, 127, 128, 131, 162
   personal liability, 54, 59, 124, 129, 130, 131
   repudiation, 38, 40, 55, 60, 129, 130, 133, 134, 137
Bank of Pensacola-Pensacola Association
   bond sale contract, 59, 123, 127, 128, 131, 162
   restructuring and financing plan, 53, 59
Bank of the United States, 13, 15, 23, 36, 37, 38, 40, 45, 46, 48, 51, 53, 55, 57, 58, 59, 60, 63, 65, 67, 68, 70, 72, 73, 74, 76, 81, 82, 83, 85, 87, 88, 89, 90, 91, 92, 93, 94, 121, 123, 127, 128, 129, 130, 131, 134, 137, 139, 142, 143, 157, 164, 184, 185, 193, 196, 198
   cashier, 40, 46, 61, 72, 73, 83, 87, 91, 105, 127, 131, 141, 195
   liquidation, 57, 73, 88, 130
      BUS Assignment (June 1841), 88, 164
      BUS Assignment (May 1841), 88, 164
      BUS Assignment (September 1841), 88, 164
Barnum, Phineas Taylor, 115
Betts, Harlan & Hollingsworth, 29, 162

*Biddle v. Morris*, 92, 162
Biddle, Edward R., 71
Biddle, Nicholas, 13, 23, 37, 38, 45, 66, 67, 70, 71, 72, 73, 74, 76, 81, 82, 83, 85, 86, 89, 91, 92, 134, 157, 162, 174, 188
Biddle, Thomas & Company, 55, 68, 121
Biddle, Thomas A., 15, 37, 55, 58, 60, 63, 64, 67, 68, 69, 70, 71, 85, 90, 121, 127, 128, 157, 159, 162
Binney, Amos, 76, 149, 152
Binney, Horace, xi, 6, 7, 11, 12, 14, 15, 16, 70, 85, 89, 90, 133, 136, 149, 152, 162
Blount, Thomas M., 46, 47, 49, 50, 58, 59, 60, 79, 103, 139, 159, 183, 188
bond markets, 36, 40
Bonus Bill, 39
Boot, Kirk, 3, 4, 14, 23, 25, 32
Booth, William L., 58, 64, 67, 116, 159
Boston & Lowell railroad, 3, 4, 14, 21, 23, 24, 27, 28, 31, 32, 33, 34, 35, 39, 84, 93
Boston & Portland railroad, 24, 28
Boston & Providence railroad, 14, 15, 23, 24, 27, 28, 31, 33, 84, 85, 93, 153, 182
Boston & Worcester railroad, 15, 24, 28, 31, 33, 144
Boston Associates, 3, 6, 7, 12, 31, 33, 34, 38, 67, 76, 85, 149, 167, 176, 190, 192
    definition, 3
Boston Manufacturing Company, 4, 17, 24, 32, 153, 182
Bradford, Samuel, 13, 15, 70, 163
Bradley & Rice, 34, 41, 161
*Bristol* locomotive engine, 21, 22, 27, 157
Brown, John A., 71, 85
Bryant & Sturgis, 38, 40
Bryant, John, 31, 38, 40, 85, 152

## C

Cadwalader, Thomas, 85
Call, Richard Keith, 49, 91, 103, 106, 120, 121, 122, 123, 127, 128, 129, 130, 131, 133, 134, 136, 137, 139, 145, 158, 163, 165, 169, 181, 183, 196

battle of Withlacoochee, 122, 131, 162
Camden & Amboy railroad, 14, 15, 21, 30, 37, 71, 91, 109, 116, 157, 176, 196
Cameron, John A., 46, 47, 48, 50, 58, 60, 100, 103, 139, 159
car and equipment trusts, 5, 151
Catlin, Clara Gregory, 46, 104, 107
Catlin, George, 46, 104, 107, 109, 161, 170, 175, 176, 177, 183, 192, 194
Catlin, James, 46, 47, 61, 117, 127, 131, 175
Central Railroad Company of New Jersey, 5, 86, 94
Chase, George E., 46, 63, 64, 65, 152
Chase, William H., 19, 35, 37, 38, 45, 46, 50, 55, 57, 59, 63, 64, 65, 79, 97, 99, 100, 103, 127, 139, 141, 142, 158, 159, 162, 165, 173, 176, 195, 197
    Chinese contract labor, 98
    Pensacola development, 97
    personal business interests, 97
    resignation from Army Corp of Engineers, 97
    slave holdings, 98
    sucession, 100, 102, 165
Chauncey, Charles, 70, 71, 85, 90, 162
Chauncey, Elihu, 38, 55, 58, 59, 60, 63, 64, 67, 70, 71, 73, 85, 90, 91, 121, 127, 131, 134, 159, 163
*Cider Making*, William Sidney Mount, 78, 79, 157, 177
Clark, Enoch W., 114, 115, 117
Clark, Thomas M., 25
Cohen, Jacob I., 114, 115, 118, 184
collateral security, 5, 13, 36, 87, 88, 150, 151
Colt, Roswell L., 85, 86, 112
conditional sale arrangements, 5, 139, 150, 151
Cooke, Jay, 114, 115, 117, 180, 184
Cope, Caleb, 71
Cowperthwaite, Joseph, 40, 59, 71, 91, 162
credit and financial intermediation, 4, 5, 35, 36, 50, 73, 93, 98, 114, 133, 150, 151
Cryder, John, 86, 94

## D

D&B Cars Contract (1842), 41, 167
D&B-F Cars Contract (1842), 41, 167
Davenport & Bridges, 34, 41, 167
Davis, Charles Augustus, 15, 38, 49, 51, 55, 58, 60, 63, 64, 65, 67, 76, 77, 78, 79, 82, 85, 86, 92, 152, 157, 159, 165, 167, 168, 178
Davis, John, 149, 152, 179
deferred payment credit mechanism, 35, 150, 151
Delaware & Hudson Canal Company, 85, 181
document accessions and collections, 155
Dorr, Albert H., 41
Duer, John, 87
Duncan, Sherman & Company, 75, 76, 92
Duval, William Pope, 45, 46, 106

## E

*E. L. Miller* locomotive engine, 21, 27
Eastern Railroad, 24
Eaton, John Henry, 53, 175
    Petticoat Affair, 53, 59, 167, 170, 190
Egeria at the Fountain, 104, 105, 107, 158
Engines Contract of L&C and P&R, 5, 12, 70, 170, 192
equipment finance, xi, 5, 6, 8, 150, 151, 209
    definition, xiii, 7, 8
Erie Canal, 109, 154, 192
Evans, Oliver, 18, 26, 174

## F

federal funding of internal improvements, 39
    Maysville Turnpike, 39, 40
    National Road, 36, 39, 161, 177, 178, 191, 193, 199
floating debt, 6, 7, 12, 149, 150
Florida
    State, 45, 49, 133, 135, 139, 140, 156, 160, 171, 172, 173
    Territory, 3, 36, 44, 45, 46, 49, 53, 55, 59, 64, 65, 67, 97, 121, 122, 123, 124, 127, 128, 129, 130, 131, 133, 134, 135, 140, 142, 143, 156, 158, 163, 165, 169, 171, 172, 173, 174, 183, 195, 196
Florida Insurance and Banking Company, 49, 103, 106, 173
Forbes, John Murray, 38, 116, 153, 154, 174
Forestall, Edmond J., 142
Fraley, Frederick, 71
Fuller, Albert, 41

## G

George's Creek Coal & Iron Company
    *Peabody v. George's Creek C&I*, 88, 94, 188
    *Tyson v. George's Creek C&I* (1911), 87, 94, 196
Gihon, John, 38, 154
Girard, Stephen, 68, 71, 184
Gowan & Marx financial firm, 56, 68, 121, 123, 127, 128
Graham, James D., 56, 58, 159
Gramercy Park, New York City, 77, 189
Gregory, Amanda Caroline Kelly, 103, 104, 106, 107
Gregory, Benjamin, 112
Gregory, Dudley S., 48, 55, 59, 60, 64, 104, 106, 107, 109, 110, 111, 112, 113, 115, 116, 117, 118, 158, 160, 178, 182, 185, 186, 194, 195
    D. S. Gregory & Co., 111, 112, 117
Gregory, James, 111, 112
    J. G. Gregory & Co., 111, 112, 117
Gregory, Walter, 38, 45, 46, 47, 48, 55, 56, 57, 58, 60, 61, 63, 64, 65, 100, 103, 104, 106, 107, 108, 109, 111, 112, 113, 114, 117, 127, 134, 137, 158, 162, 175, 183, 185, 193
Glendale Association, 103
    support for George Catlin, 104

## H

Hale, Nathan, 31
Hone, Philip, 85, 86, 176, 177, 179, 180
Howard, Charles, 63, 65, 151, 180
Humphreys & Biddle, 82, 89
Hyer, Henry, 46, 47, 58, 60, 79, 103, 106, 137, 139, 159

## I

Innerarity, John, 47

## J

Jackson, Andrew, 39, 45, 48, 53, 59, 79, 122, 167, 169, 178, 191
Jackson, Jonathan, 25, 178
Jackson, Patrick Tracy, xi, 3, 4, 5, 6, 7, 10, 11, 12, 13, 14, 15, 16, 17, 18, 19, 20, 21, 23, 24, 25, 26, 27, 29, 31, 32, 33, 34, 35, 36, 37, 38, 39, 45, 49, 53, 58, 63, 67, 68, 69, 71, 76, 78, 79, 84, 86, 89, 97, 121, 122, 137, 141, 142, 143, 149, 150, 151, 156, 157, 159, 162, 178, 181, 192, 193
    resignation from L&C, 14
    retirement, 13, 14, 32
Jaudon, Charles Bancker, 74, 75, 76
Jaudon, Lucy Ann Bainbridge, 74, 75, 76, 166
Jaudon, Mary Taylor Bainbridge, 74, 75, 76, 77, 158, 186
Jaudon, Samuel, 37, 55, 58, 63, 64, 67, 69, 71, 72, 73, 74, 75, 76, 81, 85, 88, 127, 134, 143, 157, 159, 162, 178, 188
    as London BUS agent, 37, 72, 73, 121
    as London P&R agent, 73
    *Duncan v. Jaudon*, 75, 76, 92, 169
    income, 73
Jay, Peter Augustus, 85, 133, 136, 178

## K

Kelly, Hanson, 46, 47, 48, 50, 79, 100, 103, 106, 139
Kent, James, 85, 90, 94, 133, 136, 169, 180

## L

Lee, W. Raymond, 27, 86, 149, 153, 160, 197
*Lehigh C&N v. Field*, 154, 180
Lehigh Coal & Navigation Company, 5, 37, 151, 154, 180
Lehigh Equipment Trust of Philadelphia, 5
List, Frederick, 71, 162
Little Schuylkill Navigation, Railroad & Coal, 15, 69, 71, 91
Locks & Canals (Proprietors of, on Merrimack River), xi, 3, 4, 5, 6, 7, 11, 12, 13, 14, 15, 16, 17, 18, 19, 20, 21, 23, 24, 25, 26, 27, 28, 29, 31, 32, 33, 34, 35, 36, 37, 38, 41, 45, 63, 67, 71, 84, 85, 89, 121, 139, 141, 142, 143, 144, 145, 149, 150, 151, 152, 154, 156, 158, 179, 181, 184
    machine shop, 3, 6, 17, 18, 20, 24, 26, 31, 32, 67, 85, 156
London Bond Agreement, 123, 125, 126, 127, 128, 158, 181
Loring, Joseph F., 31
lotteries, 61, 103, 110, 111, 112, 113, 114, 115, 116, 117, 118
Lowell Machine Shop, 85
Lowell, Francis Cabot, 3, 17, 18, 24, 26, 34
Lowell, John A., 14, 33, 86, 157, 163
LTCB Mortgage, 154, 181
Lycoming Coal Company, 4, 14, 19, 70, 71, 90, 182, 187
Lyman, George, 31

## M

Major Jack Downing, 78, 92
McCalmont Brothers, 38, 41, 154
McIntyre, Archibald, 55, 59, 64, 109, 110, 111, 117, 194

McKee, William, 12, 71, 154, 170, 181
McNeill, Anna Matilda, 23
McNeill, William Gibbs, 23, 84, 158
Merrimack Manufacturing Company, 17, 18, 25, 26, 32, 182
Montgomery Railroad, 47
Moody, Paul, 17, 18, 25, 153, 161
Morse, John T., 14, 149
Mount, William Sidney, 71, 76, 78, 92, 157, 166, 177, 185

## N

National City Bank of New York, 75, 76, 92, 178
National Road, 36, 39, 161, 177, 178, 191, 193
Neal, David A., 38, 150, 152
    report to P&R investors, 150, 154, 185
New Bedford & Taunton road, 24
New Castle Manufacturing, 162
Norris Locomotive Works, 23, 29, 198

## O

*Old Ironsides* locomotive engine, 21, 198
Oliver, Peggy, 86

## P

Panic of 1837, Crisis of 1839, Collapse of 1842, xi, 4, 6, 7, 12, 13, 24, 29, 35, 36, 37, 40, 115, 121, 133, 150, 159, 162, 183, 189, 191, 192, 197
*Patrick* locomotive engine, 21
Pawtucket Canal and Falls, 17, 18, 25
Peabody, George, 75, 86, 88, 92, 154, 176
Pemberton Square real estate project, 4, 14, 19
Pennsylvania Railroad Company, 50, 190
Pensacola & Perdido, 100, 101, 145
Pensacola Association, 45, 55, 56, 59, 63, 64, 67, 82, 84, 89, 121, 123, 127, 128, 129, 132, 134, 139, 143, 159, 163

Pensacola City Company, 45, 58, 60, 173, 188
Pensacola Land Company, 45, 57, 58, 60, 99
Pensacola land development project, 19, 46, 47, 50, 51, 57, 63, 145, 169
Pensacola Railroad, xi, 3, 4, 6, 7, 12, 13, 15, 16, 17, 19, 21, 23, 24, 27, 28, 31, 32, 33, 35, 36, 37, 38, 45, 46, 47, 49, 50, 53, 54, 56, 57, 58, 59, 65, 77, 79, 85, 86, 89, 97, 98, 99, 100, 101, 103, 106, 116, 121, 124, 134, 135, 137, 139, 141, 142, 143, 144, 145, 150, 178
    AF&G, 28, 46, 47, 100, 172, 189
    commissioner's report on fate of engines, 24, 38, 48, 49, 51, 59, 60, 65, 106, 107, 117, 131, 141, 144, 145, 163
    FA&G, 46, 47
    fate of L&C engines and debt, 13, 139, 143, 145, 150
    loans, 56, 60
    original conception, 47, 56, 57, 158
    share ownership, 56, 60
performance-based payments, 151
Philadelphia & Reading railroad, xi, 5, 6, 7, 11, 12, 13, 14, 15, 31, 33, 34, 37, 38, 40, 41, 45, 59, 68, 69, 71, 73, 85, 86, 91, 143, 149, 150, 151, 152, 153, 156, 157, 161, 162, 167, 170, 175, 176, 181, 184, 185, 186, 187, 190, 192
    debt, 6, 7, 12, 14, 149, 152
    debt restructuring, 18, 149
*Planet* class locomotives, 20, 21
Poinsett, Joel, 122, 131, 165, 191
PR-BW Engines Contract (1844), 28, 190
PR-BW Engines Contract (1845), 28, 190
PR-BW Engines Contract (1846), 28, 190
PR-Dotterer Lycoming Engines Contract (1842), 4, 14, 19, 70, 71, 90, 182, 187

## R

Railroad Car Trust of Philadelphia, 5
railroad system infrastructure, 4, 35, 36, 100, 209

Reid, Richard R., 139, 142, 145, 164, 171, 195
Robinson, Moncure, 69, 71, 91, 171, 186
Robinson, Morris, 55, 63, 64, 67, 76, 82, 83, 85, 86, 87, 89, 134, 143, 158, 159
Robinson, Wirt, 34, 71
Rolling Stock Contracts, 5, 6, 11, 12, 13, 14, 15, 33, 41, 143, 149, 151, 154, 192
Running Gear Contract of L&C and P&R, 5, 13, 34, 192

## S

Schuyler, Robert, 149, 152, 193, 199
Schuylkill Navigation Company, 5, 151, 154, 156, 193
   Boat Loan Proposal, 154, 193
   boat loans, 5, 151, 154
   minutes, 154, 156, 193
Seba Smith, 78
SNC Creditors Act (1852), 151, 193
Southern Life & Trust Company, 83, 103, 106, 122, 133, 135, 137, 139, 140, 172
Southern Life and Trust Company, 103, 106, 122, 133, 135, 137, 139, 140
sovereign bond issuances, 36
sovereign credit, 36
   enhancement, 32, 37, 109, 151
   substitution, 36, 37
Spencer, Lilly Martin, 104
state bonds, 36
Steele, Henry, 63, 64, 65, 67, 104
Stephenson, Robert, 3, 20, 21, 27, 157, 193
*Strong v. Taylor*, 154, 194
Strong, Jasper, 47, 50, 60, 99, 100, 103, 154, 173, 194
Sturgis, William, 12, 14, 31, 33, 38, 40, 85, 86, 152, 164, 180, 181, 184, 195

## T

Tappan, John, 81, 82
Tappan, Lewis, 82
Taylor, William B., 131, 141, 142, 195
Thayer, John Elliott, 33, 34, 38, 41, 152, 154

Thayer, Nathaniel, 38
*The Rabbit Trappers*, William Sidney Mount, 78
Thompson, John, 114, 115
Thomson Hankey & Co., 56, 68, 123
Traunton Branch railroad, 24
trust structures, 5, 12, 25, 51, 57, 58, 63, 64, 65, 67, 73, 75, 76, 77, 81, 86, 88, 92, 136, 151, 152, 153
trustees, 12, 15, 25, 51, 58, 60, 63, 64, 67, 68, 75, 77, 88, 92, 139, 151, 181, 188, 199
Tucker, John, 12, 38, 50, 195
*Tuthill v. Wheeler*, 154, 195

## U

Underhill, Fred A., 50, 99
Union Bank of Florida, 58, 59, 60, 68, 89, 90, 91, 103, 106, 122, 133, 134, 135, 136, 137, 139, 140, 145, 159, 172, 196
United New Jersey Railroad and Canal Company, 109, 116
United New Jersey Railroad and Transportation Company, 109

## V

Van Buren, Martin, 85, 122, 167

## W

Wales, Thomas B., 31
Walker, Jonathan, 140, 176, 179, 186
Walker, Jonathn, 140, 144, 176, 179, 186
Webster, Daniel, 73, 76, 85, 133, 142, 174, 190, 199
Western Railroad, 21, 23, 24, 27, 28, 31, 32, 34, 40, 84, 93, 171, 175, 198
Wetmore, William S., 86, 87, 94, 182, 192, 198
Whistler, George Washington, 3, 21, 24, 28, 31, 32, 84, 93, 197
Whistler, James Abbott McNeill, 23, 28
Whyte, Frederick Methvan, 21, 27

Wilder, Sampson Vryling Stodard, 58, 60, 63, 79, 80, 81, 82, 87, 92, 93, 121, 131, 157, 159, 191, 198
    Duc de Broglie claim, 79, 80, 92
Wilder, Sampson Vryling Stoddard, 55, 64, 67, 86, 134, 157, 160, 186, 198
Winans, Ross, 28, 32, 153, 192
Woolworth Building, 85, 94, 164

## Y

Yates & McIntyre, 55, 109, 110, 111, 115, 116
Yates, Henry, 55, 59, 64, 110, 111, 117
Yates, John Barentse, 110, 117
Yates, Joseph C., 111, 117

## ABOUT THE GRAPHIC DESIGNER

## CATHERINE DABBAGE

Catherine Dabbage is an English graphic designer with over thirty years of experince in the publishing industry. Catherine moved to Pennsylvania in 2013 and now freelances in graphics, fine art, sculpture, and illustration. Her transferable skills have led to her involvements in fundraising events for her childrens' schools, including advertising, design concepts, and decorations.

# About the Author

## Michael J.T. McMillen

Michael J.T. McMillen is a member of the Bar of the State of New York. He serves as a Partner in the international law firm of Curtis, Mallet-Prevost, Colt & Mosle LLP and an Adjunct Professor at the University of Pennsylvania Carey Law School. His legal practice is global and focuses on project, infrastructure, and equipment finance and Islamic finance. Michael teaches Islamic finance at the University of Pennsylvania Carey Law School and other institutions.

Michael was the founding chair, and twice served as chair, of the Islamic Finance Section of the American Bar Association. He has twice been honored as a recipient of Euromoney's award for Best Legal Advisory in Islamic Finance. He has also been honored as a recipient of the Sheikh Mohammed Bin Rashid Al Maktoum award in Special Recognition for Regional Continuing Contributions to Islamic Finance.

Academic degrees awarded to Michael are a Doctor of Medicine (M.D.) from the Albert Einstein College of Medicine, a Juris Doctor (J.D.) from the University of Wisconsin Law School, and a Bachelor of Business Administration (B.B.A.) from the University of Wisconsin – Madison.

Michael is married to Karin Laine McMillen. Their children are Addison L. McMillen, Alexandra L. (McMillen) Toles, and Antonio Borrero. Michael, Karin, and Addison reside at the family farm in Washington Township, Pennsylvania.

Figure 27: *Still Engine #1*

www.ingramcontent.com/pod-product-compliance
Lightning Source LLC
Chambersburg PA
CBHW082038230426
43670CB00016B/2700

# LOST IN FLORIDA

## *Prelude to Equipment Finance*

In 1836 The Proprietors of Locks and Canals on Merrimack River sold two locomotives to a start-up railroad in the Territory of Florida. The Pensacola Railroad never built an inch of track or a whit of system infrastructure.

The railroad was mere conception. Part of a grandiose scheme of a group of Floridians, led by William H. Chase, to channel cotton and lumber from Alabama and Georgia through Pensacola Bay. The Floridians would reap benefits through a Pensacola real estate development project and the new Bank of Pensacola. The bank controlled the railroad. It was intended to control U.S. federal government largess for building forts and military installations in Pensacola and the Gulf of Mexico.

The Bank of Pensacola issued bonds to finance the scheme. The Florida Territory guaranteed the bonds. Northern financiers were enlisted to purchase the bonds. Those financiers took control of the Bank of Pensacola and the real estate development project.

The Bank of Pensacola collapsed in the Panic of 1837. Florida repudiated its bond guarantee. The two locomotive engines disappeared.

Patrick Tracy Jackson, the Locks & Canals treasurer, took his lessons from the Pensacola Railroad debacle. In subsequent transactions for sales of engines, cars, and rolling stock, Jackson developed the core elements of an equipment finance structure. The structure was refined in rolling stock sales to the Baltimore & Susquehanna and Philadelphia & Reading. It was the core of Schuylkill Navigation's boat loans and the car and equipment trusts of Lehigh Coal & Navigation, the Jersey Central, and the Pennsylvania Railroad. It is used still for financing acquisitions of all manner of equipment and projects.

This book explores the intricate web of transactions surrounding the sale of locomotives to the Pensacola Railroad and the mystery of the two lost engines.

Michael J.T. McMillen is a partner of the international law firm of Curtis, Mallet-Prevost, Colt & Mosle LLP and Adjunct Professor at University of Pennsylvania Carey Law School. He has worked in project, infrastructure, and equipment finance since 1983 and Islamic finance since 1996.

ISBN 978-1-957948-01-0